OSINT Threat Intel: Investigating Hackers, Breaches, and Cyber Risks

Algoryth Ryker

Cyber threats are no longer just the concern of governments or large corporations—every individual, business, and institution is at risk. The rise of cybercriminal organizations, hacktivist movements, ransomware groups, and state-sponsored hackers has made threat intelligence (TI) a crucial field for investigators, cybersecurity professionals, and open-source intelligence (OSINT) analysts.

This book, **OSINT Threat Intel: Investigating Hackers, Breaches, and Cyber Risks**, takes you into the world of digital threat actors, where cybercriminals use sophisticated tools, dark web marketplaces, and social engineering tactics to exploit vulnerabilities. Using OSINT techniques, you'll learn how to track cybercriminal groups, investigate data breaches, identify phishing campaigns, analyze malware operations, and even map out the infrastructure of nation-state actors.

By the end of this book, you will be able to:

✓ Identify different types of threat actors, from ransomware gangs to nation-state hackers.

✓ Investigate data breaches, phishing campaigns, and malicious domains using OSINT tools.

✓ Analyze malware infrastructure, botnets, and ransomware groups using open-source data.

✓ Track cryptocurrency transactions linked to cybercrime.

✓ Map out cyber threats using frameworks like MITRE ATT&CK & the Cyber Kill Chain.

✓ Understand the future of OSINT in cyber threat intelligence.

Let's get started—because cyber threats never sleep.

Chapter Breakdown

1. Understanding Threat Intelligence & OSINT

- What is cyber threat intelligence (CTI), and why does it matter?
- How OSINT plays a crucial role in detecting and mitigating cyber threats.
- The four types of threat intelligence: Strategic, Tactical, Operational, and Technical.
- Understanding the Cyber Threat Intelligence Lifecycle.

- Challenges in threat intelligence investigations and how to overcome them.
- **Case Study**: How OSINT helped prevent a major cyber attack.

2. Tracking Cyber Threat Actors & Hacktivists

- Identifying cybercriminals, hacktivists, and state-sponsored hackers.
- Investigating threat actor aliases, online handles, and forums.
- Monitoring social media, dark web platforms, and hacker communities.
- Tracing OPSEC mistakes and de-anonymizing cybercriminals.
- **Case Study**: Unmasking a hacktivist group through OSINT.

3. Investigating Data Breaches & Leaked Credentials

- How data breaches occur: from intrusion to sale on the dark web.
- Using OSINT tools to analyze breach data.
- Searching data leak platforms and breach databases for compromised credentials.
- Identifying patterns in password reuse and credential stuffing attacks.
- **Case Study**: Tracking a corporate data breach and its aftermath.

4. Identifying Malicious Domains & Phishing Sites

- How cybercriminals use malicious domains and fake websites for attacks.
- Investigating suspicious websites using WHOIS, DNS, and Passive DNS analysis.
- Tracking phishing infrastructure and attack campaigns.
- Monitoring URL shorteners, redirects, and malicious links.
- **Case Study:** Exposing a phishing network targeting global banks.

5. Social Engineering & Phishing OSINT

- Understanding how cybercriminals manipulate people through social engineering.
- Investigating phishing emails, scam messages, and fake personas.
- Identifying deepfake attacks and social media impersonation schemes.
- **Case Study**: How OSINT stopped a CEO fraud attack.

6. Cyber Threat Intelligence (CTI) Frameworks

- Introduction to MITRE ATT&CK, Cyber Kill Chain, and the Diamond Model.
- How OSINT complements traditional cyber threat intelligence methods.
- Using STIX/TAXII for structured threat intelligence sharing.
- **Case Study**: Using the MITRE ATT&CK framework to track an APT group.

7. Ransomware Groups & Cybercriminal Tactics

- The rise of Ransomware-as-a-Service (RaaS).
- Investigating ransomware variants, operators, and dark web leak sites.
- Tracking cryptocurrency payments made to ransomware gangs.
- Understanding negotiation tactics and extortion methods used by ransomware groups.
- **Case Study**: How OSINT helped take down a ransomware gang.

8. Botnets, Malware & Virus Investigations

- Understanding botnets, C2 servers, and malware distribution networks.
- Investigating malware sample metadata, file hashes, and infection patterns.
- Using OSINT to track malware campaigns and cybercriminal infrastructure.
- **Case Study**: How OSINT tracked a botnet's global operations.

9. Advanced Persistent Threats (APTs) & Nation-State Actors

- What are APT groups, and how do they operate?
- Investigating nation-state cyber espionage campaigns.
- Tracking zero-day exploits and state-sponsored malware.
- Monitoring geopolitical cyber conflicts and state-affiliated hackers.
- **Case Study**: Using OSINT to investigate a state-sponsored attack.

10. Corporate Cybersecurity OSINT

- How corporations use OSINT for cyber threat detection and incident response.
- Investigating insider threats and employee data leaks.
- Monitoring brand reputation and cybersecurity risks on the surface and dark web.
- Identifying supply chain and third-party vulnerabilities.
- **Case Study**: How OSINT prevented a corporate espionage attack.

11. Case Study: Tracking a Cybercriminal Network

- **Initial Discovery**: Identifying suspicious threat activity.
- Gathering intel from social media, hacker forums, and dark web sources.
- Analyzing malware infrastructure and ransomware activity.
- **Mapping the network**: Identifying key players and operational patterns.
- Collaborating with law enforcement and cybersecurity teams.

- **Final Outcome**: Lessons learned from the investigation.

12. The Future of OSINT in Cybersecurity

- Emerging cyber threats and evolving hacker tactics.
- How AI and machine learning are changing cyber threat intelligence.
- The role of big data analytics and automation in OSINT.
- The future of threat intelligence sharing and cyber defense strategies.
- Legal and ethical considerations in OSINT investigations.
- **Preparing for the future**: Essential skills and tools for next-gen cyber intelligence analysts.

Final Thoughts

Cybercrime is evolving—so must threat intelligence and OSINT. This book equips you with the skills to track hackers, investigate breaches, analyze ransomware gangs, and uncover cyber threats using open-source intelligence.

By mastering OSINT-driven cyber threat intelligence, you'll be able to:

✓ Investigate cybercriminal groups, nation-state actors, and ransomware gangs.

✓ Identify malicious domains, phishing campaigns, and malware operations.

✓ Track cryptocurrency transactions linked to cybercrime.

✓ Use CTI frameworks like MITRE ATT&CK to map out cyber threats.

✓ Understand the future of OSINT in cybersecurity.

With cyber threats growing every day, the ability to gather intelligence using OSINT is no longer optional—it's essential.

Let's get started. 🚀

1. Understanding Threat Intelligence & OSINT

In this chapter, we delve into the foundational concepts of threat intelligence and Open Source Intelligence (OSINT), key components in the modern cybersecurity landscape. Understanding how threat intelligence works, including the collection, analysis, and application of data to anticipate cyber risks, is crucial for building effective security strategies. OSINT, as a subset of threat intelligence, involves gathering publicly available information from diverse sources to identify potential threats, track hacker activities, and uncover vulnerabilities. This chapter will lay the groundwork for comprehending the intricate relationship between these disciplines and highlight how they are used to detect, investigate, and prevent cyber threats.

1.1 What is Threat Intelligence? Key Concepts & Importance

In the rapidly evolving world of cybersecurity, organizations face an ever-increasing array of threats, from cybercriminals to state-sponsored actors. To mitigate the risks posed by these threats, security teams need more than just reactive measures—they need proactive, actionable insights. This is where Threat Intelligence (TI) plays a pivotal role. But what exactly is Threat Intelligence, and why is it so crucial in today's cybersecurity landscape?

Defining Threat Intelligence

At its core, Threat Intelligence is the process of gathering, analyzing, and disseminating information regarding potential or current cyber threats that could pose risks to an organization's assets, operations, and reputation. This intelligence can include a wide variety of data, including tactics, techniques, and procedures (TTPs) used by adversaries, indicators of compromise (IOCs), vulnerabilities, attack methods, and the motivations behind cyberattacks.

Unlike simple data collection, Threat Intelligence is more focused on turning raw data into actionable insights that can help an organization anticipate and prepare for possible attacks. It's not just about gathering information, but about analyzing that information to understand the enemy's behavior, intentions, and future actions.

Key Concepts in Threat Intelligence

Indicators of Compromise (IOCs): These are pieces of data that identify potentially malicious activity. IOCs can include things like suspicious IP addresses, domain names, file hashes, or unusual patterns of behavior. They are the breadcrumbs left by attackers during their campaign and can be used by cybersecurity teams to detect and prevent further incidents.

Tactics, Techniques, and Procedures (TTPs): The MITRE ATT&CK framework is an excellent example of categorizing threat actor behavior. TTPs describe the various methods and processes that adversaries use to achieve their objectives. Understanding the TTPs of known threat actors helps organizations predict how attacks will unfold and recognize early signs of compromise.

Threat Actors: These are individuals or groups responsible for cyberattacks. Threat actors can range from opportunistic cybercriminals to organized hacktivists or even state-sponsored attackers. Understanding who is behind an attack—along with their motives, resources, and techniques—helps defenders prioritize their response and develop tailored countermeasures.

Threat Campaigns and Attack Vectors: A threat campaign refers to the series of actions taken by a threat actor over time to achieve their goal (e.g., data exfiltration or system disruption). Attack vectors are the methods by which these actors enter a system, such as phishing emails, exploiting vulnerabilities, or social engineering. Recognizing the attack vector allows organizations to strengthen their defenses against known entry points.

Contextualization: One of the key aspects of effective Threat Intelligence is the ability to contextualize the gathered data. Raw IOCs or TTPs are of limited value on their own. When combined with contextual information—such as which systems are vulnerable, the specific motivations of attackers, and potential impacts—this intelligence becomes actionable and useful for decision-making.

The Importance of Threat Intelligence

Proactive Defense Against Emerging Threats:

Threat Intelligence allows organizations to anticipate and prepare for potential threats before they cause harm. In a world where cyberattacks are increasingly sophisticated and targeted, relying solely on reactive defenses (such as firewalls and antivirus software) is insufficient. Threat Intelligence provides the early warning systems needed to identify new attack vectors and threat actors, often before they can fully execute their attacks. By understanding the tactics used by threat actors, organizations can adjust their defenses to mitigate these risks ahead of time.

Informed Decision-Making:

Effective threat management is not just about having the latest tools or technologies; it's about having the right information at the right time. Threat Intelligence empowers decision-makers by providing them with data-driven insights about which threats are most pressing and which risks need immediate attention. This enables them to prioritize security efforts and allocate resources more effectively, ensuring that they address the most critical vulnerabilities first.

Enhanced Incident Response and Recovery:

In the event of an attack, Threat Intelligence plays a crucial role in speeding up response times and reducing the damage. By leveraging pre-existing intelligence about specific attack techniques or threat actor behaviors, security teams can more quickly recognize signs of compromise and deploy countermeasures. This reduces the time spent investigating and helps the team respond more effectively to limit damage, recover faster, and restore normal operations.

Intelligence Sharing Across Organizations:

Threat Intelligence isn't just useful at an individual level; it's also critical for broader collaboration within industries and sectors. Cybercriminals often target organizations within the same industry, exploiting shared vulnerabilities. By sharing Threat Intelligence, organizations can collectively defend against these common threats. Information sharing also enables the creation of industry-specific threat intelligence feeds, which provide insights into emerging trends, attack techniques, and other threats relevant to particular sectors.

Strategic Risk Management:

At the strategic level, Threat Intelligence helps organizations assess the broader risk landscape. By understanding the threat actors most likely to target their industry and the potential impact of those attacks, organizations can develop long-term strategies for cybersecurity and risk management. This intelligence helps organizations stay ahead of the curve by enabling them to align their security measures with the ever-changing cyber threat environment.

Improving Threat Detection and Automation:

Many organizations now utilize Security Information and Event Management (SIEM) systems or automated threat detection tools to spot potential attacks. However, these systems are only effective when fed with high-quality Threat Intelligence. With the right data, these tools can identify abnormal behaviors and potential threats much more effectively. Threat Intelligence enhances these systems by providing relevant, up-to-date information, improving the detection and mitigation of attacks.

Types of Threat Intelligence

Strategic Threat Intelligence: This high-level intelligence focuses on long-term threats and trends in the cybersecurity landscape. It's typically used by executives and decision-makers to inform overall organizational strategies and policies. It provides insights into the motivations of threat actors, geopolitical influences, and emerging technologies that might affect security.

Tactical Threat Intelligence: This type of intelligence focuses on understanding the tactics and techniques used by threat actors to plan and execute attacks. It provides security teams with actionable insights into specific attack methods, such as phishing campaigns or ransomware strategies. Tactical intelligence helps organizations prepare defenses against specific forms of attacks and informs the configuration of security tools.

Operational Threat Intelligence: Operational intelligence provides in-depth information about ongoing or imminent attacks. It includes real-time data such as IP addresses, domains, or file hashes that are associated with a current cyber threat. This intelligence is highly actionable and often used by security analysts to detect and respond to active attacks.

Technical Threat Intelligence: This highly detailed intelligence provides in-depth information about specific attack tools, malware signatures, vulnerabilities, and exploit techniques. Technical intelligence can be used by threat analysts and incident responders to examine the specific methods used in an attack and develop appropriate defensive measures.

Threat Intelligence is a critical component of any modern cybersecurity strategy. It transforms raw data into valuable insights that can proactively guide security measures, detect evolving threats, and improve overall risk management. By understanding the key concepts, types, and importance of Threat Intelligence, organizations can better equip themselves to anticipate, identify, and mitigate cyber threats. In a landscape where cyberattacks are growing in sophistication, Threat Intelligence is not just a useful tool—it is essential for securing the digital future.

1.2 The Role of OSINT in Cyber Threat Intelligence (CTI)

Open Source Intelligence (OSINT) has become an indispensable tool in Cyber Threat Intelligence (CTI), offering security professionals the ability to gather, analyze, and utilize publicly available information to identify and mitigate cyber threats. In an age where digital footprints are growing exponentially, OSINT provides organizations with a cost-effective, scalable, and powerful approach to monitoring cyber risks, tracking threat actors, and preventing cyberattacks before they materialize. This chapter explores the role of OSINT in CTI, highlighting its key contributions, methodologies, and the challenges associated with leveraging open-source data for threat intelligence.

Understanding OSINT in Cyber Threat Intelligence

OSINT refers to the practice of collecting and analyzing information from publicly available sources to generate actionable intelligence. Unlike classified or proprietary intelligence, OSINT relies on openly accessible data from the internet, social media, public records, news reports, forums, and even the dark web. Within the context of CTI, OSINT serves as a critical enabler in detecting cyber threats, understanding adversary tactics, and assessing vulnerabilities in real time.

By leveraging OSINT, security professionals can uncover valuable information such as leaked credentials, exposed vulnerabilities, malicious domains, and even discussions among cybercriminals in underground forums. This intelligence provides a proactive layer of defense, allowing organizations to prepare against potential attacks before they escalate.

Key Contributions of OSINT in CTI

Early Threat Detection and Warning Signs

OSINT allows cybersecurity teams to identify emerging threats before they become full-fledged attacks. By monitoring hacker forums, social media chatter, and dark web marketplaces, security analysts can detect early indicators of potential cyber threats, such as discussions about new exploits, zero-day vulnerabilities, or planned cyberattacks.

Profiling Threat Actors and Groups

Understanding the behavior, tactics, and motives of threat actors is crucial in CTI. OSINT enables analysts to track the digital footprints of cybercriminals, hacktivists, and nation-state actors by examining their online activities, affiliations, and past attack patterns. By gathering intelligence from sources such as breach disclosures, leaked chat logs, and social media accounts, OSINT helps in building comprehensive threat actor profiles.

Monitoring the Dark Web and Underground Markets

The dark web serves as a marketplace for cybercriminals to trade stolen data, hacking tools, and illicit services. OSINT tools and techniques allow analysts to infiltrate these hidden communities and monitor cybercriminal activities. Threat intelligence teams can track the sale of stolen credentials, leaked corporate data, or discussions about targeting specific organizations, allowing them to take preemptive action.

Identifying Leaked Credentials and Sensitive Data

Data breaches and credential leaks are among the most common cyber threats. OSINT helps security teams detect compromised usernames, passwords, and sensitive documents before they are exploited by malicious actors. Monitoring paste sites, GitHub repositories, and data breach dumps enables organizations to take corrective actions, such as forcing password resets or notifying affected users.

Tracking Malicious Domains and Phishing Campaigns

Cybercriminals frequently use phishing websites and malicious domains to conduct scams and steal credentials. OSINT tools can analyze domain registration records, SSL certificates, and website metadata to identify suspicious websites. By proactively detecting and blacklisting these domains, security teams can prevent phishing attacks before they reach their targets.

Assessing Third-Party and Supply Chain Risks

Organizations increasingly rely on third-party vendors, making supply chain security a critical concern. OSINT provides visibility into potential vulnerabilities in third-party networks by analyzing publicly available information about a vendor's security posture, past breaches, or potential ties to malicious actors. This intelligence helps organizations make informed decisions about their partnerships and mitigate supply chain risks.

Vulnerability Intelligence and Exploit Monitoring

Keeping track of newly discovered vulnerabilities and exploits is essential for cybersecurity teams. OSINT sources such as vulnerability databases, security blogs, and exploit repositories provide real-time updates on emerging threats. By integrating this intelligence into vulnerability management programs, organizations can prioritize patching critical flaws before attackers exploit them.

OSINT Tools and Techniques in CTI

To effectively leverage OSINT for cyber threat intelligence, security teams use a combination of manual investigation techniques and automated tools. Below are some commonly used OSINT tools and methodologies in CTI:

1. Search Engines & Advanced Querying

- **Google Dorking** – A technique used to uncover exposed databases, misconfigured servers, and sensitive files using advanced search operators.
- **Shodan & Censys** – Search engines that scan the internet for exposed devices, servers, and industrial control systems, revealing potential attack surfaces.

2. Domain & IP Intelligence

- **WHOIS Lookup** – Helps in identifying domain registrants, ownership history, and potential links to malicious actors.
- **VirusTotal** – Analyzes domains, URLs, and files for malicious activity.
- **PassiveTotal & RiskIQ** – Tools used to monitor DNS records and detect domain spoofing or phishing attempts.

3. Dark Web Monitoring

- **Tor and I2P Browsers** – Enable access to hidden forums and marketplaces where cybercriminals operate.
- **Dark Web Monitoring Services** – Services like DarkTracer or Intel471 provide insights into underground cybercriminal activities.

4. Social Media & Threat Actor Tracking

- **SOCMINT (Social Media Intelligence)** – The process of monitoring social media platforms for emerging threats, leaks, or discussions about cyberattacks.

- **Maltego** – A powerful tool for mapping relationships between entities, such as threat actors, domains, and IP addresses.

5. Paste & Breach Data Monitoring

- **Have I Been Pwned (HIBP)** – A breach notification service that tracks leaked credentials.
- **Pastebin Scrapers** – Tools that monitor paste sites for leaked data and credentials.

Challenges and Limitations of OSINT in CTI

While OSINT is a powerful tool in Cyber Threat Intelligence, it comes with its own set of challenges:

Data Overload and False Positives

OSINT generates vast amounts of data, making it difficult to filter out noise from relevant intelligence. Analysts must carefully validate and correlate findings to avoid false positives.

Legality and Ethical Considerations

The collection and use of OSINT must comply with privacy laws and ethical guidelines. Accessing certain information without authorization may cross legal boundaries, so organizations must ensure their intelligence-gathering practices remain within legal and ethical limits.

Operational Security (OPSEC) Risks

Threat actors are aware of OSINT techniques and may use deception tactics to mislead investigators. Analysts must use proper OPSEC measures, such as anonymized browsing and VPNs, to avoid detection.

Evasion by Threat Actors

Advanced cybercriminals take steps to hide their tracks, such as using encrypted communication channels, burner accounts, and anonymization tools like VPNs and Tor. This makes tracking them using OSINT more challenging.

OSINT plays a crucial role in Cyber Threat Intelligence by providing organizations with valuable insights into emerging threats, threat actor activities, and potential attack vectors. By leveraging publicly available information, security teams can proactively detect cyber threats, investigate breaches, and strengthen their defenses. However, effective use of OSINT requires a combination of the right tools, methodologies, and analytical skills to filter relevant data, assess risks, and take informed action. As cyber threats continue to evolve, OSINT will remain a cornerstone of threat intelligence, helping organizations stay one step ahead in the ever-changing cybersecurity landscape.

1.3 Types of Threat Intelligence: Strategic, Tactical, Operational & Technical

Threat intelligence (TI) is a critical component of modern cybersecurity, providing organizations with valuable insights into potential cyber threats, adversary tactics, and emerging vulnerabilities. However, not all intelligence is the same—different types of threat intelligence serve different purposes and cater to different audiences within an organization. To build an effective cybersecurity strategy, it's essential to understand the four main types of threat intelligence: Strategic, Tactical, Operational, and Technical. Each of these plays a unique role in strengthening an organization's defense posture, from high-level decision-making to real-time threat mitigation.

1.3.1 Strategic Threat Intelligence

Definition and Purpose

Strategic threat intelligence provides high-level insights into the broader cybersecurity landscape. It is designed to inform executives, board members, and decision-makers about long-term threats, industry trends, and geopolitical risks that may affect an organization's cybersecurity strategy. Unlike technical intelligence, which focuses on immediate threats, strategic intelligence looks at the big picture, helping organizations plan, prioritize resources, and align security policies with emerging risks.

Key Characteristics of Strategic Threat Intelligence

- High-level, non-technical insights
- Focus on long-term trends rather than immediate threats
- Used by executives, CISOs, and policymakers
- Contextual analysis of threats and their business impact

- Sources of Strategic Threat Intelligence

Strategic intelligence is typically derived from:

- Government and industry reports (e.g., FBI, CISA, Europol, ENISA)
- Threat landscape reports from cybersecurity firms (e.g., CrowdStrike, Mandiant, Palo Alto Networks)
- Geopolitical intelligence from international think tanks and research organizations
- OSINT (Open Source Intelligence) sources such as cybersecurity blogs, news articles, and whitepapers

Example of Strategic Threat Intelligence in Action

A financial institution might use strategic threat intelligence to assess the risk of state-sponsored cyberattacks targeting the banking sector. If intelligence reports suggest an increase in cyber espionage activities from a particular country, the organization may increase investment in threat detection capabilities, enhance employee training, and update security policies accordingly.

1.3.2 Tactical Threat Intelligence

Definition and Purpose

Tactical threat intelligence focuses on the techniques, tactics, and procedures (TTPs) used by cyber adversaries. It is primarily used by security teams, SOC (Security Operations Center) analysts, and cybersecurity engineers to understand how attackers operate and develop defenses against known attack methods.

Tactical intelligence helps organizations improve their defensive capabilities, such as configuring firewalls, setting up intrusion detection systems (IDS), and enhancing endpoint security based on known threat actor behaviors.

Key Characteristics of Tactical Threat Intelligence

- Focuses on attacker methods, tools, and procedures
- Used by security teams and SOC analysts
- Provides insights on how to defend against known threats
- Informs security controls, SIEM (Security Information and Event Management) rules, and firewalls

Sources of Tactical Threat Intelligence

- MITRE ATT&CK framework (a globally accessible knowledge base of adversary tactics and techniques)
- Threat intelligence feeds from cybersecurity vendors
- Malware analysis reports
- Incident response case studies

Example of Tactical Threat Intelligence in Action

A cybersecurity team analyzing phishing attack patterns may use tactical intelligence to implement stronger email filtering rules, conduct user awareness training, and deploy multi-factor authentication (MFA) to mitigate credential theft.

1.3.3 Operational Threat Intelligence

Definition and Purpose

Operational threat intelligence provides real-time, actionable insights on specific ongoing or imminent threats. It is used by incident response teams, threat hunters, and SOC analysts to detect and mitigate attacks as they unfold.

Unlike strategic and tactical intelligence, which focus on broader patterns and attacker methodologies, operational intelligence is time-sensitive and specific to a current attack campaign. It helps organizations respond quickly to active threats by identifying Indicators of Compromise (IOCs), monitoring threat actor movements, and analyzing attack campaigns in real time.

Key Characteristics of Operational Threat Intelligence

- Time-sensitive and directly actionable
- Used for active threat detection and response
- Includes indicators of compromise (IOCs) such as IP addresses, file hashes, and domains
- Supports incident response, forensics, and real-time monitoring
- Sources of Operational Threat Intelligence
- SIEM systems (collect logs and detect anomalies in network traffic)
- Dark web monitoring (tracking cybercriminal activities)
- Threat intelligence sharing communities (e.g., ISACs – Information Sharing and Analysis Centers)

- Real-time threat feeds and honeypots

Example of Operational Threat Intelligence in Action

A SOC team receives an alert from a threat intelligence feed that a newly discovered malware strain is actively targeting financial institutions. The team cross-references the reported IOCs (e.g., suspicious IPs, malicious file hashes) with their internal logs and immediately blocks those indicators at the firewall level, preventing a potential breach.

1.3.4 Technical Threat Intelligence

Definition and Purpose

Technical threat intelligence is the most granular form of intelligence, focusing on specific artifacts of cyber threats such as malware signatures, exploit codes, and attack tools. It is primarily used by security researchers, malware analysts, and digital forensic teams to understand the inner workings of cyber threats and develop countermeasures.

Technical intelligence is essential for reverse engineering malware, analyzing zero-day exploits, and creating security patches.

Key Characteristics of Technical Threat Intelligence

- Highly detailed, focused on specific cyber artifacts
- Used by security researchers and forensic analysts
- Includes malware signatures, exploit kits, and attack payloads
- Helps in patching vulnerabilities and creating detection signatures
- Sources of Technical Threat Intelligence
- Malware analysis reports from security firms
- Threat hunting platforms (e.g., VirusTotal, Hybrid Analysis)
- Exploit databases (e.g., CVE databases, Exploit-DB)
- Cybersecurity research publications

Example of Technical Threat Intelligence in Action

A malware researcher detects a new variant of ransomware spreading through email attachments. By analyzing the malware's code and encryption mechanism, the researcher identifies a weakness in the decryption process and develops a free decryption tool, allowing victims to recover their files without paying a ransom.

Conclusion: The Interconnection of Threat Intelligence Types

Each type of threat intelligence—Strategic, Tactical, Operational, and Technical—serves a different purpose, but they all work together to create a comprehensive cybersecurity strategy.

- Strategic intelligence informs decision-making at the executive level, helping organizations align security policies with emerging threats.
- Tactical intelligence helps defenders understand and counteract common attack techniques, improving security defenses.
- Operational intelligence provides real-time, actionable data to security teams, enabling rapid incident response.
- Technical intelligence dives deep into malware and attack tools, supporting forensic investigations and mitigation strategies.

By leveraging all four types of threat intelligence, organizations can stay ahead of cyber adversaries, reduce risks, and build a robust cybersecurity defense strategy in an increasingly hostile digital environment.

1.4 The Cyber Threat Intelligence Lifecycle

The Cyber Threat Intelligence (CTI) Lifecycle is a structured process used by cybersecurity professionals to collect, analyze, and disseminate actionable intelligence. This lifecycle ensures that intelligence is relevant, accurate, and timely, enabling organizations to proactively detect, mitigate, and prevent cyber threats. The CTI lifecycle consists of six core stages:

- Planning & Direction
- Collection
- Processing & Exploitation
- Analysis & Production
- Dissemination & Sharing
- Feedback & Refinement

Each stage plays a critical role in converting raw data into meaningful intelligence that supports decision-making and strengthens an organization's security posture.

1.4.1 Stage 1: Planning & Direction

Definition and Purpose

The first stage of the intelligence lifecycle involves defining the objectives, scope, and priorities of the CTI process. Cybersecurity teams work with key stakeholders (e.g., executives, SOC teams, IT security) to establish what threats they need to monitor and what intelligence is most valuable to their organization.

Key Activities in This Stage

- Identifying critical assets (e.g., customer data, intellectual property, financial records)
- Defining intelligence requirements (e.g., monitoring APT groups, tracking phishing campaigns)
- Understanding the organization's risk profile and industry-specific threats
- Setting priorities based on threat severity and potential impact

Example in Action

A financial institution may determine that its top intelligence priority is detecting phishing attacks targeting customers. The CTI team focuses its intelligence efforts on monitoring malicious domains, phishing kits, and threat actor discussions on underground forums.

1.4.2 Stage 2: Collection

Definition and Purpose

The collection phase involves gathering raw data from various sources to support the intelligence objectives defined in the planning stage.

Key Sources of Intelligence Collection

- **Open Source Intelligence (OSINT):** Social media, news reports, security blogs, and forums
- **Dark Web Intelligence**: Criminal marketplaces, hacker forums, and paste sites
- **Technical Sources**: Threat intelligence feeds, malware analysis reports, honeypots
- **Internal Logs & Telemetry**: Security Information and Event Management (SIEM) data, firewall logs, and intrusion detection system (IDS) alerts

Challenges in Collection

- Ensuring data accuracy and credibility
- Avoiding information overload and filtering out noise
- Adhering to legal and ethical guidelines while collecting intelligence

Example in Action

A CTI analyst monitoring ransomware groups may collect intelligence from dark web leak sites, Telegram channels, and underground marketplaces to identify stolen corporate data and ransomware tactics.

1.4.3 Stage 3: Processing & Exploitation

Definition and Purpose

Once raw data is collected, it must be cleaned, organized, and structured into a usable format. This stage transforms unstructured data (e.g., raw logs, forum posts, news articles) into structured intelligence that can be analyzed.

Key Processing Activities

- Filtering relevant vs. irrelevant data
- Extracting Indicators of Compromise (IOCs) such as malicious IPs, domains, and hashes
- Normalizing data into structured formats like STIX/TAXII (cyber threat intelligence sharing standards)
- Enriching threat intelligence with contextual metadata

Example in Action

A cybersecurity team may extract IOCs from a malware sample, such as command-and-control (C2) server IPs, and convert them into machine-readable formats for automatic blocking in firewalls and endpoint detection systems.

1.4.4 Stage 4: Analysis & Production

Definition and Purpose

The analysis phase involves interpreting processed intelligence to generate meaningful insights that can support security operations and decision-making.

Key Questions in the Analysis Phase

- **Who is behind the threat?** (Attribution to threat actors)
- **What tactics and techniques are being used?** (MITRE ATT&CK framework mapping)
- **What is the threat's potential impact?** (Risk assessment)
- **How urgent is the threat?** (Prioritization based on severity)

Types of Intelligence Reports Produced

- **Strategic Reports**: High-level analysis for executives (e.g., threat actor trends, geopolitical risks)
- **Tactical Reports**: Attack patterns and TTPs for security teams (e.g., malware trends, phishing tactics)
- **Operational Reports**: Real-time threat bulletins for SOC analysts (e.g., active ransomware campaigns)
- **Technical Reports**: Detailed malware and exploit analysis for threat researchers

Example in Action

An intelligence team analyzing a phishing campaign may uncover common attack techniques, such as fake Microsoft login pages and social engineering tactics. This insight is used to improve email filtering rules and train employees on recognizing phishing attempts.

1.4.5 Stage 5: Dissemination & Sharing

Definition and Purpose

Once intelligence is analyzed, it must be shared with the right stakeholders in a timely manner. This ensures that actionable intelligence reaches those who need it most, such as SOC teams, IT security personnel, and executive leadership.

Methods of Dissemination

- **Internal Reports & Dashboards** (For SOC teams and security analysts)
- **Threat Intelligence Platforms** (TIPs) (Automated sharing with SIEM and security tools)

- **Industry Sharing Communities** (e.g., Information Sharing and Analysis Centers - ISACs)
- **Government & Law Enforcement** Collaboration (e.g., sharing with CISA, Europol, or FBI)

Challenges in Dissemination

- Ensuring intelligence is actionable and tailored to the right audience
- Avoiding information overload with too much technical detail for non-technical stakeholders
- Balancing transparency and security when sharing intelligence externally

Example in Action

A CTI team detecting a new malware strain targeting healthcare organizations may alert hospitals and security vendors through industry-specific ISACs, enabling them to implement preventative measures.

1.4.6 Stage 6: Feedback & Refinement

Definition and Purpose

The final stage ensures that the CTI lifecycle continuously improves based on feedback from stakeholders. Threat intelligence must be adaptable, as cyber threats constantly evolve.

Key Feedback Loops

- Reviewing effectiveness of past intelligence reports
- Updating collection priorities based on new threats
- Improving processing and analysis methods
- Adapting dissemination strategies to meet stakeholder needs

Example in Action

A company that suffered a ransomware attack may review its CTI reports to identify gaps in intelligence collection and analysis, leading to an improved monitoring strategy for future ransomware threats.

Conclusion: The Importance of the CTI Lifecycle

The Cyber Threat Intelligence Lifecycle ensures that cybersecurity teams systematically collect, analyze, and act on intelligence to defend against cyber threats proactively. Each stage plays a critical role in transforming raw data into actionable intelligence that helps organizations:

- Identify and mitigate emerging threats
- Improve their security defenses
- Make informed decisions on cybersecurity strategies

By implementing a structured CTI lifecycle, organizations can stay ahead of threat actors and reduce the risk of cyberattacks in an increasingly complex digital landscape.

1.5 Common Challenges in Threat Intelligence Investigations

Threat intelligence (TI) plays a crucial role in identifying, analyzing, and mitigating cyber threats. However, conducting effective threat intelligence investigations is not without its challenges. The dynamic nature of cyber threats, the sheer volume of data, and the complexity of adversarial tactics make it difficult for intelligence teams to stay ahead of cybercriminals.

In this section, we will explore some of the most common challenges faced by threat intelligence analysts, security operations teams, and cybersecurity professionals when investigating cyber threats.

1.5.1 Data Overload and Noise

The Problem:

Cybersecurity teams often struggle with information overload, as they must process vast amounts of threat intelligence from multiple sources, including:

- Threat intelligence feeds (commercial and open-source)
- Internal security logs (SIEM, IDS, and firewalls)
- OSINT (Open Source Intelligence) from social media, forums, and news sources
- Dark web intelligence (leak sites, hacking forums)

While this data can be valuable, sifting through large volumes of irrelevant information (noise) to identify meaningful threats can be time-consuming and resource-intensive.

Possible Solutions:

- Use threat intelligence platforms (TIPs) to filter and correlate data from multiple sources.
- Leverage AI and machine learning to detect patterns and reduce false positives.
- Prioritize intelligence based on business relevance and risk level.

Example in Action:

A SOC (Security Operations Center) analyst receives thousands of threat alerts daily. By implementing automated filtering tools, they reduce the number of irrelevant alerts and focus on high-risk threats, such as ransomware attacks targeting their industry.

1.5.2 Attribution and Identifying Threat Actors

The Problem:

One of the most difficult aspects of threat intelligence is accurately attributing attacks to specific threat actors. Cybercriminals often use proxy servers, VPNs, compromised accounts, and darknet communication channels to conceal their identities. Nation-state actors, in particular, employ false flag operations to mislead investigators.

Possible Solutions:

- Cross-reference multiple intelligence sources to identify common patterns in attack methodologies (TTPs).
- Utilize the MITRE ATT&CK framework to link known tactics to specific threat groups.
- Monitor darknet forums and underground marketplaces to gather intelligence on threat actor activities.

Example in Action:

A financial institution detects a sophisticated phishing campaign. By analyzing malware signatures and attack techniques, analysts determine the attack shares similarities with a well-known Russian-speaking cybercrime group.

1.5.3 Lack of Contextual Intelligence

The Problem:

Raw threat data—such as IP addresses, hashes, and domain names—is often lacking context. Without context, security teams struggle to determine:

- The intent of the attack (e.g., espionage vs. financial gain).
- The potential impact on their organization.
- The most effective mitigation strategies.

Possible Solutions:

- Correlate technical indicators (IOCs) with real-world attack campaigns.
- Utilize industry-specific threat intelligence to understand targeted attacks.
- Engage in intelligence sharing with ISACs (Information Sharing and Analysis Centers).

Example in Action:

An enterprise detects an IP address flagged as malicious in a threat feed. However, upon deeper analysis, they discover the IP belongs to a compromised business server, not a known cybercriminal group. Without proper context, they might have taken unnecessary defensive actions.

1.5.4 Rapidly Evolving Threats

The Problem:

Cyber threats are constantly evolving, with new attack vectors, malware variants, and exploitation techniques emerging daily. Security teams struggle to keep up with:

- Zero-day vulnerabilities
- Emerging ransomware strains
- New phishing tactics and social engineering schemes

Threat actors adapt quickly, often modifying their tactics as soon as defensive measures are put in place.

Possible Solutions:

- Continuous monitoring of cyber threat landscapes through intelligence feeds and security blogs.
- Implementing behavior-based detection methods instead of relying solely on signature-based defenses.
- Using deception techniques, such as honeypots, to study new attack methods in real time.

Example in Action:

A company blocks a known phishing domain, but within hours, attackers register a slightly modified domain name and launch a new attack. The company adopts AI-powered anomaly detection to identify similar phishing attempts in real-time.

1.5.5 Threat Intelligence Sharing Limitations

The Problem:

Sharing threat intelligence is crucial for collaborative defense against cyber threats, but organizations often face obstacles, such as:

- **Legal and compliance concerns** (GDPR, CCPA, data privacy laws).
- **Trust issues between organizations** (fear of exposing vulnerabilities).
- **Inconsistent threat intelligence formats** (lack of standardization).

Possible Solutions:

- Participate in trusted threat intelligence sharing groups (e.g., FS-ISAC for financial institutions, MS-ISAC for government agencies).
- Use standardized formats like STIX/TAXII to ensure seamless data exchange.
- Anonymize sensitive intelligence before sharing with external partners.

Example in Action:

A retail company detects a credit card skimming attack on its website but hesitates to share intelligence with industry peers due to reputational concerns. By using an anonymous threat-sharing platform, they warn others without revealing their identity.

1.5.6 False Positives and Misleading Intelligence

The Problem:

Not all threat intelligence is accurate or reliable. False positives—incorrectly flagged threats—can lead to:

- Wasted time and resources on non-existent threats.
- Unnecessary security measures that disrupt operations.
- Alert fatigue, causing analysts to overlook real threats.

Possible Solutions:

- Validate intelligence against multiple sources before acting on it.
- Apply risk-based prioritization to avoid unnecessary responses.
- Use automation and AI-driven threat scoring to filter out false positives.

Example in Action:

A threat intelligence feed lists an IP as malicious, prompting a security team to block it. Upon investigation, they realize it's a legitimate cloud service provider, disrupting their own operations.

1.5.7 Resource Constraints and Skill Gaps

The Problem:

Many organizations lack the skilled personnel and resources needed to conduct in-depth threat intelligence investigations. Common challenges include:

- Shortage of trained cybersecurity professionals.
- Limited budgets for threat intelligence tools and infrastructure.
- Time constraints for in-depth analysis.

Possible Solutions:

- Automate routine intelligence tasks (e.g., IOC collection, correlation, and enrichment).
- Invest in training and certification programs for cybersecurity teams.
- Leverage third-party intelligence services when internal resources are insufficient.

Example in Action:

A small business without a dedicated threat intelligence team subscribes to a managed threat intelligence service, allowing them to stay informed about emerging threats without hiring additional staff.

Conclusion: Overcoming Threat Intelligence Challenges

Threat intelligence investigations are complex and dynamic, requiring continuous adaptation to emerging threats. By addressing these common challenges—such as data overload, attribution difficulties, evolving threats, and resource constraints—organizations can enhance their cybersecurity posture and proactively mitigate risks.

A well-structured threat intelligence strategy, combined with automation, collaboration, and skilled analysts, can help organizations transform raw data into actionable intelligence, ensuring they stay ahead of cyber adversaries in an increasingly hostile digital world.

1.6 Case Study: How OSINT Helped Prevent a Major Cyber Attack

Open Source Intelligence (OSINT) has become a critical tool in cyber threat intelligence (CTI), allowing analysts to gather publicly available data to detect and mitigate threats before they escalate. This case study illustrates how OSINT helped prevent a major cyber attack targeting a global financial institution. By leveraging OSINT techniques, threat intelligence analysts identified a coordinated phishing campaign, traced the threat actors, and neutralized the threat before it could cause significant damage.

Phase 1: Initial Discovery – Suspicious Dark Web Chatter

OSINT Detection

A cybersecurity researcher monitoring dark web forums discovered discussions about a planned attack on a major bank. Threat actors were offering phishing kits and stolen employee credentials to other cybercriminals, signaling an imminent attack.

OSINT Sources Used

- **Dark Web Monitoring**: Forums, marketplaces, and Telegram channels.
- **Pastebin & Leak Sites**: Searching for dumped credentials.

- **Threat Intelligence Feeds**: Indicators of compromise (IOCs) from past financial sector attacks.

Key Findings

- A threat actor was selling valid login credentials of employees from the targeted bank.
- The actor also advertised custom phishing kits designed to mimic the bank's login page.
- Conversations suggested the attack was scheduled to launch within days.

Phase 2: Deep Investigation – Identifying the Attack Infrastructure

Tracking the Phishing Campaign

Using OSINT, analysts identified several newly registered domains resembling the bank's official website. These domains were designed to steal login credentials from employees and customers.

OSINT Techniques Used

- **WHOIS Lookup**: To find registration details of suspicious domains.
- **Passive DNS Analysis**: To track connected malicious infrastructure.
- **Google Dorking**: Searching for indexed phishing pages.
- **Social Media Analysis**: Identifying fake customer support accounts targeting victims.

Key Findings

- Several typosquatting domains (e.g., bank-logins[.]com) were registered within the last week.
- The phishing sites used SSL certificates to appear legitimate.
- A Twitter account impersonating the bank's support team was directing customers to the fake login page.

Phase 3: Identifying the Threat Actors

Tracing the Cybercriminals

Analysts used OSINT to link the threat actor's alias to real-world identities by cross-referencing usernames, email addresses, and IP logs.

OSINT Methods Applied

- **Alias and Handle Analysis**: Searching for the hacker's username on different forums.
- **Pwned Credential Checks**: Checking if the attacker's email appeared in past data breaches.
- **Blockchain Analysis**: Tracing cryptocurrency transactions related to phishing kit purchases.

Key Findings

- The hacker had previously sold credentials from other banks.
- Their email address was linked to an old forum post revealing a personal blog.
- A Bitcoin wallet used for phishing kit transactions had ties to a well-known cybercriminal marketplace.

Phase 4: Preventing the Attack

Coordinated Action with Law Enforcement & Security Teams

Armed with intelligence gathered through OSINT, the bank's security team worked with law enforcement and domain registrars to disrupt the attack before it could be launched.

Actions Taken

- **Takedown Requests**: Malicious domains were reported and deactivated.
- **Threat Alerts**: Employees and customers were warned about phishing attempts.
- **Account Resets**: Stolen employee credentials were reset, preventing unauthorized access.
- **Law Enforcement Engagement**: The attacker's real identity was passed to authorities.

Outcome

- The phishing infrastructure was disabled before the attack went live.
- The attacker lost access to compromised credentials.
- The bank prevented millions in potential fraud losses.

Conclusion: OSINT's Role in Proactive Cyber Defense

This case study highlights how OSINT can be a powerful weapon against cyber threats. By continuously monitoring dark web activity, phishing campaigns, and hacker forums, cybersecurity teams can detect, investigate, and neutralize threats before they materialize.

In today's evolving threat landscape, proactive intelligence gathering is essential for preventing cyber attacks—and OSINT is a key component of that strategy.

2. Tracking Cyber Threat Actors & Hacktivists

In this chapter, we explore the methods and tools used to track cyber threat actors, including hackers, hacktivists, and organized cybercriminal groups. These actors can range from individuals exploiting vulnerabilities for personal gain to politically motivated groups disrupting global systems. By examining tactics such as digital footprinting, social media monitoring, and behavioral analysis, we reveal how OSINT can be leveraged to identify patterns, motives, and connections within cyber threat landscapes. Understanding the profiles and activities of these actors is essential for anticipating attacks, mitigating risks, and developing proactive defenses.

2.1 Identifying Threat Actors: Cybercriminals, Hacktivists & Nation-State Groups

Cyber threats come from various adversaries, each with distinct motivations, tactics, and levels of sophistication. Understanding the different types of threat actors—cybercriminals, hacktivists, and nation-state groups—is essential for effective cyber threat intelligence (CTI) and proactive defense.

This section explores how OSINT and CTI analysts identify and track these adversaries by analyzing their tactics, techniques, and procedures (TTPs), online footprints, and digital behaviors.

2.1.1 Cybercriminals: Profit-Driven Threat Actors

Who Are They?

Cybercriminals operate with a primary goal: financial gain. They target businesses, individuals, and governments using tactics such as:

- Ransomware attacks (e.g., LockBit, Conti, BlackCat).
- Phishing and credential theft.
- Dark web fraud (credit card skimming, identity theft, banking fraud).

Common Cybercriminal Groups & Motivations

- **Organized Cybercrime Syndicates**: Highly structured groups engaging in large-scale financial fraud and ransomware operations.
- **Lone Cybercriminals ("Script Kiddies")**: Less sophisticated individuals using pre-built hacking tools.
- **Insider Threats**: Employees who leak data or facilitate cybercrime for personal profit.

How OSINT Helps Track Cybercriminals

- **Dark Web Monitoring**: Tracking hacker forums, marketplaces, and Telegram channels for stolen data and exploits.
- **Bitcoin & Cryptocurrency Analysis**: Tracing ransom payments and illicit transactions.
- **Phishing Kit & Malware Analysis**: Identifying common tools used in attacks.
- **Social Media & Alias Tracking**: Uncovering hacker identities through usernames, emails, and behavioral patterns.

Example: Ransomware Gang Identification

A financial institution detects a ransomware attack encrypting its systems. By analyzing ransom notes, Bitcoin wallet addresses, and malware signatures, OSINT analysts trace the attack back to a Russian-speaking cybercriminal group operating on darknet forums.

2.1.2 Hacktivists: Ideology-Driven Cyber Actors

Who Are They?

Hacktivists conduct cyber attacks to promote political, social, or ideological causes. Unlike cybercriminals, their primary goal is disruption and awareness, rather than financial gain.

Common Hacktivist Tactics

- **DDoS Attacks**: Overloading websites to disrupt services (e.g., Anonymous' operations).
- **Website Defacements**: Altering websites to spread propaganda.
- **Data Leaks & Doxxing**: Exposing private information of governments or corporations.

Notorious Hacktivist Groups & Their Motivations

- **Anonymous**: Targets governments, corporations, and extremist groups for social justice causes.
- **LulzSec**: Disrupts organizations "for the lulz" (entertainment and exposure).
- **Pro-Russian & Pro-Ukraine Hacktivist Groups**: Engage in cyber conflicts during geopolitical crises.

How OSINT Helps Track Hacktivists

- **Monitoring Social Media & Dark Web Forums**: Tracking attack announcements and target discussions.
- **Doxxing & Leak Analysis**: Identifying compromised data before it spreads.
- **Website Defacement Databases**: Detecting digital graffiti and attack attribution.

Example: Anonymous' Attack on a Government Agency

Following a controversial law, a government website is taken offline by a DDoS attack claimed by Anonymous. OSINT analysts monitor hacktivist Telegram groups and Twitter discussions, linking the attack to a specific activist campaign.

2.1.3 Nation-State Groups: Cyber Warfare & Espionage

Who Are They?

Nation-state threat actors are government-sponsored hackers engaging in cyber warfare, espionage, and sabotage. These groups operate with significant resources and capabilities, often targeting critical infrastructure, military systems, and high-profile corporations.

Common Nation-State Cyber Tactics

- **Espionage & Data Theft**: Stealing intellectual property, defense secrets, and political intelligence.
- **Disinformation & Psychological Warfare**: Manipulating public perception via fake news and social media campaigns.
- **Supply Chain Attacks**: Compromising third-party vendors to infiltrate larger targets.

Notorious Nation-State APT Groups & Their Sponsors

- **Russia (APT28 / Fancy Bear, APT29 / Cozy Bear):** Engaged in political hacking, election interference, and cyber warfare.
- **China (APT41, Mustang Panda, Hafnium):** Conducts industrial espionage and cyber spying on global businesses.
- **North Korea (Lazarus Group, Kimsuky):** Focuses on cryptocurrency theft, financial fraud, and espionage.
- **Iran (Charming Kitten, OilRig, APT33):** Targets critical infrastructure and political adversaries.

How OSINT Helps Track Nation-State Actors

- **Malware & Infrastructure Analysis**: Tracking malware signatures, command-and-control (C2) servers, and attack patterns.
- **Attribution via MITRE ATT&CK Framework**: Linking attacks to known APT groups based on tactics.
- **Geopolitical Analysis**: Monitoring international tensions that may trigger cyber conflicts.
- **Social Engineering & Diplomatic Leaks**: Uncovering nation-state tactics via leaked diplomatic documents.

Example: Tracking a Chinese APT Espionage Operation

A U.S. defense contractor detects an advanced cyber intrusion. OSINT analysts trace the attack back to a known Chinese APT group by analyzing malware samples, IP addresses, and historical attack patterns. Intelligence is shared with government agencies to mitigate further threats.

Conclusion: Profiling Cyber Threat Actors with OSINT

Identifying and tracking cyber threat actors requires a deep understanding of their motivations, methods, and attack infrastructures. OSINT is a powerful tool that helps CTI teams monitor dark web activity, analyze attack patterns, and correlate intelligence across multiple sources.

By distinguishing between cybercriminals, hacktivists, and nation-state actors, security professionals can develop tailored threat intelligence strategies—enhancing their ability to detect, prevent, and respond to cyber threats effectively.

2.2 Investigating Threat Actor Handles & Aliases

Threat actors rarely use their real names when engaging in cybercrime, espionage, or hacktivism. Instead, they create handles, aliases, and pseudonyms to mask their identities. However, through OSINT techniques, investigators can uncover the real individuals behind these digital personas.

This section explores how cyber threat intelligence (CTI) analysts track threat actor handles, aliases, and usernames across the dark web, social media, and hacker forums. By cross-referencing publicly available data, analysts can unmask cybercriminals, link them to past activities, and attribute cyber threats to specific groups or individuals.

2.2.1 Understanding Threat Actor Handles & Online Identities

What Are Handles & Aliases?

- **Handles (Usernames):** Unique online identifiers used on hacker forums, dark web marketplaces, social media, and communication platforms.
- **Aliases**: Alternative names or variations of handles used to avoid detection or create multiple identities.
- **Monikers & Signatures**: Custom signatures used in malware, hacking tools, or leaked data dumps.

Why Threat Actors Reuse Handles

Despite efforts to remain anonymous, many cybercriminals reuse handles or patterns across different platforms, making it possible to track their activities. Reasons for reuse include:

- **Reputation & Trust** – In cybercriminal forums, reputation matters. Established hackers need consistent handles to maintain credibility.
- **Operational Mistakes** – Threat actors often accidentally link personal and anonymous accounts.
- **Tool & Forum Limitations** – Some platforms require unique usernames, forcing hackers to keep similar patterns.

Example: A Hacker's Handle Reuse Across Multiple Platforms

A cybercriminal using the handle "DarkWolf77" is found:

- Selling stolen credentials on a dark web marketplace.
- Asking for malware help on a hacker forum.
- Commenting on a public cybersecurity blog using a similar username.
- Registering on a social media platform with an email linked to their dark web activities.

2.2.2 OSINT Techniques for Investigating Threat Actor Handles

1. Username Enumeration & Correlation

By searching for a handle across multiple platforms, investigators can connect accounts and track threat actors.

Tools & Methods:

Google Dorking:

- "DarkWolf77" site:raidforums.com → Finds mentions on hacker forums.
- "DarkWolf77" site:pastebin.com → Checks for leaked data.

OSINT Username Search Engines:

- **WhatsMyName** – Finds usernames across social media and forums.
- **Namechk, KnowEm** – Checks username availability across platforms.
- **Dehashed** – Searches for emails and passwords linked to a username.

Telegram & Discord Scraping:

- Many threat actors use Telegram or Discord for communication. Searching for handles in public groups can expose their activities.

2. Tracking Pseudonyms on Dark Web Forums & Marketplaces

Many cybercriminals discuss hacking, malware, and exploits on darknet forums. Analysts can monitor these forums for:

- Handles linked to illicit activities (e.g., selling stolen data, offering hacking services).

- Transaction histories on underground markets (e.g., Bitcoin payments linked to a handle).
- Patterns in writing styles that match posts across different forums.

3. Cross-Referencing Handles with Data Breaches

Many hackers use the same email, password, or handle across different platforms. Analysts can:

- **Check breach databases** (e.g., HaveIBeenPwned, Dehashed, LeakCheck) to find email-address leaks connected to hacker handles.
- **Search past forum leaks** (e.g., RaidForums database dumps) to uncover real-world identities.

Example: A Cybercriminal Caught by OSINT Handle Tracking

A ransomware operator using "ShadowX" was found selling stolen credentials on a dark web forum. Investigators used OSINT techniques to:

- **Find his email from a leaked database** → It linked to an old GitHub profile.

- **Check GitHub repositories** → Found code similar to malware used in the attack.

- **Cross-check social media** → Discovered his real name on a forgotten LinkedIn profile.

2.2.3 Unmasking Threat Actors Using Behavioral Analysis

Even when hackers change handles, they often:

- Use the same writing style, language, and slang across forums.
- Maintain similar posting times and habits, revealing their time zone or location.
- Reuse profile pictures, avatars, or unique symbols.

Tools for Behavioral Analysis:

- **Stylometry Analysis (Writeprint Tools, JStylo)** – Compares writing styles.
- **Metadata Extraction (ExifTool, FOCA)** – Analyzes hidden data in images or documents posted by hackers.

- **Time Zone Tracking (Hunchly, SpiderFoot HX)** – Estimates location based on post timing.

Example: Linking a Hacker's Multiple Identities

A threat actor known as "GhostByte" on one forum also posted as "CyberPhantom" on another. By analyzing their:

✅ **Writing patterns** – Same phrases and slang were used.
✅ **Time zones** – Posts always appeared between 2 AM - 6 AM UTC, indicating a possible Eastern European location.
✅ **Email footprint** – Both handles were linked to an old email from a leaked breach.

Through these methods, the investigator confirmed both handles belonged to the same hacker.

2.2.4 Investigating Nation-State & APT Handles

Unlike cybercriminals, Advanced Persistent Threat (APT) groups linked to governments often use structured alias systems. These aliases are:

- Used across different attacks but with slight variations.
- Connected to past nation-state campaigns (e.g., malware signatures, tactics).

Examples of APT Handles & Their Groups:

Threat Actor Handle	APT Group	Country	Known Operations
Fancy Bear	APT28	Russia	Election interference, NATO espionage
Cozy Bear	APT29	Russia	SolarWinds hack, government spying
Deep Panda	APT19	China	Intellectual property theft
Lazarus	APT38	North Korea	Cryptocurrency theft, ransomware

OSINT Tracking Techniques for APTs:

- **Malware Hash Analysis (VirusTotal, Hybrid Analysis)** – Checking attack signatures.
- **Infrastructure Fingerprinting (Shodan, Censys)** – Finding C2 servers.
- **Geopolitical Tracking** – Monitoring attacks during political events.

Example: Tracking a Nation-State Hacker's Handle

A handle "RedPhoenix" appeared in cyber espionage campaigns targeting U.S. defense contractors.

- Analysis of malware signatures revealed similarities to past Chinese APT attacks.
- Cross-referencing leaks showed the handle linked to discussions in a Chinese-speaking hacking forum.
- Infrastructure analysis uncovered a C2 server in Beijing, confirming nation-state involvement.

Conclusion: Using OSINT to Expose Threat Actor Identities

Investigating cybercriminals, hacktivists, and nation-state actors starts with tracking their handles and aliases. Using OSINT techniques, analysts can:

✅ Correlate usernames across platforms.

✅ Analyze dark web activity and transaction histories.

✅ Cross-reference data breaches to uncover real identities.

✅ Use behavioral analysis to link multiple aliases.

By effectively unmasking digital adversaries, organizations can better understand cyber threats, attribute attacks, and take action to disrupt malicious actors before they cause damage.

2.3 Monitoring Social Media & Dark Web Communications

Cybercriminals, hacktivists, and nation-state actors frequently use social media and dark web platforms to coordinate attacks, sell stolen data, and share tactics. OSINT analysts and cybersecurity professionals must monitor these channels to detect threats, gather intelligence, and prevent cyber incidents before they escalate.

This chapter explores OSINT techniques for monitoring social media and dark web activity, tools for tracking cyber threats, and real-world case studies demonstrating how threat intelligence can uncover malicious operations.

2.3.1 The Role of Social Media in Cyber Threat Intelligence (CTI)

Why Social Media Matters in Threat Intelligence

Social media platforms—such as Twitter, Facebook, Telegram, Reddit, and Discord—are widely used by:

- Hacktivists to promote cyber campaigns and recruit members.
- Cybercriminals to sell stolen data, malware, and hacking services.
- Nation-state actors to spread disinformation and psychological warfare.
- Insider threats to leak corporate data or discuss vulnerabilities.

Common Cyber Threat Activities on Social Media

- Ransomware groups posting victim data leaks.
- Phishing campaigns disguised as customer support accounts.
- Malware distributors sharing download links via Twitter or Telegram.
- Hacktivists coordinating DDoS attacks in Telegram groups.
- Disinformation campaigns manipulating public opinion.

Example: How Twitter Helped Expose a Cybercriminal Group

A ransomware gang leaked stolen data on Twitter as part of their extortion tactics. OSINT analysts:

- Tracked the group's Twitter activity.
- Identified linked Telegram and dark web forums.
- Collected TTPs (Tactics, Techniques, and Procedures) for attribution.
- This intelligence helped security teams prepare defenses against future attacks.

2.3.2 OSINT Techniques for Monitoring Social Media

1. Keyword & Hashtag Monitoring

Tracking specific keywords, hashtags, and phrases can reveal cyber threats early.

Tools for Social Media Monitoring:

- **TweetDeck, Twitter API** – Real-time keyword tracking.
- **CrowdTangle** – Facebook & Instagram monitoring.

- **Social Searcher** – Searches across multiple social platforms.
- **Hootsuite, Sprinklr** – Automated social media monitoring.

Common Threat Keywords to Track:

- **"#databreach" / "leaked credentials"** – Indicates stolen data being shared.
- **"DDoS-for-hire" / "stresser service"** – Used for hiring cyberattack services.
- **"Ransomware victim list"** – Leaked victim names from ransomware groups.
- **"0-day exploit"** – Discussions about new vulnerabilities.

2. Tracking Threat Actor Accounts & Groups

Cybercriminals often use alternative social media accounts or private groups to coordinate.

Methods for Finding Threat Actor Accounts:

- Reverse image search (Google Lens, Yandex) to track reused profile pictures.
- Username correlation (WhatsMyName, Namechk) to find matching handles across platforms.
- Telegram & Discord group searches for cybercrime discussions.
- OSINT tools (Maltego, SpiderFoot HX) for mapping connections between accounts.

3. Geolocation & Time Zone Analysis

Threat actors' posting patterns, language, and timestamps can reveal:

- Their geographical location.
- Their active time zones.
- Possible links to nation-state actors.

Example: Tracking Hacktivist Activity via OSINT

A hacktivist group threatened to launch cyberattacks on a government website.

- Telegram messages showed attack coordination.
- Analysis of timestamps suggested they were operating in UTC+3 (Eastern Europe).
- Matching usernames on Twitter linked them to past Anonymous operations.

- This intelligence helped cybersecurity teams prepare for the attack in advance.

2.3.3 Investigating Cyber Threats on the Dark Web

What is the Dark Web & Why is it Important?

The dark web is a hidden part of the internet where cybercriminals sell stolen data, discuss hacking techniques, and trade exploits. It requires special tools like Tor and I2P to access.

Dark web forums and marketplaces are key sources for cyber threat intelligence, often revealing:

- Leaked credentials & sensitive corporate data.
- Zero-day exploits & hacking tools for sale.
- Discussions about upcoming cyberattacks.
- Ransomware negotiations & extortion threats.

Common Dark Web Forums & Marketplaces

Platform	Primary Use
RaidForums (defunct)	Data breaches & leaked credentials
Exploit.in	Malware, exploits, and hacking services
BreachForums	Stolen databases & cybercrime discussions
RAMP (Ransomware Marketplace)	Ransomware-as-a-Service (RaaS)
Hydra (defunct)	Darknet financial fraud & illegal goods

OSINT Techniques for Dark Web Monitoring

1. Dark Web Search Engines

- **Ahmia.fi** – Searches indexed Tor websites.
- **OnionLand** – Finds onion links to dark web forums.
- **Dark.fail** – Lists updated dark web marketplace links.

2. Forum & Market Scraping

- **Hunchly** – Captures dark web pages for investigation.

- **TOR Browser + Manual Monitoring** – Investigates hacker discussions.
- **Cybersixgill, DarkOwl, Recorded Future** – Commercial dark web intelligence tools.

3. Cryptocurrency Transaction Analysis

Many cybercriminals use Bitcoin, Monero, or Ethereum for payments. OSINT analysts track:

- Bitcoin wallets linked to ransomware payments.
- Monero transactions used for money laundering.
- Blockchain analysis (via Chainalysis, Elliptic, CipherTrace) to trace illicit funds.

2.3.4 Case Study: Detecting a Ransomware Attack via Dark Web Intelligence

Scenario:

A healthcare company was targeted by a ransomware gang. Before the attack was publicly reported, OSINT analysts identified:

- A dark web forum post offering "access to a major hospital network."
- A Telegram group discussion mentioning an upcoming ransomware operation.
- A Bitcoin wallet transaction linked to previous ransomware payments.

Outcome:

- The company strengthened its security defenses before the attack.
- Law enforcement tracked the threat actors via their cryptocurrency transactions.
- The OSINT team prevented patient data from being leaked.

Conclusion: Leveraging OSINT for Social Media & Dark Web Threat Monitoring

Monitoring social media and dark web communications is critical for cyber threat intelligence. By leveraging OSINT tools and techniques, analysts can:

✓ Detect cyber threats early through social media tracking.

✓ Uncover ransomware, phishing, and hacking operations.

✓ Investigate cybercriminal forums and dark web marketplaces.

✓ Track cryptocurrency transactions linked to cybercrime.

By combining social media OSINT, dark web intelligence, and real-time monitoring, cybersecurity teams can stay ahead of cyber threats, protect organizations, and prevent major cyber incidents before they happen.

2.4 Analyzing OPSEC Mistakes & Tracing Online Identities

Cybercriminals and threat actors go to great lengths to remain anonymous, using VPNs, Tor, burner emails, and encrypted messaging. However, even the most sophisticated adversaries make operational security (OPSEC) mistakes that expose their real identities.

This chapter explores how OSINT analysts leverage these mistakes to track cybercriminals, hacktivists, and nation-state actors. By analyzing digital footprints, reused credentials, and poor security practices, investigators can unmask hidden identities and attribute attacks.

2.4.1 Understanding OPSEC & Why It Fails

What is OPSEC?

Operational Security (OPSEC) refers to practices and strategies used to hide identities, activities, and intentions. Cybercriminals use OPSEC to:

- Avoid detection by law enforcement and cybersecurity researchers.
- Maintain anonymity while engaging in illicit activities.
- Prevent digital and physical attribution.

Common OPSEC Failures by Threat Actors

Despite using privacy-enhancing tools, many cybercriminals make mistakes such as:

- **Username and email reuse** – Using the same alias across multiple platforms.
- **Metadata leaks** – Leaving identifying details in documents, images, or forum posts.
- **Poor VPN or Tor hygiene** – Accidentally accessing accounts from real IP addresses.

- **Using personal accounts for cybercrime** – Mixing real-life and criminal activities.
- **Leaving digital breadcrumbs** – Connecting fake identities with real-world information.

2.4.2 Tracking Cybercriminals Through OPSEC Mistakes

1. Username & Alias Correlation

Threat actors often reuse usernames, handles, and emails across forums, social media, and hacking platforms.

OSINT Tools for Username Correlation:

- **WhatsMyName** – Searches username occurrences across sites.
- **Namechk, KnowEm** – Checks username availability.
- **Dehashed, LeakCheck** – Finds emails linked to username breaches.

Example:

A hacker using the alias "DarkPhantom99" was found:

✅ Selling exploits on a dark web forum.

✅ Asking for hacking advice on a Reddit thread.

✅ Using the same handle on a Twitter account with personal photos.

By correlating these accounts, investigators linked the alias to a real identity.

2. Email & Password Reuse in Data Breaches

Hackers often use the same email address or slightly modified versions across different accounts.

Tracking Methods:

- **HaveIBeenPwned, Dehashed** – Check if an email appears in past breaches.
- **Hunter.io** – Find professional email variations.

Google Dorking:

- **"@gmail.com" site:pastebin.com** – Finds exposed emails.
- **"DarkPhantom99" filetype:txt** – Searches leaked credential dumps.

Example:

A cybercriminal using "hackerx@protonmail.com" was found in a data breach with an old Yahoo email. Searching that Yahoo email uncovered a LinkedIn profile revealing his real name.

3. Image & Metadata Analysis

Hackers unknowingly expose personal details through profile pictures, screenshots, and document metadata.

OSINT Tools for Image & Metadata Analysis:

- **ExifTool, FOCA** – Extract metadata from images/documents.
- **Google Reverse Image Search, Yandex** – Find reused profile pictures.
- **TinEye** – Reverse search for image duplicates.

Example:

A ransomware gang uploaded a "proof of breach" screenshot. Metadata analysis revealed:

✓ Computer username: "Alex-Win10"

✓ Timezone: Eastern European Standard Time

✓ Editor Used: Photoshop 2022 (Russian version)

This information suggested a Russian-based attacker and helped investigators narrow down the suspects.

2.4.3 IP, VPN & Tor Mistakes Leading to Attribution

1. Forgetting to Enable VPN or Tor

Many cybercriminals make a critical mistake by:

- Logging into an anonymous account from their real IP.
- Accessing a dark web market without Tor enabled.
- Posting on a forum while using a traceable home network.

OSINT Tools for IP Tracking:

- **Shodan, Censys** – Scans open servers and exposed IPs.
- **IPinfo.io, MaxMind GeoIP** – Checks IP location details.
- **Hunchly, Maltego** – Maps connections between digital assets.

Example:

A ransomware operator using Tor accidentally accessed his Bitcoin wallet from a home IP. Law enforcement subpoenaed the ISP and linked the wallet to a real person.

2. Leaked Server Infrastructure & Hosting Mistakes

Threat actors hosting phishing sites, malware, or C2 (command-and-control) servers often:

- Forget to mask WHOIS registration details.
- Use personal hosting accounts.
- Reuse hosting services traced to their real identity.

OSINT Techniques to Trace Infrastructure:

- **Whois Lookup (WhoisXML API, ViewDNS.info)** – Finds domain ownership data.
- **Shodan, Censys** – Identifies servers linked to threat actors.
- **PassiveTotal, RiskIQ** – Tracks digital footprints across threat infrastructure.

Example:

A phishing campaign's email headers revealed an IP. Using Shodan, analysts discovered a misconfigured server with an admin login page, exposing the hacker's personal website.

2.4.4 Case Study: Unmasking a Hacker Through OPSEC Failures

Scenario:

A cybercriminal operating under the alias "ShadowRoot" was responsible for multiple credit card fraud schemes.

OSINT Investigation Steps:

Username Reuse

"ShadowRoot" appeared on a hacker forum selling stolen cards.

A similar handle, "ShadowRoot99," was found on a gaming forum with a real email.

Data Breach Cross-Referencing

The email from the gaming forum appeared in a 2017 breach with a real name attached.

Image Analysis

"ShadowRoot" used the same profile picture across multiple platforms.

Reverse image search linked it to an old personal Instagram account.

IP Address Leak

The hacker once logged into the forum without a VPN, exposing a home IP in Canada.

MaxMind GeoIP linked the IP to a specific city and ISP.

Outcome:

✓ Law enforcement identified and arrested "ShadowRoot."
✓ His personal details matched leaked forum credentials.
✓ Bitcoin transactions linked him to fraud activities.

Conclusion: Using OSINT to Trace Cybercriminal Identities

Despite their best efforts, cybercriminals often leave behind small, traceable digital footprints. By leveraging OPSEC mistakes, OSINT analysts can:

✓ Correlate usernames, emails, and leaked credentials.

✓ Analyze image metadata and document leaks.

✓ Track IP addresses and server misconfigurations.

✓ Uncover real identities through behavioral analysis.

By combining multiple OSINT techniques, cybersecurity professionals can unmask cybercriminals, prevent attacks, and attribute cyber threats with high confidence.

2.5 Tracking Hacker Forums & Underground Communities

Hacker forums and underground communities serve as the backbone of the cybercriminal ecosystem. These platforms enable threat actors to exchange hacking tools, sell stolen data, discuss exploits, and coordinate cyberattacks. OSINT analysts and cybersecurity professionals must monitor and infiltrate these spaces to gather intelligence on emerging threats, identify cybercriminals, and predict future attacks.

In this chapter, we will explore OSINT techniques for tracking hacker forums, understanding dark web marketplaces, and extracting valuable intelligence from underground communities.

2.5.1 Understanding the Structure of Hacker Forums

Hacker forums can be classified into three categories:

Forum Type	Description	Examples
Clear Web Forums	Openly accessible forums discussing hacking, exploits, and cybersecurity topics.	XSS.is, HackForums, BreachForums (defunct)
Deep Web Private Forums	Requires registration, vetting, or invitations; often encrypted.	Exploit.in, Cracked.to, RAMP
Dark Web Marketplaces & Forums	Accessible only via Tor or I2P; used for illicit trade (stolen data, malware, ransomware).	Hydra (defunct), AlphaBay, RAMP

These platforms are used by:

- Cybercriminals selling malware, ransomware, and hacking tools.

- Hacktivists organizing attacks and spreading propaganda.
- Nation-state actors recruiting hackers for espionage operations.
- Fraudsters engaging in financial crimes and identity theft.

Understanding forum structures, hierarchy, and reputation systems helps analysts assess the credibility of members and identify high-profile cybercriminals.

2.5.2 OSINT Techniques for Tracking Hacker Forums

1. Identifying & Accessing Underground Communities

Some forums are open, while others require special invites or reputation-based access.

Methods for Discovering Hacker Forums:

Google Dorking:

- **"index of /" "hacking forum"** – Searches for hacking directories.
- **site:pastebin.com "forum invite code"** – Finds forum invitation links.
- **"hacking forums" "Tor link"** – Locates underground Tor-based communities.
- **Telegram & Discord Groups**: Many hacking communities have invite-only Telegram or Discord servers that link back to underground forums.

Dark Web Search Engines:

- **Ahmia.fi** – Searches Tor network for hidden forums.
- **OnionLand Search** – Finds dark web sites.

2. Passive OSINT Monitoring of Forums

Instead of actively participating, analysts can monitor discussions, track emerging threats, and collect intelligence without engaging.

Tools for Passive Monitoring:

- **Hunchly** – Captures and organizes web activity for investigations.
- **Wayback Machine (Archive.org)** – Retrieves deleted forum posts.
- **Cybercrime Intelligence Platforms (DarkOwl, Intel471, Cybersixgill)** – Provides automated tracking of underground communities.

Example:

An OSINT analyst monitoring BreachForums detected a new ransomware group selling access to a corporate database. This intelligence helped the affected company strengthen its security before an attack occurred.

3. Infiltrating Private & Dark Web Forums

Some forums require active engagement to gain access. OSINT investigators may create sock puppet accounts (fake identities) to blend in.

Best Practices for Safe Forum Infiltration:

✅ Use virtual machines (VMs) and sandbox environments to isolate activity.

✅ Always connect through Tor, VPNs, or proxies.

✅ Avoid reusing identifiable usernames, emails, or metadata.

✅ Maintain a consistent backstory to avoid suspicion.

✅ Do not engage in illegal activities—strictly collect intelligence.

Example:

An analyst created a low-profile account on a ransomware forum by engaging in non-suspicious discussions. Over time, they gained access to a restricted section, revealing details about an upcoming cyberattack on a U.S. financial institution.

2.5.3 Extracting Intelligence from Underground Forums

1. Tracking Data Breaches & Leaked Credentials

Hacker forums often leak stolen databases, credentials, and personally identifiable information (PII).

OSINT Techniques for Breach Monitoring:

- **HaveIBeenPwned, Dehashed** – Check if emails or credentials have been exposed.
- **Pastebin & Dark Web Scrapers** – Detect fresh data leaks.
- **Maltego, SpiderFoot** – Visualize connections between leaked accounts.

Example:

A cybercriminal leaked 10,000 corporate email addresses in a Telegram channel. OSINT teams alerted affected companies, preventing phishing attacks.

2. Identifying New Malware & Exploits

Many underground forums serve as marketplaces for zero-day exploits, rootkits, and ransomware.

Tracking Malware Discussions:

- **VirusTotal & Hybrid Analysis** – Scan malware samples from hacker forums.
- **YARA Rules** – Detect new malware strains linked to threat actors.
- **Shodan & Censys** – Identify servers hosting malicious payloads.

Example:

A hacking forum advertised a new banking trojan targeting European financial institutions. Security researchers obtained a malware sample and created signatures to detect and block the threat before widespread attacks.

3. Monitoring Ransomware-as-a-Service (RaaS) Operations

Many hacker forums provide Ransomware-as-a-Service (RaaS), where cybercriminals rent ransomware tools for attacks.

OSINT Techniques for Ransomware Tracking:

- **Follow Bitcoin Transactions**: Blockchain analysis (Elliptic, Chainalysis) tracks ransomware payments.
- **Monitor Negotiation Forums**: Many ransomware groups discuss payments on dark web forums.
- **Identify Affiliates**: RaaS models involve multiple affiliates distributing ransomware.

Example:

A ransomware affiliate mistakenly posted his email in a dark web forum. OSINT teams cross-referenced it with previous cybercrime activity, identifying the attacker.

2.5.4 Case Study: Detecting a Hacker Forum Planning a Cyberattack

Scenario:

A government cybersecurity team detected chatter about a potential cyberattack on critical infrastructure in a hacker forum.

Investigation Process:

Passive OSINT Monitoring:

- Analysts monitored dark web forums and Telegram groups discussing industrial control system (ICS) attacks.

Forum Infiltration:

- An investigator joined a private hacking forum under a sock puppet account.
- They gained access to a restricted section where attack plans were discussed.

Identifying Threat Actors:

- Forum discussions revealed a small group of attackers.
- One member accidentally shared a personal email in a PGP key, linking them to a real-world identity.

Preventing the Attack:

- The intelligence was shared with national cybersecurity agencies.
- The attack was mitigated before it could cause damage.

Outcome:

✓ Threat actors identified.

✓ Attack prevented.

✓ Forum discussions flagged for future monitoring.

Conclusion: Leveraging OSINT to Track Underground Communities

Tracking hacker forums and underground communities is crucial for proactive cybersecurity. By monitoring these spaces, OSINT analysts can:

✓ Detect data breaches and leaked credentials.

✓ Identify emerging malware, exploits, and attack methods.

✓ Monitor ransomware operations and cybercrime trends.

✓ Infiltrate underground networks to gather intelligence.

By using advanced OSINT tools, secure investigative methods, and strategic monitoring, cybersecurity professionals can stay ahead of cybercriminal activities and prevent major cyber threats before they materialize.

2.6 Case Study: Unmasking a Hacktivist Group Through OSINT

Hacktivist groups operate in the shadows, leveraging anonymity to conduct cyberattacks for political, ideological, or social causes. These groups often target governments, corporations, and institutions through DDoS attacks, website defacements, and data leaks. However, despite their efforts to remain anonymous, OSINT techniques can uncover their identities, infrastructure, and operational tactics.

This case study explores how OSINT analysts unmasked a hacktivist group responsible for multiple cyberattacks by analyzing digital footprints, social media activity, OPSEC mistakes, and leaked data.

2.6.1 Background: A Hacktivist Group's Cyber Campaign

A hacktivist group known as "Red Dawn" gained attention for:

✓ Defacing government websites with political messages.

✓ Leaking sensitive corporate emails.

✓ Launching DDoS attacks on critical infrastructure.

Their attacks were widely publicized, but their real identities remained hidden behind pseudonyms, VPNs, and encrypted communications.

Objective:

OSINT analysts aimed to identify key members of Red Dawn, map their online activities, and attribute attacks to real-world identities.

2.6.2 OSINT Investigation Process

Step 1: Analyzing Digital Footprints & Social Media Activity

Hacktivist groups often use Twitter, Telegram, and dark web forums to claim responsibility for attacks.

Methods Used:

🔎 Twitter & Telegram Monitoring

- Analysts tracked hashtags and mentions related to Red Dawn.
- The group's Telegram channel contained coded messages hinting at upcoming attacks.

🔎 Google Dorking for Public Mentions

- "Red Dawn" site:pastebin.com – Searched for leaked data.
- "Red Dawn" filetype:txt – Found manifestos and internal documents.

🔎 Hashtag & Forum Analysis

Using Maltego, investigators mapped interactions between Red Dawn supporters and known hacktivists.

Breakthrough:

One of Red Dawn's social media accounts posted attack details seconds before they happened, suggesting insider knowledge.

Step 2: Tracking OPSEC Mistakes & Alias Reuse

Despite using anonymous handles, Red Dawn members made critical OPSEC errors.

Common OPSEC Mistakes Found:

1️ Username Reuse Across Platforms

- One member used the alias "ShadowX99" on Twitter.
- A similar handle appeared on a gaming forum with a real email.

2️ Leaked Email & IP Logs from Past Breaches

- The email linked to a 2018 data breach containing a personal IP address.
- OSINT tools like Dehashed and HaveIBeenPwned helped correlate the email with real-world accounts.

3️ Metadata in Leaked Files

Red Dawn's manifesto PDF contained metadata revealing:

✅ **Time zone** – Eastern European Standard Time.
✅ **Computer name** – "Sergei-Laptop".
✅ **Software used** – Russian-language PDF editor.

Breakthrough:

The alias "ShadowX99" was linked to a real email from a previous breach, revealing the hacker's real name and location.

Step 3: Identifying Infrastructure & Tracing Servers

Red Dawn hosted leaked data and hacking tools on Tor hidden services and bulletproof hosting providers.

OSINT Techniques Used:

🔎 Whois Lookup & Passive DNS Analysis

- WhoisXML API & ViewDNS were used to track Red Dawn's malicious domains.
- A misconfigured server exposed backend admin credentials.

🔎 Shodan & Censys for IP Tracking

- Analysts scanned the IP infrastructure for links to past cyberattacks.
- A forgotten subdomain linked Red Dawn's darknet site to a real-world hosting provider.

🔎 Bitcoin & Cryptocurrency Tracing

- Red Dawn accepted Bitcoin donations for their hacktivist campaigns.
- Using blockchain analysis tools (Elliptic, Chainalysis), analysts traced transactions to a centralized exchange requiring KYC (Know Your Customer) verification.

Breakthrough:

One hacker accidentally accessed a Red Dawn server without using a VPN, exposing a real IP address traced to a specific country.

Step 4: Correlating Data & Identifying Key Members

By combining all findings, analysts mapped connections between Red Dawn members.

Key Findings:

🔎 **Alias Correlation**: "ShadowX99" was linked to a real identity through past data breaches.

🔎 **Server & Hosting Traces**: A forgotten subdomain revealed a hosting provider tied to a real account.

🔎 **Bitcoin Transactions**: Ransom payments were withdrawn to an exchange requiring ID verification.

🔎 **OPSEC Mistakes**: One hacker forgot to use a VPN, exposing a real IP address.

Outcome:

✅ Law enforcement identified key members of Red Dawn.

✅ Their real-world identities were matched with aliases.

✅ Authorities disrupted the group's operations, preventing future attacks.

2.6.3 Lessons Learned: How OSINT Defeated Hacktivist Anonymity

Key Takeaways from the Investigation:

✅ Hackers always make OPSEC mistakes. Even experienced actors reuse usernames, leak metadata, or forget VPNs.

✅ Monitoring social media & hacker forums provides intelligence. Hacktivists often brag about attacks, leaving breadcrumbs for investigators.

✅ Infrastructure analysis is crucial. WHOIS lookups, passive DNS, and server misconfigurations can unmask hidden networks.

✅ Cryptocurrency transactions can lead to real identities. Many hackers cash out Bitcoin through exchanges that require ID verification.

Conclusion: The Power of OSINT in Cyber Threat Attribution

This case study demonstrates how open-source intelligence (OSINT) can successfully unmask hacktivist groups. Despite using Tor, VPNs, and encrypted communication, Red Dawn members made small OPSEC mistakes that, when combined, revealed their true identities.

By leveraging OSINT tools and techniques, cybersecurity professionals can:

✅ Track hacktivist groups before they launch attacks.

✅ Analyze alias reuse, leaked data, and server infrastructure.

✅ Correlate digital footprints to real-world identities.

✅ Disrupt cyber threats before they escalate.

This case proves that no cybercriminal is truly anonymous—they always leave a trail of evidence waiting to be uncovered.

3. Investigating Data Breaches & Leaked Credentials

In this chapter, we focus on the critical task of investigating data breaches and exposed credentials, which remain some of the most common and devastating cyber threats. By utilizing OSINT techniques, we will uncover how data from breaches spreads across the dark web, social media, and hacker forums, often leading to further exploitation. We'll examine how to track stolen data, assess the scope of breaches, and understand the implications of leaked credentials. This chapter equips you with the skills to identify compromised information, verify its authenticity, and take action to mitigate the risks associated with such breaches.

3.1 The Lifecycle of a Data Breach: From Initial Intrusion to Sale

Data breaches are a lucrative business for cybercriminals, with stolen data fueling a vast underground economy. The lifecycle of a data breach follows a structured process, from the initial intrusion to the sale and exploitation of stolen data. Understanding this lifecycle is crucial for cybersecurity professionals, OSINT analysts, and organizations aiming to prevent, detect, and mitigate breaches before they cause irreparable damage.

This chapter explores the key stages of a data breach, highlighting hacker methodologies, OSINT tracking techniques, and real-world examples of how stolen data moves through the cybercriminal ecosystem.

3.1.1 Stage 1: Initial Intrusion – How Hackers Gain Access

The first step in a data breach is gaining unauthorized access to a system. Cybercriminals use various methods to infiltrate networks, including:

Common Attack Vectors:

☐ **Phishing & Social Engineering** – Attackers trick employees into revealing credentials through fake emails or websites.
☐ **Exploiting Vulnerabilities** – Hackers scan for outdated software with unpatched security flaws.

☐ **Credential Stuffing** – Cybercriminals use leaked usernames/passwords from previous breaches to access other accounts.
☐ **Insider Threats** – Employees may sell access to hackers or leak data intentionally.
☐ **Brute Force Attacks** – Automated tools guess weak passwords to gain entry.

Case Study: Phishing Attack Leads to Data Breach

A hacker sent an email posing as an IT administrator, requesting an employee to "reset their password" via a fake company portal. Once the employee entered credentials, the hacker gained direct access to internal systems, allowing them to extract sensitive customer data.

🔎 **OSINT Tip**: Monitor paste sites (Pastebin, Ghostbin) and underground forums for leaked credentials, as they often surface before a full-scale breach is detected.

3.1.2 Stage 2: Establishing Persistence & Lateral Movement

Once inside, hackers work to maintain access and move deeper into the network to maximize data theft.

Tactics Used by Cybercriminals:

🚩 **Creating Backdoors & Persistence Mechanisms** – Attackers install remote access tools (RATs) or modify system settings to regain entry.
🚩 **Privilege Escalation** – Gaining admin-level access by exploiting misconfigured permissions.
🚩 **Lateral Movement** – Using stolen credentials to navigate from one system to another.
🚩 **Exfiltration Planning** – Identifying the most valuable data (e.g., customer records, financial information, intellectual property).

Case Study: Ransomware Gang Escalates Privileges

A ransomware group infiltrated a company's file server using a weak VPN password. Once inside, they exploited unpatched software to elevate privileges, gaining full administrative control. The attackers remained undetected for weeks before launching their attack.

🔎 **OSINT Tip**: Use tools like Shodan and Censys to scan for exposed systems that hackers might target.

3.1.3 Stage 3: Data Exfiltration – Stealing Sensitive Information

Hackers extract data without triggering security alarms by using stealth techniques.

Methods of Data Theft:

 Encrypted Tunneling – Attackers use VPNs or Tor to mask data transfers.
 Cloud-Based Storage – Stolen files are uploaded to Dropbox, Mega, or OneDrive.
 Slow Drip Exfiltration – Data is leaked in small chunks to avoid detection.
 Remote Command & Control (C2) Servers – Hackers use C2 servers to control data flow.

Case Study: Credit Card Data Stolen via Web Skimming

Hackers compromised an online store by injecting malicious JavaScript that stole customer credit card details at checkout. The stolen data was sent to a remote server in real time and later sold on dark web markets.

 OSINT Tip: Track emerging data leaks on Telegram and hacker forums to detect breaches early.

3.1.4 Stage 4: Monetization – Selling or Ransoming Stolen Data

Once data is exfiltrated, cybercriminals monetize it through various illegal markets.

How Stolen Data is Sold:

 Dark Web Marketplaces – Sites like AlphaBay and Hydra host stolen credentials, credit card data, and full identity profiles.
 Ransomware & Extortion – Attackers demand a ransom from victims in exchange for not leaking sensitive data.
 Corporate Espionage – Stolen trade secrets are sold to competitors or nation-states.
 Financial Fraud & Identity Theft – Criminals use stolen data for bank fraud, fake loans, and SIM swapping.

Case Study: Healthcare Records Sold on the Dark Web

A hacker infiltrated a hospital's electronic medical records system and stole patient data. The stolen records were later sold on a dark web forum for $50 per patient profile, allowing buyers to commit insurance fraud.

🔎 **OSINT Tip**: Use dark web crawlers (e.g., DarkOwl, Intel471) to monitor forums and marketplaces where stolen data appears.

3.1.5 Stage 5: Post-Breach Impact & Incident Response

The final stage of a breach involves victims discovering the attack, responding, and recovering.

Impact of Data Breaches:

📉 **Financial Losses** – Regulatory fines, lawsuits, and business losses.
☐ **Reputational Damage** – Loss of customer trust.
☐ **Operational Disruption** – Systems taken offline for forensic analysis.
⚖️ **Legal Consequences** – GDPR, CCPA, and other data protection laws impose penalties.

Incident Response Measures:

✅ **Forensic Investigation** – Identifying attack vectors and patching vulnerabilities.
✅ **Dark Web Monitoring** – Checking if stolen data is being traded.
✅ **Threat Intelligence Sharing** – Alerting cybersecurity networks (ISACs, CERTs).
✅ **Implementing Stronger Security Controls** – Multi-factor authentication (MFA), endpoint detection and response (EDR), and stricter access controls.

Case Study: A Company Responds to a Data Breach

After a data breach exposed 5 million customer records, the affected company monitored dark web markets for its stolen data and worked with law enforcement to take down the responsible hacker group.

🔎 **OSINT Tip**: Utilize BreachAlert services to detect when your organization's data appears in leaks.

Conclusion: How OSINT Can Track & Prevent Data Breaches

By understanding the lifecycle of a data breach, cybersecurity professionals can proactively:

✅ Detect vulnerabilities before they are exploited.

✅ Track hacker activity on underground forums.

✅ Monitor for stolen credentials and leaked databases.

✅ Respond quickly to mitigate damage.

OSINT plays a critical role in identifying breaches at every stage—from early warning signs to tracking stolen data on dark web marketplaces. By leveraging OSINT tools and investigative techniques, organizations can stay ahead of cybercriminals and protect their sensitive information.

3.2 Investigating Breach Data with OSINT Tools

Data breaches expose sensitive personal and corporate information, fueling cybercrime, fraud, and identity theft. OSINT (Open-Source Intelligence) tools play a crucial role in tracking, analyzing, and mitigating breaches by identifying leaked credentials, financial data, and corporate records.

This chapter explores how cybersecurity analysts use OSINT tools to investigate breach data, uncover hacker tactics, and protect individuals and organizations from further exploitation.

3.2.1 Understanding Breach Data & Its Impact

Types of Data Found in Breaches:

🔐 **Credentials** – Emails, usernames, and passwords used for credential stuffing attacks.
💳 **Financial Information** – Credit card details, banking records, and payment transaction logs.
🪪 **Personal Identifiable Information (PII)** – Names, addresses, phone numbers, social security numbers.
📧 **Corporate Documents & Emails** – Internal reports, intellectual property, sensitive communications.

Impact of Breach Data Exposure:

⚠ **Identity Theft** – Stolen PII is used to create fake identities or commit fraud.

⚠ **Business Espionage** – Competitors or threat actors use stolen corporate data.

⚠ **Account Takeovers (ATOs)** – Cybercriminals exploit leaked credentials for unauthorized access.

⚠ **Extortion & Ransom Demands** – Hackers threaten to publish stolen data unless a ransom is paid.

🔎 **OSINT Tip**: Monitoring breach data in real-time helps prevent cybercriminals from exploiting stolen information before affected organizations take action.

3.2.2 OSINT Tools for Breach Data Investigation

1. Have I Been Pwned (HIBP) – Identifying Compromised Credentials

🔍 **Website**: https://haveibeenpwned.com

- Checks if an email or username appears in known data breaches.
- Allows security teams to warn affected users and enforce password resets.

Example Use Case:

An organization detects unauthorized logins on employee accounts. Using HIBP, they discover several employees' emails were exposed in a past LinkedIn breach, allowing attackers to attempt password reuse.

2. DeHashed – Deep Breach Data Search

🔍 **Website**: https://www.dehashed.com

- Searches breached data for emails, usernames, phone numbers, and passwords.
- Provides access to hashed & plaintext credentials from past breaches.

Example Use Case:

An OSINT investigator tracks a hacker alias from a Telegram forum. By searching the alias in DeHashed, they find an old email account, revealing a possible real identity linked to previous breaches.

3. IntelX – Searching Dark Web & Paste Sites

🔍 **Website**: https://intelx.io

- Indexes dark web forums, paste sites, and leaked databases.
- Useful for finding early breach data leaks before full disclosures.

Example Use Case:

A security team suspects a sensitive database was leaked but finds no evidence on mainstream platforms. Searching IntelX reveals fragments of leaked records on pastebin-style sites.

4. BreachForums (Dark Web Monitoring)

🔍 **Access**: Darknet forums (TOR needed)

- Cybercriminals sell and trade breach data on underground marketplaces.
- Monitoring these forums helps detect new breaches before they become public.

Example Use Case:

A financial institution monitors dark web forums and discovers customer credit card data for sale, indicating a recent breach. This intelligence helps the institution alert affected customers and prevent fraud.

5. Shodan & Censys – Identifying Vulnerable Systems

🔍 **Website**: https://www.shodan.io | https://censys.io

- Finds exposed servers, databases, and IoT devices that may have contributed to a data breach.
- Detects misconfigured MongoDB, Elasticsearch, and RDP services used in past attacks.

Example Use Case:

A company discovers its customer database was leaked. By searching Shodan, they find an unprotected Elasticsearch instance, confirming the breach's origin.

3.2.3 Tracing Stolen Data & Attributing Breaches

1. Reverse Image & Document Metadata Analysis

☐ **Tools**: Google Reverse Image Search, ExifTool, Tineye

- Analyzes leaked document metadata to identify the author, timestamp, and device details.
- Finds duplicate images of leaked data, tracking it across different platforms.

🔎 **OSINT Tip**: Leaked PDFs may contain hidden metadata, revealing the hacker's time zone, software used, or even the computer's username.

2. Cryptocurrency Transaction Tracking

💰 **Tools**: Chainalysis, Elliptic, BitcoinWhosWho

- Tracks ransom payments from data breach extortion cases.
- Identifies wallet addresses linked to dark web transactions.

Example Use Case:

A ransomware gang demands Bitcoin for not publishing stolen customer data. By tracing the Bitcoin address, analysts find past transactions linked to other attacks, helping law enforcement track the perpetrators.

3. Domain & Hosting Analysis

☐ **Tools**: WhoisXML API, PassiveTotal, RiskIQ

- Investigates domains hosting leaked breach data.
- Identifies threat actor infrastructure linked to previous cyberattacks.

🔎 **OSINT Tip**: Hackers often reuse infrastructure across multiple campaigns, making domain correlation a powerful attribution method.

3.2.4 Real-World OSINT Investigation: Tracking a Data Breach

Case Study: Investigating a Government Data Leak

A government agency discovered sensitive employee data leaked online. Using OSINT tools, analysts followed these steps:

1⃣ Step 1: Identifying the Breach Source

- Used Shodan to scan for exposed databases.
- Found an open MongoDB instance with weak authentication.

2⃣ Step 2: Tracking Leaked Data

- Used IntelX & DeHashed to search paste sites for matching records.
- Found leaked email/password pairs posted on BreachForums.

3⃣ Step 3: Attributing the Attack

- Used WHOIS lookup & Passive DNS to track the attacker's infrastructure.
- Found connections to past cybercriminal activity from Eastern Europe.

4⃣ Step 4: Preventing Further Damage

- Agency forced password resets and secured the exposed database.
- Intelligence was shared with law enforcement to track the threat actor.

🔎 Outcome:

✅ Early breach detection prevented further data exploitation.

✅ OSINT investigation helped identify the hacker group responsible.

✅ The agency enhanced its security posture to prevent future attacks.

Conclusion: The Power of OSINT in Breach Investigations

🔹 OSINT tools enable rapid identification and response to data breaches.
🔹 Dark web monitoring helps detect stolen data before it's widely exploited.
🔹 Tracking credentials & infrastructure provides attribution to cybercriminals.
🔹 Proactive breach investigations prevent cybercriminals from profiting at scale.

By leveraging OSINT techniques, analysts can mitigate the impact of data breaches, protect victims, and disrupt the underground economy that thrives on stolen information.

3.3 Using Data Leak Search Engines & Breach Databases

Data leak search engines and breach databases play a crucial role in investigating compromised credentials, corporate leaks, and stolen personal information. Cybercriminals trade and sell breached data on the dark web, hacker forums, and Telegram channels, making it essential for OSINT analysts and cybersecurity professionals to proactively monitor and track leaked data.

This chapter explores how to use data leak search engines, breach databases, and dark web monitoring tools to identify, analyze, and mitigate threats from exposed information.

3.3.1 Understanding Data Leak Search Engines & Their Purpose

What Are Data Leak Search Engines?

🔎 Data leak search engines index stolen or exposed data from breaches, dark web sources, and open repositories, allowing analysts to:

✓ Search compromised emails, passwords, phone numbers, and company records.

✓ Identify leaked databases before they are widely exploited.

✓ Trace hacker activity through reused credentials and aliases.

✓ Prevent account takeovers (ATOs) and unauthorized access.

How Cybercriminals Use Leaked Data

⚠ **Credential Stuffing** – Using stolen username-password pairs to access other accounts.
⚠ **Phishing & Social Engineering** – Leveraging exposed personal details to create targeted scams.
⚠ **Identity Theft & Fraud** – Using leaked PII (e.g., social security numbers, driver's license data) to create fraudulent accounts.
⚠ **Corporate Espionage** – Selling sensitive business information to competitors or nation-state actors.

🔎 **OSINT Tip**: Regularly monitoring breach databases helps organizations detect compromised credentials early and enforce security measures before attackers exploit them.

3.3.2 Top Data Leak Search Engines & Breach Databases

1. Have I Been Pwned (HIBP)

🔍 **Website**: https://haveibeenpwned.com

- One of the most widely used breach databases.
- Allows users to check if an email, username, or password has been exposed in past breaches.
- API access for corporate security teams to automate breach monitoring.

Example Use Case:

A company checks if employee emails appear in any breaches and forces password resets to prevent unauthorized access.

2. DeHashed

🔍 **Website**: https://www.dehashed.com

- Searches leaked credentials, PII, and corporate data.
- Supports queries for emails, usernames, IP addresses, and even hashed passwords.
- Useful for tracking hacker aliases across multiple breaches.

Example Use Case:

An OSINT analyst tracks a hacker alias from a dark web forum and uses DeHashed to uncover past breached email accounts linked to the same alias.

3. IntelX

🔍 **Website**: https://intelx.io

- Indexes dark web marketplaces, paste sites, and leaked documents.

- Supports searches for email addresses, domain names, phone numbers, and Bitcoin addresses.
- Archives deleted pastebin posts often used for leaking breach data.

Example Use Case:

A financial institution suspects leaked customer records. By searching IntelX, they find banking details posted on a dark web forum.

4. SnusBase

🔍 **Website**: https://snusbase.com

- Similar to DeHashed, SnusBase provides advanced breach data search capabilities.
- Allows searches for emails, usernames, IP addresses, and hashed passwords.
- Often includes breaches that are not publicly disclosed.

Example Use Case:

A cybersecurity firm uses SnusBase to find stolen login credentials of executives, allowing them to enforce immediate security actions.

5. LeakCheck

🔍 **Website**: https://leakcheck.io

- Provides real-time monitoring of leaked credentials.
- Paid API access for organizations to automate breach detection.
- Useful for tracking ongoing dark web leaks and credential dumps.

Example Use Case:

A company integrates LeakCheck into its security infrastructure, alerting employees whenever their credentials appear in new breach data.

3.3.3 Using Dark Web Monitoring for Breach Data Investigations

Many high-profile breaches first appear on dark web forums and marketplaces before they are publicly disclosed. Monitoring these sources allows early detection of stolen data.

1. Monitoring Dark Web Forums

🔦 **Key Dark Web Marketplaces:**

☐ **BreachForums (formerly RaidForums)** – Used by cybercriminals to sell and trade stolen databases.
☐ **Genesis Market** – Specializes in stolen browser fingerprints and login credentials.
☐ **Exploit.in & XSS** – Russian-language forums focused on selling corporate breach data.

🔎 **OSINT Tip**: Use TOR-based crawlers like DarkOwl or Flashpoint to track stolen databases in underground communities.

2. Telegram Channels & Discord Servers

📢 Many cybercriminals now use Telegram and Discord to sell breach data in private groups.

🔍 **Tools to Monitor:**

▦ **TgScanBot** – Monitors public Telegram groups for breach-related keywords.
▦ **Hunchly** – Captures investigative screenshots of Telegram leaks before they disappear.
▦ **Cytelligence Dark Web Monitoring** – Automates breach detection across Telegram, Discord, and private forums.

Example Use Case:

A cybersecurity firm tracks Telegram channels selling fresh breach data and reports the findings to affected organizations.

3.3.4 Investigating Leaked Data for Attribution & Response

1. Identifying Threat Actor Patterns

- Many cybercriminals reuse email addresses and usernames across breaches.
- OSINT analysts cross-reference leaked credentials to track the same hacker across multiple attacks.

🔎 **OSINT Tip**: Use BreachDB searches to correlate threat actor aliases with historical breaches.

2. Monitoring for New Data Leaks

- Security teams should proactively monitor breached data to detect compromised accounts before cybercriminals exploit them.
- Automated API integrations allow organizations to receive breach alerts in real-time.

🔎 **Example Tool**: The HIBP API enables automated alerts when a new breach affects corporate email domains.

3.3.5 Case Study: Stopping a Cyberattack Using Breach Data Search

Incident:

A financial services firm discovered suspicious login attempts on executive accounts.

Investigation Steps:

1️ Breach Database Search:

- The firm's CISO used DeHashed to search executive emails.
- Found that several credentials were exposed in a LinkedIn breach.

2️ Dark Web Forum Monitoring:

- Analysts searched BreachForums and found a hacker selling company login credentials.
- The forum post revealed corporate emails and hashed passwords.

3️ Mitigation & Response:

✅ Immediate password resets for all affected accounts.

✅ Enabled Multi-Factor Authentication (MFA) for executive logins.

☑️ Threat intelligence report shared with law enforcement to track the attacker.

🔎 **Outcome**: The attack was stopped before cybercriminals could exploit the stolen credentials, preventing financial loss and data exposure.

Conclusion: Why OSINT-Driven Breach Investigations Are Critical

✔ Proactively monitoring breach databases prevents cyberattacks before they happen.

✔ Dark web and Telegram tracking help detect stolen data before public disclosure.

✔ Using OSINT tools like HIBP, DeHashed, and IntelX strengthens breach investigations.

✔ Investigating leaked credentials can lead to threat actor attribution and law enforcement action.

By leveraging data leak search engines and breach databases, security professionals can stay ahead of cybercriminals, mitigate risks, and protect both individuals and organizations from exploitation.

3.4 Analyzing Stolen Credentials & Their Impact

Stolen credentials are one of the most valuable commodities in cybercrime. Hackers use compromised usernames and passwords to gain unauthorized access to corporate networks, financial accounts, and critical infrastructure. Analyzing stolen credentials is crucial for understanding the scope of a breach, identifying attack vectors, and mitigating further risks.

This chapter explores how OSINT tools and techniques can be used to analyze leaked credentials, their impact on individuals and organizations, and how attackers exploit them for financial gain, espionage, and cyber extortion.

3.4.1 How Credentials Are Stolen & Traded

Common Ways Credentials Are Compromised

🔒 **Phishing Attacks** – Users are tricked into entering login details on fake websites.

🔒 **Malware & Keyloggers** – Trojans, spyware, and infostealers capture keystrokes and login data.

🔒 **Data Breaches** – Massive leaks expose usernames, emails, and passwords.

🔒 **Credential Stuffing Attacks** – Hackers use previously stolen credentials to access other accounts.

🔒 **Dark Web Marketplaces** – Criminals buy and sell login details in underground forums.

How Cybercriminals Exploit Stolen Credentials

⚠ **Account Takeover (ATO):** Hackers access personal and corporate accounts for fraud.

⚠ **Ransomware Deployment:** Attackers use stolen credentials to move laterally in networks.

⚠ **Business Email Compromise (BEC):** Stolen executive credentials are used to launch phishing and wire fraud schemes.

⚠ **Espionage & Blackmail:** Nation-state actors target high-profile individuals for intelligence gathering.

🔎 **OSINT Tip:** Monitoring leaked credentials on breach databases and the dark web helps identify at-risk accounts before attackers exploit them.

3.4.2 Using OSINT Tools to Analyze Stolen Credentials

1. Have I Been Pwned (HIBP) – Checking for Breached Credentials

🔍 **Website:** https://haveibeenpwned.com

- Identifies if an email or username has appeared in past breaches.
- Helps organizations force password resets for affected employees.

Example Use Case:

A company runs its domain through HIBP and finds that several employee emails were exposed in a past Dropbox breach, leading to unauthorized VPN access attempts.

2. DeHashed – Searching for Stolen Passwords

🔍 **Website:** https://www.dehashed.com

- Searches breach databases for leaked passwords, emails, and usernames.

- Identifies historical breaches linked to a specific user.

Example Use Case:

A cybersecurity team searches a suspected hacker's alias in DeHashed and finds old passwords linked to an unsecured PayPal account, leading to financial fraud investigations.

3. IntelX – Dark Web & Paste Site Analysis

🔍 **Website**: https://intelx.io

- Searches leaked credentials on paste sites and the dark web.
- Useful for early breach detection before stolen credentials are widely exploited.

Example Use Case:

A financial institution finds customer account details leaked on a dark web forum via IntelX, allowing them to warn customers and prevent fraud.

4. SnusBase – Advanced Credential Analysis

🔍 **Website**: https://snusbase.com

- Searches leaked usernames, emails, and IP addresses in breach databases.
- Supports reverse lookup for phone numbers linked to stolen accounts.

Example Use Case:

An OSINT investigator tracks a cybercriminal's phone number found in a SnusBase query, linking it to multiple compromised accounts on gaming platforms.

3.4.3 Identifying Credential Reuse & Password Weaknesses

1. Credential Stuffing & Password Recycling

Many users reuse the same password across multiple sites, making credential stuffing a major threat.

● **Example**: A password leaked from a 2019 Dropbox breach might still work for a user's Netflix or banking account today.

🔎 **OSINT Tip**: Use Pwned Passwords API (https://haveibeenpwned.com/Passwords) to check if a password has been previously exposed in breaches.

2. Hash Cracking & Weak Passwords

Many breaches contain hashed (encrypted) passwords. If an attacker cracks the hash, they can use the plaintext password to access other accounts.

🔒 Hash Cracking Tools Used by Hackers:

◆ **Hashcat** – Fast password recovery and brute-force tool.
◆ **John the Ripper** – Cracks weak password hashes from breaches.
◆ **Rainbow Tables** – Precomputed hash lists for fast cracking of common passwords.

Example Use Case:

A leaked database contains MD5-hashed passwords. A hacker uses Hashcat to crack weak hashes, revealing the plaintext passwords and leading to further exploitation.

3.4.4 Case Study: How Stolen Credentials Led to a Major Cyberattack

Incident:

A Fortune 500 company suffered a massive data breach after attackers gained unauthorized access to their VPN.

Investigation Steps:

1️⃣ Credential Leak Discovery

- OSINT analysts searched breach databases (DeHashed, SnusBase) for stolen employee credentials.
- Found that an IT administrator's email was exposed in a past breach.

2️⃣ Password Reuse & Credential Stuffing Attack

- The IT admin had reused the same password across multiple accounts.
- Hackers used credential stuffing to access the company's VPN.

3️⃣ Data Exfiltration & Ransomware Deployment

- Attackers exfiltrated sensitive corporate data.
- Later, they deployed ransomware to encrypt critical business files.

🔎 Outcome:

✅ The breach investigation revealed poor password management policies.

✅ The company enforced two-factor authentication (2FA) to prevent future attacks.

✅ Incident response teams worked with law enforcement to track the cybercriminal group.

3.4.5 Mitigating the Impact of Stolen Credentials

Best Practices for Individuals & Organizations

🔐 **Use Unique Passwords** – Never reuse passwords across different accounts.
🔐 **Enable Multi-Factor Authentication (MFA)** – Prevents attackers from logging in with stolen credentials.
🔐 **Monitor for Breaches** – Use HIBP, DeHashed, and IntelX to check if your credentials have been leaked.
🔐 **Rotate Compromised Passwords** – Immediately reset passwords found in breach databases.
🔐 **Educate Employees on Phishing Risks** – Prevents credentials from being stolen in the first place.

🔎 **OSINT Tip**: Regular breach monitoring and dark web intelligence gathering help organizations detect threats early and prevent large-scale cyberattacks.

Conclusion: Why Credential Analysis Is Critical for Cybersecurity

✔ Stolen credentials fuel cybercrime, leading to account takeovers, fraud, and espionage.

✓ OSINT tools like DeHashed, IntelX, and SnusBase help track and investigate breached passwords.

✓ Analyzing password reuse patterns helps prevent credential stuffing attacks.

✓ Mitigating credential leaks through strong authentication and security awareness is essential.

By leveraging OSINT-driven credential analysis, cybersecurity teams can reduce risks, strengthen defenses, and prevent attackers from exploiting compromised accounts.

3.5 Identifying Patterns in Credential Reuse & Password Cracking

Credential reuse is one of the most exploited weaknesses in cybersecurity. Many individuals and even organizations reuse passwords across multiple accounts, making them vulnerable to credential stuffing attacks, brute-force attempts, and password cracking techniques. Threat actors leverage previously breached credentials, weak password patterns, and automated tools to gain unauthorized access to accounts and corporate networks.

This chapter explores how to identify credential reuse patterns, analyze stolen passwords, and understand password cracking techniques used by hackers. By leveraging OSINT tools and methodologies, cybersecurity professionals can detect vulnerabilities, prevent unauthorized access, and mitigate the impact of exposed credentials.

3.5.1 Understanding Credential Reuse & Its Risks

What is Credential Reuse?

Credential reuse occurs when a user or an organization uses the same username-password combination across multiple platforms. If one account is compromised, all accounts using the same credentials become vulnerable.

How Attackers Exploit Credential Reuse

● **Credential Stuffing Attacks**: Hackers use stolen username-password pairs to access multiple services.

● **Account Takeovers (ATO):** Cybercriminals gain control of personal or business accounts.

● **Business Email Compromise (BEC):** Attackers use compromised corporate emails for phishing and financial fraud.

● **Espionage & Lateral Movement**: Nation-state actors use breached credentials to infiltrate networks.

🔎 **OSINT Tip**: Monitoring breach data for reused passwords helps organizations detect security risks before attackers exploit them.

3.5.2 Identifying Credential Reuse Patterns

1. Tracking Password Reuse Across Data Breaches

OSINT tools can cross-reference email addresses and usernames across multiple breaches to identify reused passwords.

🔍 **Example:**

A user's credentials were exposed in a LinkedIn breach in 2012. If the same password is used on Facebook or a corporate VPN, hackers can gain access through credential stuffing.

☐ **Tools to Detect Credential Reuse:**

✓ **Have I Been Pwned (HIBP)** – Checks if an email or password appears in past breaches.

✓ **DeHashed** – Searches breach databases for email-password reuse.

✓ **SnusBase** – Tracks usernames and hashed passwords across multiple leaks.

🔎 **OSINT Tip**: Organizations should force password resets for employees whose credentials have been exposed in past breaches.

2. Identifying Common Password Patterns

Many users create passwords based on predictable patterns, making them easy to crack.

🔑 Common Weak Password Patterns:

- **Personal Information**: Birthdays, names, addresses (e.g., John1987, Miami123).
- **Keyboard Sequences**: Simple patterns (qwerty, 123456, abcdef).
- **Common Phrases**: Repeated words (password1, letmein, iloveyou).
- **Site-Specific Variations**: Using the same root password with slight modifications (GooglePass123, FacebookPass123).

🔎 **OSINT Tip**: Password entropy analysis can reveal how users construct their passwords and predict reused variations.

3.5.3 How Hackers Crack Passwords

1. Brute Force Attacks

Hackers attempt every possible password combination until they find the correct one.

◆ Tools Used:

✓ **Hydra** – Automated brute-force tool for SSH, FTP, and web logins.

✓ **Medusa** – Performs large-scale brute-force attacks.

✓ **Ncrack** – Targets remote authentication services like RDP and MySQL.

🔎 **Defense**: Enforce account lockouts after multiple failed login attempts.

2. Dictionary Attacks

Instead of trying every combination, attackers use precompiled lists of common passwords.

◆ Popular Wordlists:

✓ **RockYou.txt** – Contains millions of leaked passwords.

✓ **SecLists** – Open-source password dictionary for penetration testing.

✓ **CrackStation** – Huge database of common passwords.

🔎 **Defense**: Use passwords that do not exist in leaked datasets.

3. Hash Cracking

When passwords are stored as hashes, attackers use hash cracking tools to decrypt them.

◆ **Hash Cracking Tools:**

✓ **Hashcat** – GPU-accelerated password recovery tool.

✓ **John the Ripper** – Cracks weak password hashes.

✓ **Rainbow Tables** – Precomputed hash values used to break encrypted passwords.

🔎 **Defense**: Use strong encryption algorithms (bcrypt, PBKDF2, Argon2) for password hashing.

3.5.4 Case Study: Tracking a Cybercriminal Using Password Reuse

Incident:

An OSINT investigation revealed that a cybercriminal was using the same password across multiple services.

Investigation Steps:

1️ Breach Data Search

- Investigators used DeHashed to find the hacker's email in multiple leaks.
- Found that the same password appeared in different breaches.

2️ Dark Web Analysis

- The hacker's credentials were found on BreachForums.
- Investigators linked the same password to different usernames across multiple platforms.

3️ Attribution & Law Enforcement Action

- The reused password helped OSINT analysts track the hacker's activity across multiple websites.
- Law enforcement linked the credentials to illegal activities and arrested the cybercriminal.

🔎 **Outcome**: Identifying password reuse helped investigators unmask the hacker's real identity.

3.5.5 Best Practices to Prevent Credential Reuse & Password Attacks

For Individuals

✅ **Use a Password Manager** – Generates and stores unique passwords for every account.

✅ **Enable Multi-Factor Authentication (MFA)** – Prevents unauthorized access even if a password is stolen.

✅ **Monitor for Leaked Credentials** – Regularly check HIBP and DeHashed for breach alerts.

For Organizations

✅ **Implement Strong Password Policies** – Require long, complex passwords that do not follow predictable patterns.

✅ **Regularly Rotate Credentials** – Prevents attackers from using old breached passwords.

✅ **Use Breach Monitoring Services** – Detects stolen corporate credentials before they are exploited.

🔎 **OSINT Tip**: Automating breach monitoring and enforcing MFA can stop credential stuffing attacks before they happen.

Conclusion: Why Credential Reuse Analysis Is Critical

✔ Credential reuse remains one of the biggest cybersecurity risks.

✔ Hackers exploit reused passwords to take over accounts and infiltrate networks.

✔ Analyzing leaked credentials helps track cybercriminals and prevent further attacks.

✓ Using OSINT tools for breach monitoring can detect threats before they escalate.

By identifying password reuse patterns, strengthening authentication security, and leveraging OSINT-driven breach analysis, organizations and individuals can mitigate cyber risks and protect sensitive accounts from exploitation.

3.6 Case Study: Tracking a Corporate Data Breach & Its Aftermath

Corporate data breaches can have devastating consequences, leading to financial losses, reputational damage, regulatory fines, and cyber extortion. Tracking how a breach occurs, how stolen data spreads, and how organizations respond provides valuable insights into cyber threat intelligence (CTI) and OSINT techniques.

In this case study, we will analyze a real-world corporate data breach, step through the investigative process using OSINT tools and methodologies, and examine the aftermath, including mitigation efforts, legal consequences, and long-term impact.

3.6.1 The Incident: A Fortune 500 Company Breach

Background

A multinational corporation in the financial sector suffered a massive data breach, exposing millions of customer records, sensitive financial data, and internal communications.

◆ **Target**: Fortune 500 Financial Services Company
◆ **Attack Vector**: Compromised employee credentials
◆ **Data Exposed**: Personally Identifiable Information (PII), financial transactions, and internal emails
◆ **Threat Actor**: A cybercriminal group specializing in ransomware and data leaks

3.6.2 Initial Signs of the Breach

The breach first became evident when:

● Customers reported unauthorized transactions linked to their accounts.

● Security researchers detected leaked corporate emails on dark web forums.
● A threat actor advertised stolen data on a ransomware extortion website.

OSINT Discovery

Investigators used dark web monitoring tools to locate posts about the breach.

☐ **Tools Used:**

✓ **IntelX & DarkOwl** – Found leaked employee credentials and internal documents.

✓ **DeHashed & SnusBase** – Checked for reused passwords and employee email leaks.

✓ **Twitter & Telegram Monitoring** – Detected hackers discussing the breach.

🔎 **OSINT Tip**: Tracking early signs of a breach on underground forums can help companies respond before widespread exploitation.

3.6.3 Investigating the Attack: How the Breach Happened

Step 1: Identifying the Initial Attack Vector

🔍 **Findings**: Hackers gained access through a compromised VPN account belonging to an IT administrator.
🔍 **Cause**: The password was exposed in a previous data breach and reused for remote access.

Step 2: Lateral Movement & Data Exfiltration

After breaching the VPN, the attackers:

● Escalated privileges using outdated software vulnerabilities.
● Exfiltrated sensitive customer and financial records to an offshore server.
● Deployed ransomware to encrypt internal files and demand payment.

🔎 **Key Indicator**: The attackers operated undetected for weeks, exploiting weak security policies.

3.6.4 Tracing Stolen Data on the Dark Web

Tracking the Sale of Breached Data

After the data theft, the cybercriminals:

- Posted samples of stolen customer data on dark web marketplaces.
- Advertised the breach on Telegram hacker channels and Twitter leak accounts.
- Attempted to sell full databases to other threat actors.

OSINT Investigation Findings

☐ **Dark Web Tools Used:**

✓ **IntelX** – Found employee emails in past breaches.

✓ **DarkOwl & Recon-ng** – Tracked mentions of stolen data.

✓ **Tor & Onion Services** – Located ransomware extortion messages.

🔎 **OSINT Tip**: Analyzing metadata in leaked documents can reveal attacker details and infrastructure.

3.6.5 The Aftermath: Impact on the Company & Response Efforts

1. Financial & Legal Consequences

● **Stock Price Drop** – The company's stock fell 15% within days of the breach.
● **Regulatory Fines** – The company faced a $20 million penalty for data protection failures.
● **Customer Lawsuits** – Victims filed a class-action lawsuit over exposed financial records.

2. Mitigation Efforts & Cybersecurity Improvements

✓ **Incident Response Team Activation** – Engaged forensic experts to contain the attack.
✓ **Mandatory Password Resets** – Forced all employees to update credentials.
✓ **Multi-Factor Authentication (MFA) Enforcement** – Eliminated password-only access to sensitive systems.
✓ **Dark Web Monitoring Contracts** – Partnered with intelligence firms to track stolen data resale attempts.

3.6.6 Lessons Learned & Preventative Measures

Key Takeaways from the Case

✓ **Credential Reuse is a Major Weakness** – Attackers exploited password reuse from old breaches.

✓ **Dark Web Monitoring is Critical** – Early detection of leaked data can reduce damage.

✓ **Ransomware Prevention Requires Strong Security Controls** – MFA, segmentation, and endpoint protection could have prevented lateral movement.

✓ **Timely Response Reduces Financial Losses** – Faster breach detection minimizes regulatory fines and legal impact.

Best Practices for Organizations

✓ **Regularly Audit Employee Credentials** – Use breach monitoring tools like HIBP & DeHashed.

✓ **Enforce Strong Password Policies** – Require unique, complex passwords with MFA.

✓ **Monitor the Dark Web for Early Breach Signs** – Use IntelX, DarkOwl, and Telegram OSINT.

✓ **Strengthen Incident Response Plans** – Conduct regular cyberattack simulations.

Conclusion: The Role of OSINT in Corporate Breach Investigations

◆ OSINT tools play a crucial role in tracking stolen credentials and leaked data.

◆ Dark web intelligence helps organizations detect and respond to breaches faster.

◆ Threat intelligence frameworks (MITRE ATT&CK, Cyber Kill Chain) improve breach analysis.

◆ Proactive cybersecurity measures reduce the risk of future attacks.

By leveraging OSINT, monitoring breach data, and strengthening authentication security, organizations can minimize cyber risks and prevent large-scale data breaches.

4. Identifying Malicious Domains & Phishing Sites

In this chapter, we dive into the critical task of identifying malicious domains and phishing sites, which are commonly used in cyberattacks to deceive victims and steal sensitive information. Through OSINT techniques, we'll explore how to spot suspicious domain names, analyze website characteristics, and trace the digital footprints of attackers. We will also examine tools and methods to detect phishing schemes, from examining URL structures to recognizing social engineering tactics. By understanding these threats, you'll be better equipped to identify and neutralize malicious sites before they can cause harm, ensuring enhanced security in the digital landscape.

4.1 How Cybercriminals Use Malicious Domains in Attacks

Malicious domains play a critical role in cyberattacks, serving as command-and-control (C2) servers, phishing sites, malware distribution points, and data exfiltration hubs. Cybercriminals register deceptive domains to trick users, bypass security defenses, and evade detection by leveraging techniques such as domain spoofing, fast flux hosting, and DNS hijacking.

This chapter explores how malicious domains are used in cyberattacks, the methods hackers employ to mask their activities, and OSINT techniques for identifying and analyzing these threats.

4.1.1 The Role of Malicious Domains in Cyber Attacks

What Are Malicious Domains?

A malicious domain is a website or internet address used by cybercriminals to facilitate illegal activities. These domains can be used to:

● Host phishing pages that steal credentials.
● Distribute malware and ransomware payloads.
● Serve as Command-and-Control (C2) infrastructure for botnets.
● Exfiltrate stolen data from breached systems.

Why Hackers Use Domains Instead of IP Addresses

Cybercriminals prefer using domains over static IP addresses because:

✓ Domains are easier to register, change, and abandon.

✓ They can use domain generation algorithms (DGA) to create thousands of domains daily.

✓ Security systems may block known IP addresses, but newly registered domains evade detection.

🔎 **OSINT Tip**: Tracking recently registered domains and monitoring for suspicious keyword patterns can help detect emerging threats.

4.1.2 How Cybercriminals Create and Distribute Malicious Domains

1. Domain Spoofing & Typosquatting

Cybercriminals register look-alike domains to impersonate legitimate websites.

◆ **Examples of Spoofed Domains:**

✓ microsoft-support[.]com instead of support.microsoft.com

✓ faceb00k[.]com instead of facebook.com

☐ **OSINT Tools for Detecting Typosquatting:**

✓ **DNSTwist** – Generates and detects spoofed domain variations.

✓ **URLScan.io** – Analyzes suspicious URLs and their content.

🔎 **OSINT Tip**: Always check the WHOIS registration details to identify patterns in domain ownership.

2. Fast Flux Hosting & Bulletproof Hosting

Fast flux and bulletproof hosting allow hackers to rotate IP addresses dynamically to avoid detection.

◆ How It Works:

✓ **Fast Flux**: Domains constantly change IP addresses, making them hard to track.

✓ **Bulletproof Hosting**: Servers in unregulated regions ignore takedown requests from law enforcement.

☐ OSINT Tools for Analyzing Hosting Patterns:

✓ **RiskIQ PassiveTotal** – Maps domain-hosting relationships.

✓ **Shodan & Censys** – Identifies malicious servers and infrastructure.

🔎 **OSINT Tip**: If a domain's IP address changes frequently, it might be part of a botnet or phishing campaign.

3. Domain Generation Algorithms (DGA)

Hackers use automated domain generation algorithms to create hundreds or thousands of new domains daily for C2 communications.

◆ Example of DGA-generated domains:

✓ abx91dke3[.]com

✓ jjds92md01[.]net

☐ OSINT Tools for Detecting DGA Domains:

✓ **DGArchive** – Tracks algorithmically generated domains.

✓ **VirusTotal Graph** – Maps domain-to-IP relationships for malicious networks.

🔎 **OSINT Tip**: If a domain name is nonsensical or frequently changing, it could be DGA-generated.

4.1.3 How Malicious Domains Are Used in Cyber Attacks

1. Phishing & Credential Theft

● Hackers create fake login pages that mimic real sites (e.g., PayPal, Google, banking portals).
● Victims enter their credentials, which are harvested and sold on the dark web.

☐ **OSINT Tools for Identifying Phishing Domains:**

✓ **PhishTank** – Database of reported phishing sites.

✓ **CheckPhish.ai** – Scans URLs for phishing indicators.

🔎 **OSINT Tip**: If a domain has no historical WHOIS data or was registered very recently, it might be a phishing site.

2. Malware & Ransomware Distribution

● Malicious domains deliver drive-by downloads, trojans, and ransomware payloads.
● Hackers use exploit kits on compromised domains to infect users.

☐ **OSINT Tools for Analyzing Malware Domains:**

✓ **Hybrid Analysis & Any.Run** – Runs suspicious URLs in virtual sandboxes.

✓ **ThreatCrowd** – Maps malware domains and their associations.

🔎 **OSINT Tip**: If a domain hosts multiple malware families, it is likely part of a larger cybercriminal infrastructure.

3. Command-and-Control (C2) Servers

● Attackers use domains to communicate with infected machines in botnets and APT operations.
● C2 domains send encrypted commands to compromised devices for data theft or DDoS attacks.

☐ **OSINT Tools for Tracking C2 Domains:**

✓ **AlienVault OTX & Abuse.ch** – Lists known C2 domains.

✓ **Maltego** – Maps domain relationships in APT campaigns.

🔎 **OSINT Tip**: If a domain is linked to multiple infected devices, it may be part of a botnet C2 infrastructure.

4. Data Exfiltration & DNS Tunneling

● Hackers use DNS tunneling to exfiltrate stolen data through seemingly normal domain queries.
● Attackers encode stolen information into DNS request packets to evade network detection.

☐ **OSINT Tools for Detecting DNS Tunneling:**

✓ **Wireshark** – Analyzes DNS request anomalies.

✓ **PassiveTotal** – Identifies domains with high DNS query traffic.

🔎 **OSINT Tip**: If a domain has unusual query patterns or excessive DNS traffic, it might be used for data exfiltration.

4.1.4 Case Study: Tracking a Malicious Domain Used in a Phishing Campaign

Incident:

A financial institution discovered multiple employees received phishing emails leading to a fake login page impersonating their internal portal.

Investigation Steps:

1☐ Extracted domain from phishing email

secure-login[.]bankingupdate[.]com

2☐ **Performed WHOIS lookup**

Found the domain was registered two days ago in an offshore hosting provider.

3️⃣ Checked URL reputation databases

PhishTank & VirusTotal flagged the domain as a known phishing site.

4️⃣ Analyzed hosting infrastructure

Found that the same IP hosted multiple other phishing domains impersonating banks.

5️⃣ Reported the domain for takedown

Contacted domain registrars and security vendors to blacklist the domain.

🔎 **Outcome**: The phishing domain was taken down, and email security filters were updated to prevent similar attacks.

Conclusion: The Importance of Malicious Domain OSINT Investigations

✔ Malicious domains are a core part of cybercrime, enabling phishing, malware, and C2 operations.

✔ Cybercriminals use domain spoofing, fast flux, and DGA to evade detection.

✔ OSINT tools can help track, analyze, and take down malicious domains before they cause damage.

✔ Security teams must continuously monitor new domain registrations to stay ahead of emerging threats.

By leveraging OSINT techniques, analysts can identify and neutralize malicious domains, protecting both individuals and organizations from cyber threats.

4.2 Investigating Suspicious Websites & Their Registrants

Cybercriminals use fraudulent websites for phishing, malware distribution, and financial fraud. Investigating suspicious domains and their registrants is a critical component of OSINT-driven cybersecurity. By analyzing WHOIS records, DNS history, hosting infrastructure, SSL certificates, and dark web associations, security analysts can uncover cybercriminal networks, track malicious actors, and identify attack patterns.

In this chapter, we will explore OSINT methodologies, tools, and techniques to investigate suspicious websites and their operators.

4.2.1 Identifying Suspicious Websites

Red Flags of a Malicious Website

Cybercriminals often use deceptive tactics to lure victims. Here are common indicators of a suspicious website:

● **Recently Registered Domains** – Most phishing and scam sites are created days or weeks before an attack.

● **Misspelled URLs & Typosquatting** – Domains that mimic legitimate brands (e.g., paypa1[.]com instead of paypal.com).

● **Lack of HTTPS or Self-Signed SSL Certificates** – Fraudulent sites often have unverified or expired SSL certificates.

● **Multiple Hosting IPs & Fast Flux** – Domains that frequently change IP addresses to evade detection.

● **Affiliation with Known Malicious Domains** – Connections to other blacklisted or flagged domains.

Quick OSINT Checks for a Suspicious Domain

☐ **Tools for Quick Analysis:**

✓ **VirusTotal** – Checks if a website is flagged for phishing or malware.

✓ **URLScan.io** – Renders and analyzes the webpage's structure.

✓ **CheckPhish.ai** – Detects phishing indicators.

✓ **Google Safe Browsing** – Verifies if a domain is marked as unsafe.

🔎 **OSINT Tip**: If a website was registered less than 30 days ago, has hidden WHOIS details, and uses free hosting services, it could be a phishing site.

4.2.2 Investigating Domain Registration & WHOIS Records

Step 1: Conducting a WHOIS Lookup

WHOIS databases store domain registration details, including:

- Registrant name & contact email
- Registration date & expiration
- Registrar (e.g., Namecheap, GoDaddy, etc.)

☐ **OSINT Tools for WHOIS Lookup:**

✓ **WhoisXML API** – Provides historical and reverse WHOIS data.

✓ **ViewDNS.info** – Retrieves current WHOIS details.

✓ **Whoxy** – Checks bulk WHOIS records.

🔎 **Key Findings in WHOIS Data:**

- If the registrant email appears in other domain registrations, it may belong to a cybercriminal.
- Domains with short expiration dates (<1 year) are often used for fraud.
- If the registrant address is fake or unverifiable, it could indicate a malicious entity.

🔎 **OSINT Tip**: Use reverse WHOIS searches to uncover other domains registered by the same email or company name.

4.2.3 Analyzing DNS Records & Hosting Infrastructure

Step 2: Checking DNS Records

DNS records reveal IP addresses, mail servers, and subdomains linked to a domain.

☐ **OSINT Tools for DNS Investigation:**

✓ **SecurityTrails** – Tracks historical DNS changes.

✓ **PassiveTotal by RiskIQ** – Identifies connected infrastructure.

✓ **DNSDumpster** – Maps subdomains and hosting relationships.

What to Look For:

- Frequent IP address changes (Fast Flux hosting).
- Connections to blacklisted IPs or known malware hosts.
- Shared infrastructure with other malicious domains.

OSINT Tip: If multiple fraudulent domains share the same DNS server, they may be part of a cybercriminal network.

4.2.4 Investigating SSL Certificates & Web Technologies

Step 3: Checking SSL Certificates

SSL certificates provide insights into a website's security configuration and potential threat actor affiliations.

☐ OSINT Tools for SSL Analysis:

✓ **Censys.io** – Scans SSL certificates and associated domains.

✓ **Shodan** – Finds sites using the same SSL certificate.

✓ **crt.sh** – Tracks certificate issuance records.

Key Findings from SSL Analysis:

- Self-signed certificates suggest untrustworthy or malicious activity.
- If a certificate is shared across multiple phishing domains, they likely belong to the same attacker.
- Short-lived certificates are often used for fraudulent campaigns.

OSINT Tip: If a website has an SSL certificate from a known phishing certificate authority, it may be a scam.

4.2.5 Tracking Website Ownership & Hosting Providers

Step 4: Mapping Hosting Infrastructure

Cybercriminals often use offshore hosting providers or bulletproof hosting to evade takedowns.

OSINT Tools for Hosting Analysis:

✓ **Hosting Checker** – Identifies a website's hosting provider.

✓ **HackerTarget Reverse IP Lookup** – Finds other sites hosted on the same IP.

✓ **IPinfo.io** – Retrieves geolocation and ISP details.

🔎 **Key Findings:**

- If a website shares an IP with known malware sites, it's likely malicious.
- Offshore hosting (Russia, Ukraine, etc.) is often used for cybercrime operations.
- Fast flux networks use rapidly changing IPs to avoid detection.

🔎 **OSINT Tip**: If a suspicious website changes hosting providers frequently, it may be trying to evade cybersecurity defenses.

4.2.6 Dark Web & Threat Intelligence Investigations

Step 5: Searching for Mentions on the Dark Web

Cybercriminals often discuss fraudulent websites and phishing domains on forums and Telegram groups.

Dark Web OSINT Tools:

✓ **DarkOwl** – Monitors dark web discussions about domains.

✓ **OnionScan** – Scans Tor sites for security flaws.

✓ **IntelX.io** – Searches for leaked domain-related data.

🔎 **What to Look For:**

- Hackers selling phishing kits for a domain.
- Threat actors discussing breached credentials linked to the site.
- Mentions of the domain in dark web leak databases.

🔎 **OSINT Tip**: If a domain is advertised on dark web forums as a phishing service, it should be flagged immediately.

4.2.7 Case Study: Investigating a Fake Banking Website

Incident:

Security researchers detected a website impersonating a major bank:

⬧ *secure-banking-login[.]com*

Investigation Steps:

1️⃣ **WHOIS Lookup** – The domain was registered three days ago with hidden details.
2️⃣ **DNS Analysis** – The site shared an IP with multiple phishing domains.
3️⃣ **SSL Certificate Check** – Used a self-signed certificate, indicating fraudulent activity.
4️⃣ **Dark Web Investigation** – The domain was mentioned on a cybercrime Telegram channel.
5️⃣ **URL Scan** – The site hosted a fake login page to steal banking credentials.

🔎 **Outcome**: The phishing domain was reported and blacklisted, preventing financial fraud.

Conclusion: The Importance of Website & Registrant Investigations

✔ Investigating domain registrants helps track cybercriminals and fraud networks.

✔ OSINT tools provide insights into DNS history, SSL certificates, and hosting infrastructure.

✔ Dark web monitoring can reveal hidden connections between threat actors.

✔ Early detection of fraudulent domains prevents phishing attacks and data theft.

By using OSINT techniques, analysts can uncover malicious domains, identify cybercriminal networks, and enhance cyber threat intelligence.

4.3 WHOIS, DNS, and Passive DNS Analysis for OSINT

Cybercriminals rely on malicious domains to conduct phishing campaigns, distribute malware, and execute cyberattacks. OSINT analysts and cybersecurity professionals use WHOIS, DNS, and Passive DNS analysis to investigate these domains, track their infrastructure, and uncover hidden connections between threat actors.

In this section, we will explore how WHOIS lookups, DNS records, and Passive DNS analysis provide crucial intelligence for cyber investigations.

4.3.1 Understanding WHOIS Records in OSINT

What is WHOIS?

WHOIS is a public database that stores domain registration details, including:

- Registrant name & email
- Registration & expiration dates
- Registrar (e.g., Namecheap, GoDaddy, etc.)
- Nameservers & hosting provider
- Using WHOIS for Cyber Investigations

OSINT analysts use WHOIS records to:

✓ Identify who registered a domain.

✓ Track suspicious domain patterns (e.g., bulk registrations).

✓ Link domains to known cybercriminals.

✓ Determine if a site is newly registered and suspicious.

WHOIS Lookup OSINT Tools

☐ **Recommended Tools:**

✓ **WhoisXML API** – Provides historical and reverse WHOIS data.

✓ **ViewDNS.info** – Checks current WHOIS details.

✓ **Whoxy** – Performs bulk WHOIS lookups.

Red Flags in WHOIS Data

● Recently registered domains (phishing domains are often <30 days old).
● Domains registered with free email providers (Gmail, Yahoo, etc.).
● Hidden or anonymized registrant details (indicates a potential scam).
● Frequent domain expiration & renewal cycles (suggests fraud activity).

🔎 **OSINT Tip**: If an email or phone number appears in WHOIS, use it in reverse lookup tools to find other domains registered by the same individual.

4.3.2 Investigating DNS Records for Cyber Threat Intelligence

What is DNS?

The Domain Name System (DNS) translates domain names into IP addresses. Cybercriminals exploit DNS by:

◆ Registering fraudulent domains for phishing & malware delivery.
◆ Using fast flux DNS to evade detection.
◆ Hiding behind bulletproof hosting to avoid takedowns.

Key DNS Record Types for OSINT Analysis

✓ **A Record** – Maps a domain to an IP address.

✓ **MX Record** – Identifies the email server (useful for phishing investigations).

✓ **NS Record** – Reveals the authoritative nameserver.

✓ **TXT Record** – Contains security settings (e.g., SPF for email authentication).

How to Analyze DNS for Malicious Domains

1️⃣ **Check for Frequent IP Changes** – Fast flux networks indicate a botnet or malware operation.
2️⃣ **Look for Blacklisted Domains** – Compare DNS records with threat intelligence feeds.
3️⃣ **Investigate Shared Infrastructure** – If multiple scam sites share the same DNS servers, they may be part of a cybercriminal network.

DNS OSINT Tools

Recommended Tools:

✓ **SecurityTrails** – Tracks historical DNS records.

✓ **DNSDumpster** – Maps subdomains and hosting details.

✓ **MXToolbox** – Checks MX, SPF, and TXT records.

🔎 **OSINT Tip**: If a malicious domain shares its mail server (MX Record) with other sites, those domains might also be part of a phishing operation.

4.3.3 Leveraging Passive DNS for Tracking Threat Actors

What is Passive DNS?

Unlike traditional DNS lookups, Passive DNS stores historical DNS data from multiple sources. It allows OSINT analysts to:

✓ Track past IP addresses used by a domain.

✓ Find domains that previously used the same IP (revealing hidden connections).

✓ Identify malware infrastructure and pivot between related domains.

Why Passive DNS is Critical for OSINT

✅ Detects malicious domains before they are blacklisted.

✅ Uncovers attack infrastructure linked to phishing & malware.

✅ Helps track cybercriminals across multiple operations.

Passive DNS OSINT Tools

Recommended Tools:

✓ **RiskIQ PassiveTotal** – Tracks domain and IP history.

✓ **Farsight Security Passive DNS** – Provides detailed DNS intelligence.

✓ **VirusTotal Graph** – Visualizes domain-IP relationships.

🔎 **OSINT Tip**: If multiple phishing domains share the same historical IP, they may belong to the same threat actor group.

4.3.4 Case Study: Investigating a Phishing Campaign with WHOIS & Passive DNS

Incident:

A suspicious email led to the discovery of a phishing site mimicking a bank:

◆ *secure-banking-login[.]com*

Investigation Steps:

1☐ **WHOIS Lookup** – The domain was registered 5 days ago with anonymized details.
2☐ **DNS Analysis** – The IP was previously associated with other phishing sites.
3☐ **Passive DNS Investigation** – Found 25+ other fraudulent domains using the same IP.
4☐ **OSINT Cross-Checks** – The registrar email was linked to a dark web hacker forum.

🔎 **Outcome**: The phishing site was reported and shut down, preventing financial fraud.

Conclusion: Why WHOIS, DNS, and Passive DNS Matter in OSINT

✔ WHOIS helps track domain ownership and cybercriminal networks.

✔ DNS records reveal hosting details, subdomains, and attack infrastructure.

✔ Passive DNS analysis uncovers historical domain-IP connections for deeper investigations.

✔ Combining these techniques enhances cyber threat intelligence and OSINT investigations.

By leveraging WHOIS, DNS, and Passive DNS, OSINT analysts can expose cybercriminals, prevent fraud, and strengthen cybersecurity defenses.

4.4 Identifying Phishing Kit Infrastructures & Campaigns

Phishing attacks remain one of the most effective cyber threats, leveraging fraudulent websites, deceptive emails, and cloned login pages to steal credentials and sensitive information. Cybercriminals often use phishing kits—pre-packaged tools that automate the creation of fake login pages—to conduct large-scale attacks.

By investigating phishing kit infrastructures, OSINT analysts can track threat actors, identify campaign patterns, and disrupt phishing operations before they cause damage.

4.4.1 Understanding Phishing Kits & How They Work

What is a Phishing Kit?

A phishing kit is a collection of scripts, templates, and resources that allows attackers to quickly set up fake login pages. These kits typically include:

- HTML & JavaScript files that mimic real websites
- Pre-configured email templates for mass phishing campaigns
- Backend scripts that capture and send stolen credentials
- Anti-detection mechanisms to bypass security tools

How Phishing Kits Are Distributed

- Sold on dark web marketplaces and hacker forums.
- Shared via Telegram and Discord channels among cybercriminals.
- Hosted on compromised websites or free hosting platforms.
- Used by affiliates in phishing-as-a-service (PhaaS) operations.

🔎 **OSINT Tip**: Searching for phishing kit "readme.txt" or "license.txt" files in open directories can reveal details about the kit's author and origin.

4.4.2 Investigating Phishing Domains & Hosting Infrastructure

Step 1: Identifying Phishing Domains

Most phishing campaigns rely on fraudulent domains that impersonate real brands (e.g., paypa1-login[.]com).

OSINT Techniques to Investigate Phishing Domains

✓ **WHOIS Lookup** – Identify registrant details and hosting providers.

✓ **Passive DNS Analysis** – Find connections to other phishing domains.

✓ **SSL Certificate Analysis** – Track self-signed or shared certificates.

✓ **Subdomain Enumeration** – Discover hidden infrastructure behind phishing sites.

Tools for Phishing Domain Analysis

☐ **Recommended OSINT Tools:**

✓ **WhoisXML API** – Checks domain registration history.

✓ **SecurityTrails** – Monitors DNS changes and domain relations.

✓ **Shodan & Censys** – Scans for SSL certificates linked to phishing domains.

✓ **URLScan.io** – Captures a full snapshot of a suspicious site.

🔎 **OSINT Tip**: If multiple phishing domains share the same SSL certificate or hosting IP, they may belong to the same cybercriminal network.

4.4.3 Analyzing Phishing Kit Code & Artifacts

Step 2: Extracting Phishing Kit Files

Many phishing sites leave behind unprotected directories containing phishing kit artifacts. Analysts can:

✓ Search for open directories (e.g., example.com/phishkit/).

✓ Look for forgotten ZIP or TAR files with phishing kit source code.

✓ Extract metadata from HTML and PHP files to find creator details.

Common Files Found in Phishing Kits

💼 **index.html** – Fake login page mimicking a real site.

- 📁 **post.php** – Backend script that sends credentials to attackers.
- 📁 **email.php** – Phishing email sender script.
- 📁 **config.txt** – Configuration file with attacker details.

OSINT Techniques for Code Analysis

✓ **Metadata Extraction** – Check timestamps, author names, and comments in the code.

✓ **Hash Comparison** – Use tools like VirusTotal to check if the kit has been used in past attacks.

✓ **JavaScript Fingerprinting** – Analyze phishing scripts for unique patterns.

OSINT Tools for Code Analysis

☐ **Recommended Tools:**

✓ **Hybrid Analysis** – Scans and analyzes phishing kit files.

✓ **CyberChef** – Decodes obfuscated phishing scripts.

✓ **VirusTotal** – Checks files for known malware signatures.

🔎 **OSINT Tip**: If a phishing kit's configuration file contains an attacker's email or Telegram ID, it can be used to track down other attacks linked to the same threat actor.

4.4.4 Tracking Phishing Campaigns & Attack Patterns

Step 3: Monitoring Phishing Campaigns in Real-Time

Phishing operations follow predictable attack patterns. OSINT analysts track:

✓ **Campaign Timing** – Are attacks linked to holidays or financial events?

✓ **Target Sectors** – Are campaigns aimed at banks, e-commerce, or social media?

✓ **Attack Methods** – Are phishing emails, SMS, or voice phishing (vishing) used?

Monitoring Phishing Threats Using OSINT

☐ **Real-Time Phishing Intelligence Feeds:**

✓ **PhishTank** – Community-driven phishing database.

✓ **OpenPhish** – Tracks active phishing URLs.

✓ **Abuse.ch URLhaus** – Detects malware-hosting phishing domains.

✓ **Have I Been Pwned?** – Checks if emails were compromised in phishing breaches.

🔎 **OSINT Tip**: Search for phishing domain mentions in Telegram groups, hacker forums, and Pastebin leaks to uncover ongoing campaigns.

4.4.5 Case Study: Tracking a Phishing-as-a-Service (PhaaS) Operation

Incident:

Security researchers identified a new phishing campaign targeting banking customers.

Investigation Steps:

1️⃣ **Domain Analysis** – WHOIS lookup revealed recently registered phishing domains mimicking a bank.
2️⃣ **Passive DNS Investigation** – Found dozens of other phishing sites sharing the same IP.
3️⃣ **Phishing Kit Extraction** – Open directories exposed source code with attacker email addresses.
4️⃣ **Dark Web Research** – The phishing kit was being sold on a Telegram cybercrime channel.
5️⃣ **Campaign Monitoring** – The same kit was used to attack multiple banks over 3 months.

🔎 **Outcome:**

✓ The phishing domains were reported and blacklisted.

✓ The phishing kit seller was tracked down on dark web forums.

✓ Law enforcement was alerted, leading to takedowns of associated infrastructure.

Conclusion: The Importance of Phishing Kit Investigations in OSINT

✓ Identifying phishing kits helps disrupt cybercrime operations.

✓ Investigating domain infrastructure exposes phishing campaigns.

✓ Tracking kit authors provides intelligence on future threats.

✓ Monitoring phishing attack patterns enhances cyber defenses.

By leveraging WHOIS, DNS, code analysis, and dark web monitoring, OSINT analysts can detect, track, and prevent phishing threats before they spread.

4.5 Monitoring URL Shorteners, Redirects & Malicious Links

Cybercriminals frequently use URL shorteners and redirects to conceal malicious links in phishing campaigns, malware distribution, and social engineering attacks. By leveraging OSINT techniques, analysts can unmask hidden URLs, track threat actor infrastructure, and prevent cyber threats before they escalate.

In this section, we will explore how malicious URLs operate, how attackers bypass security filters, and the OSINT tools used to investigate suspicious links.

4.5.1 Understanding URL Shorteners & Their Role in Cybercrime

What Are URL Shorteners?

URL shorteners transform long web addresses into short, simplified links (e.g., bit.ly/xyz123). While useful for marketing, they are often exploited by cybercriminals to:

◆ Obfuscate phishing and malware links
◆ Bypass security filters that detect known malicious domains
◆ Track user interactions (e.g., clicking on a phishing email)
◆ Chain multiple redirects to evade detection

Commonly Abused URL Shorteners

⚠ **Legitimate services often used by attackers:**

✓ **Bit.ly** – Widely used, offers click analytics.

✓ **TinyURL** – Allows attackers to create deceptive links.

✓ **t.co (Twitter's shortener)** – Used in social media phishing.

✓ **is.gd & cutt.ly** – Less monitored, often used in scam campaigns.

Signs of a Suspicious Shortened URL

● Sent via unexpected emails, SMS, or social media.
● No context provided about where the link leads.
● Time-sensitive wording (e.g., "Act now!" or "Your account is locked!").
● Uses multiple shortening services chained together.

🔎 **OSINT Tip**: If you suspect a shortened URL is malicious, avoid clicking it. Instead, expand and analyze it using URL preview tools.

4.5.2 Investigating Shortened URLs & Expanding Redirects

Step 1: Expanding Shortened URLs

Before clicking a suspicious link, OSINT analysts first unmask the full URL using expansion tools.

☐ **Recommended URL Expansion Tools:**

✓ **CheckShortURL** – Expands links and checks for phishing.

✓ **Unshorten.me** – Reveals the original URL and site reputation.

✓ **WhereGoes** – Traces multiple redirects and landing pages.

Step 2: Checking URL Reputation

Once expanded, the full URL is analyzed for potential threats.

☐ **Recommended URL Threat Analysis Tools:**

✓ **VirusTotal** – Scans URLs for malware and phishing indicators.

✓ **Google Safe Browsing** – Checks if the domain is flagged as dangerous.

✓ **URLHaus (Abuse.ch)** – Identifies known malware-distributing domains.

🔎 **OSINT Tip**: If a shortened URL redirects to another shortened URL, attackers may be chaining services to evade detection.

4.5.3 Analyzing HTTP Redirects & Hidden Redirection Chains

How Attackers Use Redirects to Hide Malicious Links

🔎 **Cybercriminals frequently chain multiple redirects to:**

✓ Bypass security filters that block known malicious sites.

✓ Load phishing pages dynamically to evade detection.

✓ Drop malware payloads through compromised websites.

Types of Malicious Redirects

● **301/302 Redirects**: Forward users to a phishing or malware site.
● **Meta Refresh Redirects**: Uses HTML <meta> tags to reload malicious pages.
● **JavaScript Redirects**: Automatically sends victims to an attack site.
● **Server-Side Redirects**: Hard to detect; executed on the backend.

Tracking Redirect Chains with OSINT

☐ **Recommended Redirect Analysis Tools:**

✓ **Redirect Detective** – Maps all redirections and final landing pages.

✓ **WhereGoes** – Traces complete redirect paths.

✓ **urlscan.io** – Captures website snapshots and scripts.

🔎 **OSINT Tip**: Redirects often lead to "burner" domains—disposable domains used in one attack before being discarded. Identifying shared hosting IPs can expose more linked malicious sites.

4.5.4 Investigating Malicious Links in Emails, SMS & Social Media

How Attackers Use Malicious Links

◆ **Email Phishing (Spear Phishing & Business Email Compromise)** – Links lead to fake login pages or malware downloads.

◆ **Smishing (SMS Phishing)** – Attackers send fake banking or delivery notifications with a malicious link.

◆ **Social Media Attacks** – Fake profiles spread links to scams or drive-by malware downloads.

OSINT Techniques for Analyzing Malicious Links

✓ Extract email headers to analyze sender reputation.

✓ Check URL previews without clicking the link.

✓ Look for typosquatting & homoglyph domains (e.g., micr0soft[.]com).

✓ Compare with threat intelligence feeds to see if the domain is blacklisted.

☐ **Recommended Link Investigation Tools:**

✓ **PhishTank** – Identifies active phishing URLs.

✓ **Abuse.ch URLHaus** – Tracks malware-hosting domains.

✓ **MetaDefender** – Multi-engine scan for malicious URLs.

🔎 **OSINT Tip**: Many phishing URLs use Unicode domain tricks (e.g., paypal.com vs. paypal.com). Use a Punycode decoder to reveal disguised characters.

4.5.5 Case Study: Tracking a URL Shortener in a Phishing Campaign

Incident:

A financial institution reported an increase in phishing attacks targeting its customers. Emails contained shortened URLs leading to fake login pages.

Investigation Steps:

1⬜ **Expanding the Shortened URLs** – Found multiple redirects leading to a fake banking portal.

2⬜ **Checking URL Reputation** – VirusTotal flagged the final destination as a phishing site.

3⬜ **Tracing Hosting Infrastructure** – The phishing site shared an IP with several other scam sites.

4⬜ **Dark Web Investigation** – The same phishing kit was being sold on Telegram hacker groups.

5⬜ **Campaign Attribution** – The attack infrastructure was traced back to a known threat actor group.

🔎 **Outcome:**

✓ The malicious links were blacklisted, preventing further attacks.

✓ The threat actor's phishing kit was identified, allowing security teams to monitor future campaigns.

✓ Law enforcement and CERT teams took action to dismantle the phishing infrastructure.

Conclusion: Why Monitoring URL Shorteners & Redirects is Critical

✓ Attackers use shortened URLs to disguise malicious links in phishing attacks.

✓ Redirect chains help cybercriminals bypass security filters and distribute malware.

✓ OSINT techniques can expand, analyze, and track suspicious links to uncover threat actor infrastructure.

✓ Investigating malicious URLs helps prevent phishing, fraud, and cyberattacks before they spread.

By leveraging OSINT tools for link analysis, domain tracking, and threat intelligence, security analysts can proactively detect and disrupt cyber threats hidden within shortened URLs and redirection chains.

4.6 Case Study: Exposing a Phishing Network Targeting Banks

Phishing remains one of the most effective tactics used by cybercriminals to steal banking credentials and financial information. In this case study, we will analyze how an OSINT investigation uncovered a large-scale phishing network targeting multiple banks. By tracking malicious domains, phishing kits, and attacker infrastructure, security analysts were able to disrupt the network and prevent financial fraud.

4.6.1 Incident Overview

In early 2024, multiple banks reported a rise in phishing emails impersonating their customer service teams. Victims received emails with links to fake login pages, where their credentials were stolen. The phishing network was well-organized, using:

✓ Shortened URLs to obfuscate malicious links

✓ Multiple redirections to bypass security filters

✓ Phishing kits that cloned legitimate banking portals

✓ Fast-flux hosting to evade takedowns

A coordinated OSINT investigation was launched to track down the threat actors behind the campaign.

4.6.2 Investigating the Phishing Emails & Malicious Links

Step 1: Extracting & Analyzing Phishing Email Headers

Security analysts collected phishing emails from multiple bank customers and examined their headers.

🔍 Key Findings:

✓ Spoofed sender domains (e.g., support@bank-secure[.]com)

✓ Email servers linked to known spam IPs

✓ Embedded shortened URLs leading to phishing sites

☐ **Tools Used:**

✓ **MXToolBox** – Checked email server reputation.

✓ **EmailHeaders.net** – Analyzed forged email origins.

🔎 **OSINT Tip**: Phishing emails often contain invisible tracking pixels to monitor when a victim opens the email. Disabling image loading in email settings can prevent attackers from gathering victim data.

Step 2: Expanding Shortened URLs & Unmasking Redirect Chains

The phishing emails contained Bit.ly and TinyURL links, requiring OSINT techniques to trace their final destinations.

☐ **Tools Used:**

✓ **CheckShortURL** – Expanded shortened links.

✓ **URLScan.io** – Captured full snapshots of the phishing sites.

✓ **WhereGoes** – Mapped redirect chains.

🔍 **Key Findings:**

✓ The shortened links redirected users through multiple intermediary sites before reaching the phishing page.

✓ Some intermediary domains were legitimate but compromised websites, used to hide malicious activity.

✓ The final phishing pages closely resembled real bank login portals, stealing usernames and passwords.

4.6.3 Analyzing the Phishing Site Infrastructure

Step 3: Investigating Domain Registrations & WHOIS Data

Security analysts conducted a WHOIS lookup on the phishing domains to identify connections between them.

 Tools Used:

✓ **WhoisXML API** – Retrieved domain registration details.

✓ **SecurityTrails** – Mapped linked domains and hosting history.

🔍 **Key Findings:**

✓ Most domains were recently registered and used privacy protection services to hide registrant details.

✓ Some phishing domains shared the same hosting provider, suggesting they were part of a larger campaign.

✓ Several domains were registered using disposable email addresses, often linked to free mail providers.

🔎 **OSINT Tip**: Some attackers forget to enable WHOIS privacy, exposing real email addresses that can be searched on Have I Been Pwned or hunter.io to find associated accounts.

Step 4: Extracting Phishing Kit Artifacts

Some phishing sites had open directories, exposing the source code of phishing kits. Analysts downloaded and examined the files.

 Tools Used:

✓ **HTTrack** – Cloned phishing pages for offline analysis.

✓ **CyberChef** – Decoded obfuscated scripts.

✓ **VirusTotal** – Scanned PHP scripts for known malware.

🔍 **Key Findings:**

✓ The phishing kits were pre-configured to send stolen credentials to attacker-controlled email addresses.

✓ Some files contained metadata revealing the creator's username, leading to additional OSINT discoveries.

✓ JavaScript files showed hardcoded Telegram and Discord bot IDs, used to send stolen credentials to cybercriminals in real-time.

🔎 **OSINT Tip**: Searching for phishing kit "readme.txt" or "config.php" files on indexed directories can reveal threat actor contact details.

4.6.4 Tracing the Threat Actor on the Dark Web

Step 5: Searching Hacker Forums & Marketplaces

Investigators found the same phishing kits being sold on underground forums and Telegram groups.

☐ **Tools Used:**

✓ **Dark Web Search Engines (OnionLand, Ahmia)** – Searched for related phishing kit discussions.
✓ **Telegram OSINT Bots** – Extracted user activity linked to phishing kit sales.

🔍 **Key Findings:**

✓ The phishing kits were advertised in Telegram hacking groups.

✓ The same threat actor also sold fake banking documents, suggesting involvement in financial fraud.

✓ Forum discussions revealed that the actor used Bitcoin for transactions, leading to blockchain analysis.

🔎 **OSINT Tip**: Many threat actors reuse the same usernames across different underground platforms. Searching these aliases on Dehashed, IntelligenceX, or GitHub can reveal past activity and linked accounts.

4.6.5 Disrupting the Phishing Network & Key Takeaways

Outcome of the Investigation

✔ Phishing domains were reported and taken down by hosting providers.

✔ Banking security teams implemented proactive measures to warn customers.

✔ Law enforcement agencies were provided with intelligence on the phishing operation.

✔ The phishing kits and Telegram groups were flagged, reducing their reach.

Key Takeaways for OSINT Investigators

✔ **Monitor URL shorteners & redirects** – Many phishing campaigns rely on them.

✔ **Extract and analyze phishing kit artifacts** – They often contain OPSEC mistakes.

✔ **Search the dark web for phishing kit sellers** – Tracking sellers can reveal larger cybercriminal networks.

✔ **Correlate threat actor infrastructure** – Finding shared IPs, WHOIS details, and hosting providers can expose other malicious domains.

Conclusion: The Power of OSINT in Phishing Investigations

This case study highlights how OSINT techniques can uncover large-scale phishing operations targeting financial institutions. By combining email analysis, domain tracking, phishing kit investigation, and dark web monitoring, security analysts can:

✔ Identify and dismantle phishing infrastructure.

✔ Unmask cybercriminals behind phishing attacks.

✔ Protect banks and customers from credential theft and fraud.

🔎 **Final OSINT Tip**: Continuous monitoring of phishing domains, social media threats, and underground marketplaces is essential for staying ahead of evolving phishing tactics.

5. Social Engineering & Phishing OSINT

This chapter explores the intersection of social engineering and phishing attacks, where human behavior becomes the primary vulnerability exploited by cybercriminals. We will delve into how OSINT can be used to gather personal information and craft highly targeted social engineering attacks. From profiling individuals through social media and online activities to recognizing common phishing tactics, this chapter will equip you with the tools to identify and thwart these deceptive techniques. Understanding the psychology behind social engineering and the methods used to manipulate victims is key to preventing successful phishing campaigns and safeguarding both individuals and organizations.

5.1 Understanding Social Engineering & How It's Used in Cybercrime

Social engineering is one of the most effective and dangerous tools in a cybercriminal's arsenal. Unlike traditional hacking, which relies on exploiting vulnerabilities in software or networks, social engineering targets the human element, manipulating individuals into revealing sensitive information, clicking malicious links, or granting unauthorized access.

This section explores the psychology behind social engineering, the various tactics used by cybercriminals, and real-world examples of how attackers exploit trust, fear, urgency, and authority to deceive victims. Understanding these techniques is essential for OSINT analysts, cybersecurity professionals, and organizations looking to identify, prevent, and mitigate social engineering attacks.

5.1.1 The Psychology Behind Social Engineering

At its core, social engineering exploits human emotions and cognitive biases. Cybercriminals manipulate victims by leveraging psychological triggers such as:

◆ **Authority** – Impersonating someone in power (e.g., IT support, police, CEO).
◆ **Urgency** – Creating pressure to act quickly before thinking critically (e.g., "Your account will be suspended!").
◆ **Fear** – Threatening consequences for non-compliance (e.g., "Pay now or face legal action!").

◆ **Greed** – Offering fake rewards or financial incentives (e.g., lottery scams, investment fraud).

◆ **Curiosity** – Using enticing subject lines or messages to provoke clicks (e.g., "Exclusive leaked data!").

◆ **Trust & Familiarity** – Masquerading as a known contact (e.g., spear-phishing from a compromised account).

🔎 **OSINT Tip**: Attackers often gather information from social media, data breaches, and public records to craft highly convincing social engineering attacks. Regular monitoring of personal data exposure can help mitigate risk.

5.1.2 Common Social Engineering Techniques Used in Cybercrime

1. Phishing (Email & SMS Attacks)

Phishing is the most common form of social engineering, where attackers send fraudulent emails or messages that appear to come from a trusted source.

✓ **Spear Phishing** – Highly targeted phishing attacks using personalized information.

✓ **Whaling** – Attacks targeting high-profile executives and decision-makers.

✓ **Smishing** – SMS-based phishing scams impersonating banks, delivery services, or government agencies.

✓ **Vishing** – Voice phishing via phone calls, often posing as customer support.

☐ **OSINT Tools for Phishing Analysis:**

✓ **PhishTank** – Database of known phishing URLs.

✓ **VirusTotal** – Checks URLs for malicious intent.

✓ **URLScan.io** – Captures phishing site screenshots.

2. Pretexting (Building a Fake Story to Gain Trust)

Pretexting involves creating a fabricated scenario to manipulate victims into revealing confidential data or performing unauthorized actions.

✓ Attackers pose as IT staff asking for login credentials.

✓ Fake law enforcement officers request sensitive data.

✓ Scammers impersonate HR personnel seeking employee records.

🔎 **OSINT Tip**: Always verify unexpected requests through official contact channels. Attackers often use spoofed emails and phone numbers to increase credibility.

3. Baiting (Luring Victims with Tempting Offers)

Baiting relies on enticement to trick individuals into compromising security.

✓ Malware-infected USB drives left in company parking lots.

✓ Fake job offers leading to credential theft.

✓ Free software downloads bundled with trojans or spyware.

☐ **OSINT Tools for Detecting Malware & Suspicious Files:**

✓ **Any.Run** – Interactive malware analysis.

✓ **Hybrid Analysis** – Scans files for threats.

✓ **Cuckoo Sandbox** – Virtual environment for testing malware.

4. Quid Pro Quo (Exchanging Something for Access)

In quid pro quo attacks, hackers offer a service or benefit in exchange for sensitive information.

✓ Fake tech support scams promising to "fix" non-existent computer issues.

✓ Fraudulent IT consultants tricking employees into installing malware.

✓ Attackers posing as survey researchers asking for confidential business insights.

🔎 **OSINT Tip**: Many quasi-legitimate job postings on LinkedIn and freelance sites are actually social engineering traps designed to collect sensitive information.

5. Tailgating & Physical Social Engineering

Not all attacks happen online—physical social engineering is a major cybersecurity risk.

✓ Piggybacking into office buildings by following an authorized employee.

✓ Wearing fake ID badges to gain access to restricted areas.

✓ Dumpster diving for discarded documents containing sensitive data.

🔎 **OSINT Tip**: Physical reconnaissance (checking Google Street View, social media images, and building layouts) helps attackers plan tailgating attacks.

5.1.3 Case Studies: Real-World Social Engineering Attacks

Case Study 1: The Twitter Bitcoin Scam (2020)

📠 Attackers used phone-based social engineering to compromise Twitter's internal tools.

✓ **Pretexting technique** – Hackers tricked Twitter employees into resetting credentials.

✓ Gained access to high-profile accounts (Elon Musk, Bill Gates, Apple, etc.).

✓ Launched a fake Bitcoin giveaway, stealing over $100,000 in cryptocurrency.

🔎 **Takeaway**: Even tech giants are vulnerable to well-crafted social engineering attacks.

Case Study 2: The Ubiquiti Breach (2021)

📠 A former employee used social engineering and insider access to steal company data.

✓ Posed as an external hacker to demand a ransom payment.

✓ Manipulated employees into restoring access to compromised systems.

✓ Exfiltrated gigabytes of sensitive corporate information.

🔎 **Takeaway**: Insider threats and unauthorized access pose major risks to organizations.

5.1.4 How OSINT Helps Detect & Prevent Social Engineering Attacks

1. Identifying Social Engineering Pre-Attack Indicators

☐ OSINT Techniques to Spot Social Engineering Attempts:

✓ **Monitoring leaked credentials** – Check if employee data is exposed on the dark web.

✓ **Analyzing domain spoofing** – Detect lookalike email domains used in phishing.

✓ **Tracking social media mentions** – Identify potential impersonation attacks.

🔎 Key Tools:

✓ **Have I Been Pwned** – Checks for breached emails.

✓ **DNSTwist** – Finds typosquatting domains.

✓ **SOCMINT (Social Media Intelligence) Tools** – Detect impersonation attempts.

2. Implementing Strong Social Engineering Defense Strategies

✓ **Security Awareness Training** – Employees should be trained to recognize social engineering tactics.

✓ **Multi-Factor Authentication (MFA)** – Reduces the risk of credential-based attacks.

✓ **Strict Verification Policies** – Always verify identity before sharing sensitive information.

✓ **OSINT Recon on Attackers** – Gathering intelligence on threat actors prevents future attacks.

Conclusion: Why Social Engineering Remains a Top Cybersecurity Threat

✓ Social engineering is highly effective because it exploits human psychology rather than technical vulnerabilities.

✓ Attackers use phishing, pretexting, baiting, and quid pro quo techniques to manipulate victims.

✓ Real-world cases (Twitter hack, Ubiquiti breach) show the devastating impact of social engineering.

✓ OSINT can identify social engineering pre-attack indicators by tracking leaked data, phishing domains, and impersonation threats.

✓ Education and awareness are the best defenses against social engineering tactics.

🔎 **Final OSINT Tip**: Always verify requests for sensitive information, avoid clicking unknown links, and monitor your digital footprint to minimize exposure to social engineering attacks.

5.2 Investigating Phishing Emails & Suspicious Messages

Phishing remains one of the most pervasive cyber threats, responsible for countless data breaches, financial fraud incidents, and malware infections. Cybercriminals disguise malicious emails and messages as legitimate communications, tricking victims into revealing credentials, clicking harmful links, or downloading malware.

For OSINT analysts and cybersecurity professionals, investigating phishing attempts is crucial to identifying attackers, tracking phishing campaigns, and mitigating risks. This section will break down how to analyze phishing emails, extract critical intelligence, and use OSINT tools to trace threat actors and their infrastructure.

5.2.1 Identifying Phishing Emails & Suspicious Messages

Phishing emails often exhibit telltale signs that distinguish them from legitimate messages. Some common red flags include:

🔹 **Spoofed sender addresses** – Attackers forge email headers to appear from trusted entities.

🔹 **Urgency or threats** – "Your account will be locked unless you act now!"

🔹 **Grammar and spelling errors** – Common in hastily crafted phishing attempts.

🔹 **Unusual links or attachments** – Often leading to fake login pages or malware.

🔹 **Requests for sensitive data** – Banks, IT departments, and service providers rarely ask for credentials via email.

🔎 **OSINT Tip**: Even if an email appears legitimate, always hover over links (without clicking) to inspect the actual destination URL.

5.2.2 Extracting & Analyzing Email Headers

Step 1: Viewing Email Headers

Every email contains a hidden header with metadata that reveals:

✓ Sender's actual email address

✓ Mail server IPs used to send the message

✓ Authentication results (SPF, DKIM, DMARC)

✓ Routing path of the email

🔎 **How to View Email Headers:**

✓ **Gmail**: Open the email → Click the three dots → "Show Original"

✓ **Outlook**: Open email → File → Properties → Internet Headers

✓ **Yahoo**: Click "More" → "View Raw Message"

Step 2: OSINT Tools for Email Header Analysis

☐ **Tools Used:**

✓ **MxToolBox (https://mxtoolbox.com)** – Checks mail server reputation.

✓ **IPinfo.io** – Identifies sender's IP address location.

✓ **Email Header Analyzer (https://toolbox.googleapps.com/apps/messageheader/)** – Decodes routing information.

🔍 **Key Findings:**

✓ If the email fails SPF, DKIM, or DMARC, it's likely spoofed.

✓ If the sender's IP belongs to a known spam network, it's likely malicious.

✓ If the email originated from an unexpected country, it warrants further investigation.

5.2.3 Investigating Phishing Links & Malicious URLs

Step 3: Expanding Shortened Links

Phishing emails often contain shortened or obfuscated URLs to hide their true destination.

☐ **Tools Used:**

✓ **CheckShortURL (https://checkshorturl.com/)** – Expands short links (Bit.ly, TinyURL, etc.).

✓ **Unshorten.it** – Reveals full URL before clicking.

🔍 **Key Findings:**

✓ If the expanded URL mimics a real domain (e.g., paypalsupport[.]com instead of paypal.com), it's a phishing attempt.

✓ If the link redirects multiple times before landing on a login page, it's likely fraudulent.

Step 4: Scanning URLs for Malicious Behavior

Once the full URL is revealed, the next step is analyzing it for threats.

☐ **Tools Used:**

✓ **VirusTotal (https://www.virustotal.com/)** – Scans URLs for malware and phishing indicators.

✓ **URLScan.io** – Captures screenshots and detects phishing behavior.

✓ **PhishTank (https://www.phishtank.com/)** – Checks if the URL is a known phishing site.

🔎 **OSINT Tip**: Many phishing websites look identical to real login pages. Always check the domain name carefully before entering credentials.

5.2.4 Investigating Attachments & Suspicious Files

Step 5: Checking Email Attachments for Malware

Phishing emails often contain attachments disguised as invoices, receipts, or security updates, but they may contain malware or ransomware.

☐ **Tools Used:**

✓ **VirusTotal** – Scans files for malware.

✓ **Hybrid Analysis (https://www.hybrid-analysis.com/)** – Runs files in a sandbox environment.

✓ **Any.Run (https://any.run/)** – Interactive malware analysis platform.

🔍 **Key Findings:**

✓ **.exe, .scr, .bat files** – High risk of malware execution.

✓ **Macros in Office documents** – Common vector for ransomware and keyloggers.

✓ **Encrypted ZIP/RAR files** – Attackers may use password-protected archives to bypass security filters.

5.2.5 Tracing the Phishing Infrastructure & Attackers

Step 6: Investigating the Email Domain & IP Address

If the phishing email uses a custom domain (e.g., bank-security[.]com), investigate its origin.

☐ **Tools Used:**

✓ **Whois Lookup (https://whois.domaintools.com/)** – Finds domain registration details.

✓ **SecurityTrails (https://securitytrails.com/)** – Checks historical DNS records.

✓ **DNSTwist (https://dnstwist.it/)** – Detects lookalike phishing domains.

🔍 **Key Findings:**

✓ If the domain was recently registered (less than a month old), it's suspicious.

✓ If the registrant used privacy protection, it might be a phishing operation.

✓ If the domain shares the same IP as other phishing sites, it's likely part of a larger campaign.

5.2.6 Case Study: Uncovering a Phishing Campaign Targeting Bank Customers

Incident Overview

A phishing campaign targeted customers of a major financial institution, using fake security alerts urging victims to log in and verify their accounts.

Investigation Steps & Findings

✓ **Extracted email headers** – Sender used a spoofed email impersonating bank support.

✓ **Analyzed phishing link** – URL expanded to bank-login[.]support, which looked legitimate but was a fraudulent domain.

✓ **Scanned phishing page** – URLScan.io revealed an identical clone of the bank's login portal.

✓ **Checked domain registration** – Domain was registered one week prior, indicating a recent scam operation.

✓ **Traced attacker infrastructure** – The same hosting server also hosted similar phishing sites for PayPal and Amazon.

Outcome

✓ The phishing domains were reported and taken down.

✓ Bank security teams implemented additional email filtering rules to block similar attacks.

✓ OSINT analysts continued monitoring for new phishing domains using WHOIS tracking and passive DNS analysis.

5.2.7 Key Takeaways & Defense Strategies

✓ **Always analyze email headers** – Spoofed emails often fail SPF, DKIM, and DMARC checks.

✓ **Never click on unknown links** – Expand shortened URLs and inspect domains before visiting.

✓ **Use OSINT tools to investigate phishing domains** – WHOIS, passive DNS, and malware scanners can expose attacker infrastructure.

✓ **Scan suspicious attachments** – Avoid opening unknown files without sandboxing them first.

✓ **Monitor phishing trends** – Tracking active phishing campaigns helps identify new attack patterns before they escalate.

Conclusion: How OSINT Enhances Phishing Investigations

By combining email header analysis, domain tracking, malware scanning, and OSINT tools, investigators can uncover phishing networks, trace cybercriminals, and prevent financial losses. As phishing attacks evolve, continuous monitoring and proactive intelligence gathering are essential in defending against these threats.

🔎 **Final OSINT Tip**: Phishing campaigns often reuse email templates, domains, and hosting infrastructure—tracking these elements can expose larger cybercriminal networks behind phishing attacks.

5.3 Identifying Fake Personas & Social Media Impersonation

Cybercriminals, scammers, and threat actors frequently use fake personas and social media impersonation to manipulate victims, spread misinformation, conduct espionage, or launch phishing attacks. These fabricated identities can range from completely fictional profiles to stolen identities used for fraudulent activities.

For OSINT analysts and cybersecurity professionals, detecting and investigating these fake personas is crucial to preventing fraud, disinformation campaigns, and cyber-enabled threats. In this section, we will explore techniques and tools to uncover fake profiles, verify online identities, and trace the actors behind impersonation campaigns.

5.3.1 Understanding Fake Personas & Their Uses

Fake personas are digital identities created to deceive, manipulate, or exploit others. They can be used for:

✓ **Cybercrime & Fraud** – Scammers create fake business or individual profiles to scam victims via investment fraud, romance scams, or phishing.

✓ **Espionage & Social Engineering** – Intelligence agencies or corporate spies use fabricated identities to infiltrate organizations or gain insider information.

✓ **Disinformation & Influence Operations** – Fake accounts are used to spread propaganda, manipulate public opinion, or incite conflict.

✓ **Hacker OPSEC** – Cybercriminals use fake identities to mask their real identities while conducting illicit activities.

✓ **Troll & Bot Networks** – Malicious actors create coordinated networks of fake accounts to amplify messages, harass targets, or manipulate trends.

🔎 **OSINT Tip**: Fake profiles are often reused across multiple platforms. Investigating patterns across accounts can expose entire impersonation networks.

5.3.2 Identifying Red Flags of Fake Social Media Accounts

Fake profiles can be automated (bots) or human-controlled (sock puppets). Common indicators of fake accounts include:

⬥ **Newly created profile** – Fake accounts are often recently made, with little activity history.

⬥ **Low engagement** – They have few followers, random likes, and little interaction with real users.

⬥ **Suspicious profile pictures** – Stolen images, AI-generated faces, or stock photos.

⬥ **Incomplete bios** – Lack of personal details, vague job descriptions, or mismatched information.

⬥ **Unusual posting patterns** – Bot-like behavior, such as copy-pasting content, rapid posting, or repeating the same message across different platforms.

⬥ **Impersonation of real people** – Scammers often steal identities from real individuals, celebrities, or corporate executives.

🔎 **OSINT Tip**: Reverse search profile pictures using Google Reverse Image Search or PimEyes to check if they are stolen from the web.

5.3.3 OSINT Techniques for Investigating Fake Personas

Step 1: Reverse Searching Profile Pictures

Many fake profiles use stolen images from stock photography sites, other social media accounts, or even AI-generated faces.

☐ **Tools Used:**

✓ **Google Reverse Image Search (https://images.google.com/)** – Detects duplicates of an image online.

✓ **PimEyes (https://pimeyes.com/)** – Finds faces across social media and other sites.

✓ **TinEye (https://tineye.com/)** – Compares profile pictures against a massive image database.

🔍 **Key Findings:**

✓ If the image appears on multiple unrelated websites, it was likely stolen.

✓ If the image comes from a stock photo site, the profile is fake.

✓ AI-generated faces (e.g., from ThisPersonDoesNotExist.com) have symmetrical features, distorted backgrounds, or unnatural-looking eyes.

Step 2: Verifying Profile Information & Activity

Fake personas often have contradictory, generic, or fabricated details.

☐ **Tools Used:**

✓ **Namechk (https://www.namechk.com/)** – Checks if a username is used across multiple platforms.

✓ **Spokeo (https://www.spokeo.com/)** – Searches public records for name and location verification.

✓ **LinkedIn & Company Directories** – Helps verify employment claims.

🔍 **Key Findings:**

✓ If the username is inactive on most platforms, it may be fake.

✓ If the claimed job position does not match company records, it is likely fraudulent.

✓ If the name does not appear in public records, it may be an alias.

Step 3: Analyzing Writing & Posting Patterns

Many fake accounts use scripted responses or unnatural language.

☐ **Tools Used:**

✓ **TweetBeaver (https://tweetbeaver.com/)** – Analyzes Twitter account activity.

✓ **Botometer (https://botometer.osome.iu.edu/)** – Detects bot-like behavior on Twitter.

✓ **Twitonomy (https://www.twitonomy.com/)** – Tracks hashtags and word usage patterns.

🔍 **Key Findings:**

✓ If the account posts the same message across multiple groups, it is likely automated.

✓ If the grammar and sentence structure appear robotic or inconsistent, it may be AI-generated.

✓ If the account engages with only a specific group of users, it may be part of a coordinated operation.

Step 4: Tracing Impersonation & Stolen Identities

Scammers frequently clone real profiles or create slightly modified versions of them.

☐ **Tools Used:**

✓ **Facebook Graph Search (https://www.facebook.com/graphsearch/)** – Identifies duplicate profiles.
✓ **Have I Been Pwned (https://haveibeenpwned.com/)** – Checks if an email linked to a profile has been in past breaches.
✓ **EmailRep.io (https://emailrep.io/)** – Assesses email reputation and prior use.

🔍 Key Findings:

✓ If multiple profiles exist with the same name and images, one is likely fraudulent.

✓ If the email associated with the account has been found in breaches, the profile may be compromised.

✓ If the user claims different personal details across platforms, they may be lying about their identity.

5.3.4 Case Study: Unmasking a Fake LinkedIn Persona Used for Social Engineering

Incident Overview

A cybercriminal group was using fake LinkedIn profiles to pose as recruiters from a major tech company, tricking IT professionals into downloading malware disguised as job application software.

Investigation Steps & Findings

✓ **Reverse-searched profile pictures** – Found the same images on a stock photo site.

✓ **Checked employment details** – No record of these "recruiters" in the actual company's employee database.

✓ **Analyzed posting patterns** – Each profile had very few connections, no real engagement, and generic posts.

✓ **Traced email addresses** – Emails used belonged to recent data breaches, indicating fraudulent use.

Outcome

✓ The fake profiles were reported and removed from LinkedIn.

✓ The tech company alerted job seekers about the impersonation scam.

✓ OSINT analysts tracked down other profiles from the same threat actors.

5.3.5 Key Takeaways & Defense Strategies

✓ **Always verify profile images** – Reverse image searches can expose stolen pictures.

✓ **Check for inconsistencies** – Fake profiles often use generic or contradictory details.

✓ **Analyze account activity** – Bots and impersonators exhibit suspicious posting patterns.

✓ **Monitor duplicate accounts** – Scammers often clone real profiles to gain credibility.

✓ **Use OSINT tools** – WHOIS, data breach searches, and account activity checks can uncover fraudulent social media identities.

Conclusion: How OSINT Strengthens Identity Verification

The rise of AI-generated identities, deepfake technology, and social media manipulation makes OSINT investigations more critical than ever. By using verification tools, behavioral analysis, and investigative techniques, analysts can detect fake personas, prevent fraud, and unmask threat actors before they cause harm.

🔎 **Final OSINT Tip**: Fake personas are rarely used in isolation—tracking one fraudulent account can reveal entire networks of deception.

5.4 Analyzing Common Pretexting & Scamming Tactics

Social engineering remains one of the most effective cyber attack techniques, with pretexting and scamming tactics being core components of phishing campaigns, financial fraud, and identity theft. Cybercriminals use deceptive stories (pretexts) to manipulate victims into revealing sensitive information, transferring funds, or clicking on malicious links. These scams can be highly sophisticated, leveraging OSINT-gathered intelligence to appear convincing.

In this section, we will explore the most common pretexting and scam tactics, how they exploit psychological vulnerabilities, and the OSINT techniques that can be used to detect and investigate them.

5.4.1 Understanding Pretexting in Social Engineering

What is Pretexting?

Pretexting is a social engineering technique where an attacker fabricates a false scenario (pretext) to gain the target's trust and manipulate them into divulging information or taking an action. Unlike basic phishing, pretexting involves a well-researched, personalized approach to deceive the victim.

Key Elements of Pretexting:

✔ **A Convincing Story** – Attackers create a situation that seems legitimate, such as posing as an IT technician, HR representative, or financial institution.

✔ **Psychological Manipulation** – They exploit trust, urgency, fear, or authority to pressure the victim.

✔ **Use of OSINT Data** – Pretexting scams often use publicly available information to appear more authentic (e.g., knowing an employee's recent promotion, boss's name, or company policies).

🔎 **OSINT Tip**: Attackers frequently scrape LinkedIn, company websites, and social media to craft personalized pretexts. Investigating what information is publicly exposed can help organizations mitigate these threats.

5.4.2 Common Pretexting & Scam Techniques

1. Business Email Compromise (BEC) & CEO Fraud

Cybercriminals impersonate high-ranking executives to trick employees into transferring funds or revealing sensitive data.

◆ **How It Works:**

✔ Attacker researches the target organization using OSINT (e.g., company hierarchy, executive names).

✔ They spoof the CEO's email and send a "urgent" request to an employee (usually in finance or HR).

✔ The employee, believing the email is legitimate, processes the fraudulent request.

☐ **Detection Tools:**

✓ **Email Header Analysis (MXToolbox, IP Tracker)** – Checks for domain spoofing.

✓ **OSINT Tools (Hunter.io, Have I Been Pwned)** – Verifies if an executive's email has been compromised in past breaches.

2. Tech Support & IT Helpdesk Scams

Attackers pose as IT support personnel to trick employees into revealing login credentials or installing malware.

◆ **How It Works:**

✓ The attacker calls or emails an employee claiming there's an issue with their system.

✓ They use technical jargon to sound convincing and pressure the victim into providing login details or installing remote access software.

✓ The attacker gains unauthorized access and deploys malware or steals data.

☐ **Detection Tools:**

✓ **WHOIS Lookup (WhoisXML API, DomainTools)** – Verifies if the sender's domain matches the real company.

✓ **Reverse Phone Lookup (Truecaller, Scammer.info)** – Checks if the number is flagged as fraudulent.

3. Tax & Payroll Scams

Cybercriminals target HR departments or employees by impersonating tax agencies, payroll providers, or financial institutions.

◆ **How It Works:**

✓ The attacker sends an email claiming to be from the IRS, a tax agency, or payroll service.

✓ They request sensitive payroll records, employee W-2s, or direct deposit changes.

✓ Stolen data is used for identity theft and financial fraud.

Detection Tools:

✓ **Google Dorking ("site:irs.gov" searches)** – Verifies if an email or link is from an official source.

✓ **Domain Spoofing Checks (EmailRep.io, MXToolbox)** – Detects fraudulent sender domains.

4. Social Media Impersonation & Romance Scams

Scammers create fake profiles on social media and dating apps to build trust with victims before requesting money or sensitive information.

◆ **How It Works:**

✓ Scammers use stolen or AI-generated images to create fake accounts.

✓ They build relationships over time, gaining the victim's trust.

✓ Once trust is established, they fabricate an emergency (e.g., medical bills, travel expenses) and request money.

Detection Tools:

✓ **Reverse Image Search (Google Images, PimEyes)** – Detects if the profile photo is stolen.

✓ **Social Media Analysis (Namechk, OSINT Framework)** – Identifies duplicate or suspicious profiles.

5. Fake Job & Recruitment Scams

Cybercriminals impersonate recruiters or HR personnel to steal victims' personal information or distribute malware.

◆ **How It Works:**

✓ Victims receive fake job offers via LinkedIn, email, or job boards.

✓ The "recruiter" requests personal data, banking details, or an upfront payment for training or equipment.

✓ Some scams involve sending malicious documents disguised as job applications.

☐ **Detection Tools:**

✓ **WHOIS & Domain History (WhoisXML API, DomainTools)** – Verifies if the recruitment email domain is legitimate.

✓ **VirusTotal & Hybrid Analysis** – Scans suspicious job-related attachments for malware.

5.4.3 OSINT Techniques for Investigating Pretexting & Scams

1. Reverse Engineering Scam Domains & Emails

✓ Use WHOIS Lookup to check when the domain was created and its owner.

✓ Use MXToolbox to check if an email is from a known scam domain.

✓ Use EmailRep.io to analyze email reputation and past fraudulent activity.

2. Identifying Fake Identities & Social Media Scammers

✓ Use Reverse Image Search (PimEyes, Google) to check if a profile picture is stolen.

✓ Use Namechk to verify if the username is used across multiple platforms.

✓ Use Twitonomy or Botometer to analyze posting behavior and detect fake accounts.

3. Tracing Cryptocurrency & Financial Fraud

✓ Use BitcoinAbuse.com to check if a Bitcoin wallet is linked to scams.

✓ Use Blockchain Explorer to track cryptocurrency transactions linked to fraudulent activities.

✓ Use Maltego & Intel Techniques Tools to map out fraudulent financial networks.

5.4.4 Case Study: Exposing a BEC Scam Targeting a Fortune 500 Company

Incident Overview

A finance executive received an urgent email from the CEO requesting an immediate wire transfer of $250,000 to a supplier. The email seemed legitimate but had minor discrepancies.

Investigation Steps:

✓ **Checked the email headers** – Found it was sent from a spoofed domain similar to the company's.

✓ **Used WHOIS lookup** – Domain was registered only a few days prior, indicating fraud.

✓ **Reverse-searched email address** – Found it listed in previous scam reports.

Outcome:

✓ The fraudulent transfer was prevented before any funds were lost.

✓ The company implemented additional email security measures to detect spoofing.

✓ The attacker's domain was blacklisted and taken down.

5.4.5 Key Takeaways & Defense Strategies

✓ **Train employees on pretexting tactics** – Awareness is the best defense against social engineering.

✓ **Enable email authentication protocols** – Use DMARC, DKIM, and SPF to prevent spoofing.

✓ **Monitor for domain impersonation** – Regularly check for typosquatting and lookalike domains.

✓ **Use OSINT tools for scam detection** – WHOIS, email analysis, and reverse image searches can expose fraud.

✓ **Verify financial transactions** – Always confirm wire transfer requests via phone before approving them.

Conclusion: Strengthening Cyber Defenses Against Pretexting Scams

Pretexting attacks continue to evolve, using OSINT-based intelligence to enhance deception. By combining technical analysis, behavioral monitoring, and OSINT techniques, organizations can identify, investigate, and mitigate social engineering threats before they cause damage.

🔎 **Final OSINT Tip**: Many scammers reuse emails, domains, and phone numbers—tracking these identifiers can help uncover larger fraud networks.

5.5 How OSINT Can Be Used to Defend Against Social Engineering

Social engineering attacks exploit human psychology rather than technical vulnerabilities, making them one of the most dangerous threats in cybersecurity. Attackers leverage Open-Source Intelligence (OSINT) to craft highly convincing scams, but OSINT can also be used defensively to detect, analyze, and mitigate these threats.

This section explores how OSINT techniques can help organizations and individuals protect against phishing, impersonation, pretexting, and other social engineering tactics by identifying risks, verifying identities, and uncovering fraudulent activity.

5.5.1 Understanding the Role of OSINT in Social Engineering Defense

How Attackers Use OSINT to Social Engineer Victims

Before launching an attack, cybercriminals gather intelligence to make their scams appear legitimate. They collect:

✓ **Employee Information** – Names, positions, email addresses, and phone numbers from LinkedIn, company websites, and data breaches.

✓ **Behavioral Insights** – Personal interests, routines, and connections from social media (e.g., Twitter, Facebook, Instagram).

✓ **Company Structure & Policies** – Internal processes, reporting chains, and financial details from job postings, press releases, and annual reports.

🔎 **Example**: A hacker finds an executive's vacation photos on Instagram and emails their assistant, pretending to be the CEO requesting an urgent wire transfer while "traveling abroad."

How OSINT Can Defend Against Social Engineering

Defensive OSINT can be used to:

✓ Monitor and reduce exposed personal and corporate information.

✓ Identify fraudulent websites, emails, and social media accounts.

✓ Track and investigate cybercriminal tactics to predict future attacks.

By staying ahead of attackers, organizations can minimize their risk of falling victim to social engineering schemes.

5.5.2 OSINT Techniques to Detect & Prevent Social Engineering Attacks

1. Identifying Publicly Available Information (Self-OSINT & Risk Audits)

Attackers rely on leaked and public information—conducting a self-audit can reveal what's at risk.

☐ **Key OSINT Tools for Self-Audits:**

✓ **Google Dorking** – Use advanced search queries to find exposed data (e.g., "filetype:xls site:company.com" to find spreadsheets).
✓ **Have I Been Pwned** – Check if personal or company emails have been exposed in breaches.
✓ **Maltego** – Map relationships between email addresses, social media accounts, and domains.
✓ **OSINT Framework** – Discover additional sources of leaked company or employee data.

🔎 **Defense Tip:** Organizations should regularly conduct "Red Team OSINT Exercises" to see what an attacker can learn and take proactive measures to remove or secure sensitive data.

2. Verifying Suspicious Emails & Domains (Phishing Detection)

Phishing is a common form of social engineering. OSINT techniques can help verify suspicious emails before clicking links or responding.

☐ **Key OSINT Tools for Email Verification:**

✓ **EmailRep.io** – Checks the reputation of an email sender.

✓ **MXToolbox** – Analyzes email headers to detect spoofing.

✓ **WHOIS Lookup (WhoisXML API, DomainTools)** – Verifies when and where a domain was registered.

✓ **URLScan.io & VirusTotal** – Scans URLs for phishing and malware.

🔎 **Example**: A finance department receives an email from "ceo@company-support.com" requesting an urgent wire transfer. A WHOIS lookup reveals the domain was registered only a week ago, indicating fraud.

3. Detecting Social Media Impersonation & Fake Profiles

Cybercriminals create fake personas to scam employees, executives, and even customers.

☐ **Key OSINT Tools for Social Media Investigations:**

✓ **PimEyes & TinEye** – Reverse image search to detect stolen profile pictures.

✓ **Namechk** – Checks if a username exists on multiple platforms.

✓ **Twitonomy & Botometer** – Analyzes Twitter accounts for bot-like activity.

✓ **LinkedIn Profile Audits** – Detects recently created or incomplete profiles impersonating company executives.

🔎 **Example**: An attacker creates a fake LinkedIn profile for a "new HR manager" and sends phishing messages to employees about a "payroll update." OSINT tools detect that the profile was created only days ago, raising a red flag.

4. Tracing Scammer Phone Numbers & Spoofed Calls

Attackers use VoIP services and spoofed numbers to impersonate banks, government agencies, or IT departments.

☐ Key OSINT Tools for Phone Verification:

✓ **Truecaller** – Identifies caller names and flags known scam numbers.

✓ **Scammer.info & ScamCallFighters** – Community databases of reported scam phone numbers.

✓ **Whitepages Reverse Lookup** – Checks if a phone number is linked to a real person or business.

🔎 **Example**: A scammer posing as IT support calls an employee, requesting their credentials. Truecaller reveals the number is flagged as "high risk," preventing a potential account breach.

5. Investigating Suspicious Cryptocurrency Transactions

Many scams involve cryptocurrency payments, making OSINT crucial for tracking fraud.

☐ Key OSINT Tools for Crypto Investigations:

✓ **BitcoinAbuse.com** – Reports known scam Bitcoin wallets.

✓ **Blockchain Explorer** – Tracks cryptocurrency transactions.

✓ **CipherTrace & Chainalysis** – Advanced blockchain forensics tools.

🔎 **Example**: A victim is asked to send Bitcoin to a wallet in a ransomware scam. Checking BitcoinAbuse.com shows the wallet is linked to multiple fraud cases, confirming the scam.

5.5.3 Case Study: How OSINT Prevented a Spear Phishing Attack

Incident Overview

A cybersecurity firm's CEO received an email from what appeared to be their cloud service provider, requesting a password reset due to "suspicious activity." The email contained a legitimate-looking login link.

OSINT Investigation:

✓ **WHOIS Lookup**: The domain "cloudservices-support.com" was only two days old.

✓ **Email Header Analysis**: The sender's IP address was traced to a known phishing operation in Eastern Europe.

✓ **URLScan.io**: The login page was flagged as a phishing site impersonating a major cloud provider.

Outcome:

✓ The CEO did not click the phishing link.

✓ The domain was reported and blacklisted.

✓ The company implemented a threat intelligence feed to monitor new phishing domains.

5.5.4 Best Practices for Using OSINT to Defend Against Social Engineering

✓ **Conduct Regular OSINT Audits** – Identify and reduce public exposure of sensitive information.

✓ **Train Employees on OSINT-Based Threats** – Show real-world examples of phishing, impersonation, and scams.

✓ **Monitor Company Mentions & Fake Profiles** – Use OSINT tools to detect impersonation and fraud.

✓ **Verify Every Request** – Encourage employees to verify emails, calls, and fund transfer requests before acting.

✓ **Use Multi-Factor Authentication (MFA)** – Even if credentials are stolen, MFA prevents unauthorized access.

Conclusion: OSINT as a Shield Against Social Engineering

Social engineering attacks rely on information, deception, and psychological manipulation. The same OSINT techniques that attackers use to gather intelligence on victims can be leveraged defensively to detect fraud, verify identities, and protect organizations from scams.

By integrating OSINT into cybersecurity strategies, companies can stay one step ahead of attackers, reducing their exposure and increasing resilience against social engineering threats.

🔎 **Final OSINT Tip**: Every organization should have a dedicated OSINT strategy—continuously monitoring for new threats, leaked data, and potential attack vectors.

5.6 Case Study: How OSINT Stopped a CEO Fraud Attack

CEO fraud, also known as Business Email Compromise (BEC), is a highly targeted social engineering attack where cybercriminals impersonate high-ranking executives to trick employees into transferring funds or disclosing sensitive information. These scams have caused billions of dollars in losses worldwide.

This case study explores how OSINT played a critical role in detecting and stopping a sophisticated CEO fraud attempt before financial damage could occur.

5.6.1 The Attack: A Fake CEO Email Request

A financial officer at a multinational corporation received an urgent email from the company's CEO, requesting a confidential wire transfer to a new overseas vendor. The email was marked as high priority, emphasized discretion, and included an invoice attachment with payment details.

At first glance, the email seemed legitimate:

✔ It was sent from ceo@company-email.com, appearing identical to the CEO's actual email.

✔ It used the CEO's signature, writing style, and phrasing.

✔ The invoice contained realistic formatting and financial details.

However, the finance officer had undergone OSINT-based phishing awareness training and decided to verify the request using OSINT techniques.

5.6.2 OSINT Investigation: Detecting the Red Flags

Step 1: Analyzing the Email Header

The finance officer extracted the email's header information and used MXToolbox to examine the sender's IP address.

🔎 Findings:

✔ The return path differed from the real CEO's email.

✔ The sender's IP originated from a different country than the company's headquarters.

✔ SPF, DKIM, and DMARC email authentication checks failed, suggesting spoofing.

Step 2: Investigating the Invoice Document

The invoice attachment was uploaded to VirusTotal and Intezer Analyze to check for malware or embedded tracking scripts.

🔎 Findings:

✔ No immediate malware detected, but hidden metadata in the PDF revealed it was recently created by a suspicious username.

✔ The bank details in the invoice were linked to previous fraud cases in a scammer database.

Step 3: Verifying the CEO's Email Domain

Using WHOIS lookup and Passive DNS analysis, the finance officer checked the domain company-email.com.

🔎 Findings:

✔ A typosquatting domain (company-email.com) was registered one week ago and used to send the fraudulent email.

✔ The domain used a lookalike "I" instead of an "L"—a common trick in impersonation scams.

Step 4: Checking for Executive Impersonation on Social Media

Since attackers often use social media for reconnaissance, the finance officer searched for the CEO's recent online activity and possible impersonation.

☐ **Tools Used:**

✓ **PimEyes** – Reverse image search for fake CEO profiles.

✓ **LinkedIn & Twitter audits** – Checking for recently created impersonation accounts.

🔎 **Findings:**

✓ A fake LinkedIn profile mimicking the CEO was recently created.

✓ The profile was connecting with company employees and collecting information.

✓ Attackers likely used OSINT to study the CEO's writing style and communication habits.

5.6.3 Stopping the CEO Fraud Attempt

With multiple red flags confirmed, the finance officer:

✓ Did NOT transfer the funds and immediately escalated the case to IT security.

✓ The cybersecurity team reported and blocked the fake domain.

✓ Employees were warned about the phishing attempt, preventing further attacks.

✓ The fake LinkedIn profile was reported and removed.

✓ The incident was documented, strengthening the company's fraud detection process.

5.6.4 Key Lessons: Using OSINT to Prevent CEO Fraud

1. Conduct OSINT Self-Audits to Detect Exposed Information

✓ Regularly scan for typosquatting domains mimicking company emails.

✓ Check for executive impersonation profiles on LinkedIn and social media.

✓ Monitor data leaks that expose executive emails, making them targets for phishing.

2. Train Employees to Use OSINT for Threat Verification

✓ Email header analysis – Detect spoofed or suspicious senders.

✓ WHOIS lookups – Verify sender domain registration dates and IP origins.

✓ Reverse image searches – Identify fake social media profiles used in scams.

3. Implement Multi-Factor Authentication (MFA) and Email Security

✓ MFA on executive accounts prevents unauthorized access.

✓ DMARC, DKIM, and SPF email policies block domain spoofing attempts.

✓ Threat intelligence feeds alert teams to newly registered impersonation domains.

Conclusion: OSINT as a Defense Against Executive Impersonation

This case study highlights how proactive OSINT techniques can identify and stop CEO fraud attacks before they succeed. By combining email analysis, domain investigations, and social media monitoring, organizations can detect fraud attempts early, protect their executives, and prevent financial losses.

🔎 **Final OSINT Tip**: Regularly audit and monitor executive digital footprints—attackers rely on public information to craft convincing scams. Reducing exposure and training employees to verify suspicious requests is the best defense against CEO fraud.

6. Cyber Threat Intelligence (CTI) Frameworks

In this chapter, we explore the various Cyber Threat Intelligence (CTI) frameworks that provide structured approaches to understanding and responding to cyber threats. We will examine widely recognized models such as the MITRE ATT&CK framework, the Diamond Model of Intrusion Analysis, and the Kill Chain, detailing how each helps analysts track, categorize, and analyze threat actors' tactics, techniques, and procedures (TTPs). By leveraging these frameworks, analysts can improve their ability to detect, respond to, and mitigate cyber threats in a more organized and efficient manner. This chapter will provide a solid understanding of how to apply these frameworks in real-world investigations and threat intelligence workflows.

6.1 Key CTI Frameworks: MITRE ATT&CK, Cyber Kill Chain & Diamond Model

Cyber Threat Intelligence (CTI) frameworks provide structured approaches for understanding, analyzing, and responding to cyber threats. Security professionals rely on these models to map out attacker behavior, identify vulnerabilities, and develop defensive strategies. Three of the most widely used CTI frameworks are:

- **MITRE ATT&CK** – A comprehensive knowledge base of adversary tactics and techniques.
- **Cyber Kill Chain** – A model outlining the stages of a cyberattack.
- **The Diamond Model** – A framework for analyzing threat actors, infrastructure, capabilities, and victims.

Each of these frameworks plays a critical role in threat hunting, incident response, and proactive defense strategies.

6.1.1 MITRE ATT&CK Framework

The MITRE ATT&CK (Adversarial Tactics, Techniques, and Common Knowledge) framework is a globally accessible knowledge base that categorizes real-world cyber adversary behaviors. It helps cybersecurity professionals map attacker techniques to specific tactics and improve detection, response, and mitigation efforts.

Structure of MITRE ATT&CK

MITRE ATT&CK is organized into several key components:

✓ **Tactics** – The "why" behind an attack (e.g., Initial Access, Privilege Escalation, Exfiltration).

✓ **Techniques** – The "how" an attacker achieves their goal (e.g., Phishing, Credential Dumping, Command and Control).

✓ **Sub-Techniques** – More granular details on how specific techniques work.

✓ **Procedures** – Real-world examples of how adversaries implement techniques.

Why MITRE ATT&CK is Important

◆ **Threat Hunting & Detection**: Security teams can map attack behaviors to known adversary techniques.

◆ **Adversary Emulation**: Organizations use the framework to simulate attacks and test defenses.

◆ **Incident Response**: Helps analysts understand attacker movements within a network.

Example: Using MITRE ATT&CK for Threat Analysis

A company detects PowerShell execution on an endpoint. By mapping this activity to MITRE ATT&CK:

✓ **Tactic**: Execution

✓ **Technique**: T1059 (Command and Scripting Interpreter)

✓ **Sub-Technique**: T1059.001 (PowerShell)

✓ **Possible Adversaries**: FIN7, APT29

Security teams can then investigate lateral movement and implement mitigations based on known attack patterns.

6.1.2 Cyber Kill Chain Framework

The Cyber Kill Chain, developed by Lockheed Martin, describes the stages of a cyberattack from reconnaissance to exfiltration. It helps security teams identify where an attack can be detected and disrupted before significant damage occurs.

Seven Stages of the Cyber Kill Chain

1☐ **Reconnaissance** – Attackers gather intelligence on the target (e.g., OSINT, social media research, scanning).

2☐ **Weaponization** – Creating a malicious payload (e.g., exploit development, malware packaging).

3☐ **Delivery** – Sending the weapon to the victim (e.g., phishing emails, drive-by downloads).

4☐ **Exploitation** – Gaining access by exploiting a vulnerability.

5☐ **Installation** – Establishing persistence on the victim's system (e.g., installing malware or backdoors).

6☐ **Command & Control (C2)** – Attackers establish remote control over the infected system.

7☐ **Actions on Objectives** – The final goal (e.g., data theft, ransomware deployment, system disruption).

Why the Cyber Kill Chain is Important

◆ **Proactive Defense**: Security teams can disrupt an attack at various stages before completion.

◆ **Incident Response**: Helps structure forensic analysis of an attack's progress.

◆ **Detection Strategy**: Enables SOC teams to align monitoring efforts with attack stages.

Example: Stopping an Attack at the Delivery Stage

A phishing email (Delivery stage) contains a malicious attachment. Analyzing the sender domain and scanning the attachment with VirusTotal reveals malware. The security team blocks the sender, preventing Exploitation and Installation stages.

6.1.3 The Diamond Model of Intrusion Analysis

The Diamond Model is a four-dimensional framework for analyzing cyber threats. It helps connect different elements of an attack to improve attribution and response.

Four Core Components of the Diamond Model

- **Adversary** – The attacker or threat group behind the operation.
- **Capability** – The tools, exploits, and malware used.
- **Infrastructure** – The C2 servers, phishing domains, and infected machines.
- **Victim** – The targeted organization, individual, or system.

Why the Diamond Model is Important

- **Threat Attribution**: Helps link attackers to specific campaigns based on shared tactics.
- **Infrastructure Tracking**: Maps out how adversaries communicate with compromised machines.
- **Predictive Analysis**: Helps forecast an attacker's next move based on past behaviors.

Example: Mapping a Phishing Campaign with the Diamond Model

A cybercriminal sends a phishing email containing a malicious PDF attachment. The Diamond Model would analyze:

✓ **Adversary**: Threat actor using phishing.

✓ **Capability**: Weaponized PDF exploiting CVE-2023-12345.

✓ **Infrastructure**: Fake domain hr-portal-login[.]com used for credential harvesting.

✓ **Victim**: Employees of a financial institution.

Using this analysis, security teams can track similar phishing campaigns, block related domains, and predict attacker actions.

6.1.4 Comparing MITRE ATT&CK, Cyber Kill Chain & Diamond Model

Framework	Purpose	Strengths	Use Cases
MITRE ATT&CK	Maps attacker tactics and techniques	Granular threat intelligence, real-world attack examples	Threat hunting, adversary emulation, SOC investigations
Cyber Kill Chain	Tracks the stages of a cyberattack	Helps detect and stop attacks at different phases	Incident response, intrusion detection, proactive defense
Diamond Model	Analyzes and attributes cyber threats	Focuses on relationships between attacker, tool, infrastructure, and victim	Attribution, infrastructure tracking, predictive analysis

6.1.5 Best Practices for Applying CTI Frameworks

✓ **Combine multiple frameworks** – Use MITRE ATT&CK for tactical mapping, Cyber Kill Chain for detection, and the Diamond Model for threat attribution.

✓ **Integrate frameworks into SIEM & SOC workflows** – Enhance detection rules, automated alerts, and forensic investigations.

✓ **Use threat intelligence feeds** – Enrich analysis with real-time threat indicators mapped to frameworks.

✓ **Continuously update attacker profiles** – Adapt security measures based on evolving threat techniques.

MITRE ATT&CK, the Cyber Kill Chain, and the Diamond Model each offer unique perspectives on cyber threats. When used together, they help cybersecurity teams understand, detect, and respond to attacks more effectively.

By leveraging these CTI frameworks, organizations can proactively defend against cyber threats, strengthen incident response, and enhance overall security posture.

6.2 How OSINT Complements Traditional CTI Methods

Cyber Threat Intelligence (CTI) traditionally relies on internal security telemetry, threat feeds, and structured frameworks to detect and mitigate cyber threats. However, Open-Source Intelligence (OSINT) has become an essential component of modern CTI, providing real-time insights, external threat monitoring, and adversary tracking beyond an organization's perimeter.

This chapter explores how OSINT enhances traditional CTI methods, improves cyber threat investigations, and provides security teams with deeper visibility into attacker behaviors, infrastructure, and intent.

6.2.1 The Limitations of Traditional CTI Methods

Traditional CTI relies on internal security tools such as:

✓ **SIEMs (Security Information and Event Management)** – Aggregates logs and alerts.

✓ **Endpoint Detection & Response (EDR)** – Monitors endpoints for malicious activity.

✓ **Threat Intelligence Feeds** – Provides IOCs (Indicators of Compromise).

✓ **Closed-Source Intelligence (CSTI)** – Paid reports from private vendors.

● **Challenges in Traditional CTI:**

- **Limited External Visibility**: Threat actors often operate outside the organization's monitored network (e.g., dark web forums, hacker marketplaces).
- **Slow IOC Updates**: Some threat feeds rely on historical attack data, making them reactive rather than proactive.
- **Attribution Gaps**: Identifying real-world actors behind an attack is difficult using internal logs alone.

This is where OSINT fills the intelligence gaps.

6.2.2 How OSINT Strengthens CTI

OSINT provides a wider scope of intelligence by analyzing publicly available data, including:

✓ Threat actor discussions on forums, Telegram, and dark web marketplaces.

✓ Leaked credentials and breach data from data leak repositories.

✓ Malicious domains and phishing campaigns tracked via WHOIS and passive DNS.

✓ Social media intelligence (SOCMINT) to monitor hacker activity.

By incorporating OSINT, CTI teams gain real-time external insights into emerging threats before they impact the organization.

Key Benefits of OSINT in CTI:

◆ **Early Threat Detection** – Identifies hacker chatter, leaked credentials, and upcoming attacks.

◆ **Attribution & Actor Profiling** – Tracks threat actor aliases, OPSEC mistakes, and infrastructure.

◆ **Incident Enrichment** – Provides context to internal alerts using external intelligence.

6.2.3 OSINT Use Cases in Cyber Threat Intelligence

1. Threat Actor Tracking & Attribution

🔍 **OSINT Tools:**

- **Social Media Monitoring**: Identifying hacker aliases and fake personas.
- **Dark Web Crawlers**: Analyzing underground forums for cybercrime discussions.
- **PimEyes & ExifTool**: Reverse image searching and metadata extraction for attacker profiling.

✅ **Example**: An APT group discusses an upcoming ransomware campaign on a dark web forum. OSINT helps link the actors to previous attacks, enabling proactive threat hunting.

2. Monitoring Dark Web & Data Breaches

🔍 **OSINT Tools:**

- **BreachForums & RaidForums Monitoring**: Tracking stolen credentials and corporate data leaks.
- **Have I Been Pwned (HIBP):** Checking exposed emails/passwords linked to enterprise domains.
- **DeHashed & IntelX**: Searching for leaked credentials used in credential stuffing attacks.

✅ **Example**: A leaked database with employee logins is found on a dark web marketplace. OSINT helps prevent account takeovers by enforcing password resets and MFA.

3. Identifying Malicious Domains & Phishing Sites

🔍 **OSINT Tools:**

- **WHOIS Lookups & Passive DNS**: Investigating suspicious domains.
- **URLScan.io & PhishTank**: Checking phishing sites in real time.
- **Email Header Analysis**: Detecting spoofed domains used in phishing attacks.

✅ **Example**: A typosquatting domain mimicking a bank is discovered via OSINT before a phishing campaign is launched. Security teams block the domain, preventing fraud.

4. Analyzing Ransomware & Malware Infrastructure

🔍 **OSINT Tools:**

- **Malware Bazaar & VirusTotal**: Identifying malware hashes and C2 servers.
- **Hybrid Analysis & Any.Run**: Analyzing sandboxed malware behavior.
- **Shodan & Censys**: Finding exposed C2 servers and compromised IoT devices.

✅ **Example**: A new ransomware variant appears on VirusTotal with unique IOCs. OSINT helps threat researchers identify similarities to past ransomware strains, improving detection.

6.2.4 Integrating OSINT with Traditional CTI Workflows

To maximize effectiveness, OSINT should be automated and integrated into existing CTI workflows.

1. Automating OSINT Data Collection

☐ **Tools for Automation:**

✓ **SpiderFoot & Maltego** – Automate reconnaissance and infrastructure mapping.

✓ **TheHarvester & Recon-ng** – Collect domain, email, and IP intelligence.

✓ **Mitaka & IntelX API** – Automate threat lookup queries via browser extensions.

◆ **Example**: Automating dark web monitoring to alert SOC teams when company credentials are leaked.

2. Correlating OSINT with Internal Threat Intelligence

🔗 **Combining OSINT with Traditional CTI Data:**

✓ Linking leaked credentials (OSINT) to failed login attempts (SIEM logs).

✓ Correlating domain WHOIS data (OSINT) with phishing email sources (SOC alerts).

✓ Identifying attacker TTPs (OSINT) and mapping them to MITRE ATT&CK (CTI framework).

◆ **Example**: A new phishing domain detected via OSINT is cross-checked against internal email logs to identify if employees have received phishing attempts.

3. Enhancing Threat Attribution with OSINT

🔎 **How OSINT Helps in Attribution:**

✓ Tracking threat actor aliases across multiple forums.

✓ Identifying repeat infrastructure use (IP addresses, C2 domains).

✓ Uncovering attacker OPSEC mistakes (e.g., reused usernames, metadata leaks).

◆ **Example**: A hacker's alias from a data breach forum matches an identity on a gaming website, revealing personal details and connections to past cybercrime activities.

6.2.5 Challenges & Risks of Using OSINT in CTI

While OSINT is valuable, it comes with certain challenges and risks:

1. Data Accuracy & False Positives

● Publicly available data may be outdated, manipulated, or misleading.
✅ **Solution**: Cross-validate OSINT findings with traditional CTI data.

2. Ethical & Legal Considerations

● Some OSINT methods (e.g., scraping dark web forums) may violate platform policies.
✅ **Solution**: Ensure legal compliance when collecting intelligence.

3. Operational Security (OPSEC) Risks

● Investigating threat actors openly may alert them to your monitoring efforts.
✅ **Solution**: Use sock puppet accounts and VPNs for anonymous intelligence gathering.

OSINT is a critical force multiplier for Cyber Threat Intelligence. By complementing traditional CTI methods, OSINT provides real-time visibility, early threat detection, and deeper insights into cybercriminal activities.

Security teams that integrate OSINT with SIEMs, threat feeds, and CTI frameworks can proactively defend against cyber threats, track adversaries more effectively, and strengthen overall cybersecurity posture.

6.3 Mapping OSINT Findings to Threat Intelligence Frameworks

Cyber Threat Intelligence (CTI) frameworks provide structured methodologies for analyzing, categorizing, and responding to cyber threats. By integrating Open-Source Intelligence (OSINT) with these frameworks, security analysts can connect real-world OSINT findings to established threat models, improving threat attribution, risk assessment, and response strategies.

This chapter explores how OSINT can be mapped to key CTI frameworks, including MITRE ATT&CK, the Cyber Kill Chain, and the Diamond Model of Intrusion Analysis, to enhance cyber threat investigations.

6.3.1 The Importance of Mapping OSINT to CTI Frameworks

OSINT provides real-time insights into cyber threats from external sources such as:

✓ Dark web forums and underground marketplaces.

✓ Leaked data repositories and breach databases.

✓ Social media platforms used by threat actors.

✓ Phishing sites and malicious domain infrastructures.

However, OSINT findings often appear disconnected without proper contextualization. By mapping OSINT to standardized frameworks, analysts can:

◆ Correlate intelligence with known attacker behaviors and techniques.
◆ Improve attribution by linking OSINT data to established threat actor TTPs.
◆ Strengthen incident response with structured, actionable intelligence.

6.3.2 Mapping OSINT to MITRE ATT&CK

Overview of MITRE ATT&CK

The MITRE ATT&CK (Adversarial Tactics, Techniques, and Common Knowledge) framework is a globally recognized model that categorizes attacker TTPs (Tactics, Techniques, and Procedures) based on real-world cyber intrusions.

✔ **Tactics** – The high-level goals attackers aim to achieve (e.g., Initial Access, Credential Access).

✔ **Techniques** – Specific methods used to achieve those goals (e.g., Phishing, Brute Force).

✔ **Procedures** – The detailed execution steps attackers follow.

How OSINT Maps to MITRE ATT&CK

OSINT findings can be linked to specific ATT&CK techniques based on the intelligence collected:

OSINT Finding	Mapped MITRE ATT&CK Technique
Hacker forum post selling breached credentials	T1555 – Credentials from Password Stores
Newly registered phishing domain	T1566 – Phishing
Leaked RDP access on dark web	T1078 – Valid Accounts
Social media impersonation attack	T1585 – Establish Accounts (Social Engineering)
Malware C2 IP found via OSINT scanning	T1071 – Application Layer Protocol

✅ **Example**: An OSINT investigation identifies a new phishing site targeting a financial institution. The site is mapped to T1566 (Phishing) in ATT&CK, allowing analysts to apply relevant mitigation strategies.

6.3.3 Using the Cyber Kill Chain for OSINT Investigations

Overview of the Cyber Kill Chain

Developed by Lockheed Martin, the Cyber Kill Chain outlines the stages of a cyberattack, from reconnaissance to exploitation and data exfiltration. The model is widely used in threat intelligence and defense planning.

Mapping OSINT to the Cyber Kill Chain Stages

Kill Chain Phase	Relevant OSINT Findings
Reconnaissance	Hacker discussions about future attacks, exposed employee emails, leaked credentials.
Weaponization	Discovery of malware loaders, phishing kits, or exploit tools on underground forums.
Delivery	Identification of phishing emails, malicious attachments, or drive-by download links.
Exploitation	OSINT findings on exploited vulnerabilities (e.g., CVE discussions on forums).
Installation	Tracking malware C2 servers and infected endpoints using OSINT tools.
Command & Control (C2)	Passive DNS analysis revealing C2 infrastructure for malware.
Actions on Objectives	Stolen data being sold on dark web marketplaces.

✅ **Example**: A security team discovers a hacker forum thread discussing vulnerabilities in a company's VPN service. This OSINT finding maps to the Reconnaissance phase, allowing proactive mitigation before an attack occurs.

6.3.4 Applying the Diamond Model of Intrusion Analysis

Overview of the Diamond Model

The Diamond Model of Intrusion Analysis helps structure cyber threat intelligence by focusing on four key elements of an attack:

- **Adversary** – The threat actor behind the attack.
- **Capability** – The tools and exploits used.
- **Infrastructure** – The command-and-control (C2) servers, domains, and IPs.
- **Victim** – The targeted individual, organization, or sector.

How OSINT Supports the Diamond Model

Diamond Model Element	OSINT Contribution
Adversary	Identifying hacker aliases, OPSEC mistakes, and connections between accounts.
Capability	Discovering exploit kits, malware samples, and attack tools on dark web forums.
Infrastructure	Mapping malicious IPs, domains, and phishing websites to attacker activity.
Victim	Analyzing breach databases to identify compromised companies and individuals.

✅ **Example**: OSINT research links multiple phishing sites to a single threat actor by analyzing WHOIS data and server IPs. This maps to the Infrastructure and Adversary elements in the Diamond Model, helping analysts track the attack campaign.

6.3.5 Automating OSINT Mapping to Frameworks

Using Threat Intelligence Platforms (TIPs)

Threat Intelligence Platforms (TIPs) such as MISP, Anomali ThreatStream, and IBM X-Force Exchange allow analysts to:

✓ Correlate OSINT findings with ATT&CK techniques.

✓ Map phishing domains to Cyber Kill Chain phases.

✓ Visualize adversary activity using the Diamond Model.

Automated OSINT Collection & Analysis

◆ **ThreatFox & VirusTotal** – Identify malware hashes and map them to known attack techniques.
◆ **Maltego & SpiderFoot** – Automate OSINT investigations and infrastructure mapping.
◆ **Shodan & Censys** – Find attacker-controlled servers and match them to C2 techniques.

✅ **Example**: An OSINT scanner detects a new phishing domain registered with a suspicious email. The domain is automatically mapped to ATT&CK T1566 (Phishing) within a TIP, triggering an alert for security teams.

6.3.6 Challenges in OSINT Mapping

1. Data Overload & False Positives

● Large volumes of OSINT data can lead to false positives and irrelevant intelligence.
✅ **Solution**: Use machine learning-based threat correlation tools to filter out noise.

2. OPSEC & Ethical Considerations

● Certain OSINT activities, such as interacting with threat actors, may pose OPSEC risks.
✅ **Solution**: Ensure investigations follow ethical hacking principles and legal guidelines.

3. Dynamic TTPs & Evolving Threats

● Attackers frequently change tactics, making static mapping less effective.
✅ **Solution**: Continuously update threat mappings with real-time OSINT feeds.

Mapping OSINT findings to MITRE ATT&CK, the Cyber Kill Chain, and the Diamond Model significantly enhances cyber threat intelligence. By integrating OSINT with CTI frameworks, security teams can:

✓ Better understand attacker behaviors and motives.

✓ Strengthen attribution efforts and incident response.

✓ Proactively detect and mitigate cyber threats.

Using automation tools and TIPs, OSINT-driven intelligence can be efficiently correlated with known attack patterns, improving overall cybersecurity posture.

6.4 Using STIX/TAXII for Sharing Threat Intelligence

Threat intelligence is most effective when it is shared across organizations, cybersecurity teams, and governments in a structured and actionable format. To facilitate this, two widely adopted standards—STIX (Structured Threat Information Expression) and TAXII (Trusted Automated Exchange of Indicator Information)—enable organizations to exchange real-time cyber threat intelligence (CTI) in a machine-readable way.

In this chapter, we explore how STIX/TAXII enhance OSINT-driven threat intelligence, how security teams can leverage these protocols, and how automated sharing of threat indicators strengthens cyber defenses.

6.4.1 Understanding STIX: Structured Threat Information Expression

What is STIX?

STIX (Structured Threat Information Expression) is a standardized language developed by MITRE and OASIS to describe and share cyber threat intelligence in a structured format. It enables cybersecurity teams to organize, analyze, and communicate threat intelligence efficiently.

Key Components of STIX

STIX models threat intelligence using nine core objects, each representing a key aspect of cyber threats:

STIX Object	Description
Threat Actor	Identifies a cybercriminal, hacktivist, or nation-state group.
Indicator	Describes an observable pattern (e.g., a phishing domain, malware hash).
Attack Pattern	Defines a specific TTP (e.g., spear-phishing, SQL injection).
Malware	Documents known malware variants and their characteristics.
Tool	Captures tools used by threat actors (e.g., Cobalt Strike, Mimikatz).
Vulnerability	Identifies exploited software flaws (e.g., CVE-2023-23397).
Observed Data	Logs evidence of an attack (e.g., logs of a malicious IP connection).
Incident	Documents a real-world security event.
Course of Action	Provides mitigation strategies for identified threats.

Example STIX Representation of a Phishing Attack

A phishing domain (example-bank-login[.]com) impersonating a legitimate banking site can be structured in STIX format like this:

```
{
  "type": "indicator",
  "id": "indicator--12345",
  "created": "2025-02-19T10:30:00Z",
  "modified": "2025-02-19T10:30:00Z",
  "pattern": "[domain-name:value = 'example-bank-login.com']",
```

```
"valid_from": "2025-02-19T00:00:00Z",
"labels": ["phishing"],
"description": "Phishing site targeting banking customers"
}
```

✅ **Benefit**: Security teams can automatically ingest and correlate this data within threat intelligence platforms (TIPs) to block malicious domains before they cause harm.

6.4.2 Understanding TAXII: Trusted Automated Exchange of Indicator Information

What is TAXII?

TAXII (Trusted Automated Exchange of Indicator Information) is a protocol for securely sharing STIX-formatted intelligence over networks. It enables organizations to distribute, request, and receive CTI in real time.

TAXII acts as the communication channel for STIX, providing a structured way to send and pull intelligence from threat-sharing communities and security vendors.

Key TAXII Concepts

TAXII Concept	Description
Collections	Groups of STIX objects containing shared intelligence.
Channels	Mechanisms for real-time sharing of STIX data.
Clients & Servers	Entities requesting and providing threat intelligence.

TAXII Sharing Models

TAXII supports two primary models for threat intelligence distribution:

- **Push Model** – A TAXII server sends intelligence updates to subscribers.
- **Pull Model** – A TAXII client requests specific intelligence when needed.

✅ **Example Use Case**: A financial institution subscribes to a TAXII feed from a cybersecurity vendor, receiving real-time alerts on newly discovered banking malware and phishing domains.

6.4.3 How OSINT Integrates with STIX/TAXII

Using OSINT for Structured Threat Intelligence

OSINT findings can be structured into STIX objects and shared via TAXII feeds to benefit the wider cybersecurity community. Common OSINT sources include:

✔ Phishing domains discovered via WHOIS lookups.

✔ Dark web threat actor aliases and TTPs.

✔ Compromised credentials from data breach dumps.

✔ Malware hashes identified in virus analysis.

OSINT Finding	Mapped STIX Object	Shared via TAXII?
Phishing site	Indicator	Yes
Breached database	Observed Data	Yes
Hacker alias from dark web	Threat Actor	Yes
Malware sample	Malware	Yes
Exploited software vulnerability	Vulnerability	Yes

✅ **Benefit**: Organizations can share OSINT-based intelligence automatically, preventing other security teams from becoming victims of the same threats.

6.4.4 Setting Up a STIX/TAXII Threat Intelligence Workflow

Step 1: Collect OSINT Data

✔ Gather intelligence from dark web forums, phishing sites, malware sandboxes, and breach databases.

Step 2: Structure Data in STIX Format

✔ Convert raw OSINT into STIX objects (Indicators, Threat Actors, Malware, etc.).

Step 3: Share via a TAXII Server

✓ Publish structured intelligence via TAXII feeds for consumption by security teams.

Step 4: Automate Threat Ingestion

✓ Use Threat Intelligence Platforms (TIPs) like MISP, Anomali, or IBM X-Force Exchange to automate ingestion and correlation of shared threat intelligence.

✓ **Example:**

- A new ransomware strain is detected through OSINT research.
- The malware hash and C2 IPs are structured in STIX format.
- The intelligence is shared via a TAXII feed to global security teams.
- Other organizations automatically ingest the data and block the threat.

6.4.5 Challenges in STIX/TAXII Implementation

1. Data Quality & False Positives

● **Problem**: Poorly structured or inaccurate OSINT may lead to false alerts.
✓ **Solution**: Use validated sources and automated threat correlation tools.

2. Operational Complexity

● **Problem**: STIX/TAXII integration requires technical expertise.
✓ **Solution**: Leverage managed TAXII services for easier deployment.

3. Legal & Privacy Considerations

● **Problem**: Sharing OSINT-based intelligence may expose sensitive data.
✓ **Solution**: Follow GDPR and cybersecurity compliance guidelines when sharing threat data.

STIX and TAXII are powerful frameworks that allow organizations to structure and share cyber threat intelligence efficiently. By integrating OSINT findings with STIX/TAXII, security teams can:

✓ Enhance real-time threat intelligence sharing.

✓ Improve automated detection and response to cyber threats.

✓ Strengthen collective defense against emerging cyber risks.

Adopting STIX/TAXII in OSINT-driven CTI operations allows organizations to collaborate globally, ensuring that cyber threats are detected, shared, and mitigated before they cause widespread damage.

6.5 Leveraging Threat Intelligence Platforms (TIPs) for OSINT Investigations

Threat Intelligence Platforms (TIPs) are centralized systems that collect, analyze, and manage cyber threat intelligence (CTI) from multiple sources. For OSINT investigations, TIPs provide automated threat correlation, real-time alerts, and integration with external data sources, helping analysts detect and track cyber threats more efficiently.

This chapter explores how TIPs enhance OSINT investigations, their core functionalities, and how security teams can use them to uncover cybercriminal activities, track threat actors, and prevent cyberattacks.

6.5.1 What is a Threat Intelligence Platform (TIP)?

A Threat Intelligence Platform (TIP) is a centralized software solution that collects, analyzes, and shares threat intelligence across an organization. It helps security teams aggregate OSINT, commercial, and internal threat data into one system for actionable intelligence.

Key Functions of a TIP

- **Data Collection**: Ingests intelligence from OSINT feeds, dark web forums, security blogs, and structured feeds (STIX/TAXII, MISP, VirusTotal, etc.).
- **Threat Correlation**: Links indicators of compromise (IOCs) to threat actors, malware, and attack campaigns.
- **Automated Threat Detection**: Flags malicious domains, phishing attempts, and breach data in real time.
- **Collaboration & Sharing**: Enables teams to share OSINT findings with trusted partners via STIX/TAXII.

- **Incident Response Support**: Helps SOC teams and threat hunters quickly triage and respond to emerging cyber threats.

6.5.2 How TIPs Enhance OSINT Investigations

1. Automating OSINT Collection

TIPs can automatically pull data from OSINT sources, reducing manual effort. Examples include:

- **Phishing site tracking** (URLScan, PhishTank)
- **Dark web monitoring** (Tor forums, Telegram groups)
- **Breach databases** (Have I Been Pwned, DeHashed)
- **Malware repositories** (VirusTotal, Hybrid Analysis)

Example: A TIP detects a new ransomware variant and correlates its C2 servers, malware hashes, and attack patterns using OSINT and structured intelligence feeds.

2. Correlating Threat Intelligence from Multiple Sources

TIPs integrate OSINT, commercial threat feeds, and internal intelligence to identify attack trends.

Threat Source	Data Collected	Used For
Dark Web Markets	Leaked credentials, stolen credit cards	Fraud prevention
Phishing Databases	Fake login pages, phishing emails	Phishing detection
WHOIS & DNS Records	Malicious domain registrations	Threat attribution
Breach Dumps	Compromised employee accounts	Security monitoring

Example: An OSINT-based TIP correlates leaked credentials from a data breach with known hacker activity on dark web forums, helping analysts identify the attacker.

3. Real-Time Threat Alerts & Incident Response

- TIPs monitor live OSINT sources for emerging cyber threats.
- Security teams receive real-time alerts when a new exploit, phishing campaign, or hacker activity is detected.

- TIPs help SOC teams respond to threats faster by automating IOC detection, blocking malicious IPs, and blacklisting phishing domains.

Example: A TIP detects a phishing campaign impersonating a financial institution and automatically alerts security teams, enabling faster mitigation before customers fall victim.

6.5.3 Key Threat Intelligence Platforms for OSINT Investigations

1. MISP (Malware Information Sharing Platform)

- Open-source TIP for sharing threat intelligence (IOCs, TTPs, attack patterns).
- Supports STIX, TAXII, and JSON-based intelligence feeds.
- Used by CERTs, government agencies, and enterprises.

Best For: Cyber threat sharing, IOC correlation, SOC investigations.

2. Anomali ThreatStream

- AI-powered TIP that automates OSINT collection and threat correlation.
- Provides integrated dark web monitoring and threat actor tracking.
- Supports commercial, OSINT, and internal intelligence feeds.

Best For: Enterprise threat hunting, SOC integration, automated threat detection.

3. Recorded Future

- Uses machine learning to analyze OSINT, dark web chatter, and hacker forums.
- Provides real-time risk scores for domains, IPs, and threat actors.
- Supports TTP mapping using MITRE ATT&CK.

Best For: Dark web monitoring, hacker profiling, risk assessment.

4. IBM X-Force Exchange

- Cloud-based TIP for investigating cyber threats using OSINT, IBM threat feeds, and AI-based analytics.
- Offers automated threat intelligence sharing via TAXII/STIX.
- Integrates with SIEMs like Splunk and QRadar.

Best For: Corporate threat intelligence, AI-driven threat analysis.

5. ThreatConnect

- Combines OSINT, commercial threat feeds, and security telemetry for advanced threat hunting.
- Features graph-based analysis to visualize attack campaigns.
- Enables custom threat intelligence workflows for enterprise security teams.

Best For: Enterprise CTI operations, SOC automation, advanced threat correlation.

6.5.4 Setting Up a TIP for OSINT Investigations

Step 1: Select a TIP

- Choose a TIP that supports OSINT sources, STIX/TAXII, and real-time threat analysis.
- **Options**: MISP (open-source), Anomali, Recorded Future, IBM X-Force.

Step 2: Integrate OSINT Feeds

- Connect dark web monitoring tools, phishing feeds, and breach databases.
- **Examples**: PhishTank, Have I Been Pwned, URLScan, VirusTotal, Hybrid Analysis.

Step 3: Automate Threat Detection

- Configure real-time alerts for phishing sites, ransomware campaigns, leaked credentials.
- Use machine learning models for behavioral analysis of emerging threats.

Step 4: Share Intelligence Using STIX/TAXII

- Distribute structured intelligence to security teams, SOCs, and industry partners.

Step 5: Use TIPs for Incident Response

- Correlate OSINT findings with malware indicators, threat actor profiles, and attack tactics (TTPs).
- Use MITRE ATT&CK integration to map adversary behaviors.

6.5.5 Case Study: Using a TIP to Track a Ransomware Campaign

Scenario

- A cybersecurity team detects a suspicious dark web post advertising stolen data.
- The threat actor claims to sell corporate credentials stolen via ransomware.
- The team uses a Threat Intelligence Platform (TIP) to investigate.

Investigation Process

TIP Ingests OSINT Data:

- Monitors dark web marketplaces for stolen data.
- Collects ransomware samples from malware repositories.

Correlates Threat Intelligence:

- Links leaked credentials to a known ransomware variant.
- Matches threat actor alias to previous attacks.

Provides Real-Time Defense:

- Blocks associated IPs, domains, and hashes before attacks spread.
- Alerts affected companies about their compromised data.

Outcome: Security teams prevent follow-up attacks, mitigate ransomware risks, and protect organizations from data theft.

Threat Intelligence Platforms (TIPs) are essential for enhancing OSINT-driven cyber investigations. By integrating OSINT sources, dark web intelligence, and automated threat analysis, TIPs enable security teams to track cybercriminals, correlate attack patterns, and prevent cyber threats more effectively.

Key Takeaway: Leveraging TIPs reduces investigation time, improves incident response, and strengthens cybersecurity defenses against evolving cyber threats.

6.6 Case Study: Using the MITRE ATT&CK Framework to Identify an APT Group

Advanced Persistent Threats (APTs) are among the most sophisticated cyber adversaries, often backed by nation-states or highly organized cybercriminal groups. These actors employ stealthy, prolonged attacks, leveraging a combination of malware, exploits, social engineering, and operational security (OPSEC) techniques to achieve their objectives.

In this case study, we explore how OSINT investigators and cybersecurity analysts used the MITRE ATT&CK framework to track, attribute, and disrupt an APT group targeting a financial institution. By mapping the attackers' tactics, techniques, and procedures (TTPs) to the ATT&CK framework, the security team was able to identify the group behind the attack and strengthen defenses against future threats.

6.6.1 Background: The Cyberattack on a Financial Institution

In early 2023, a major financial institution detected unauthorized network access originating from an external IP address. The initial indicators suggested a potential phishing campaign, but further investigation revealed a coordinated attack leveraging multiple intrusion techniques.

The security team conducted a comprehensive OSINT-driven investigation and mapped the attack patterns to the MITRE ATT&CK framework, which ultimately led to the attribution of the attack to APT38, a cyber espionage group linked to North Korea.

6.6.2 Step 1: Identifying Initial Access & Intrusion Tactics

Suspicious Activity Detected

- Employees reported receiving phishing emails masquerading as urgent payment requests.
- Security logs showed attempts to exploit a known vulnerability (CVE-2022-XXXX) in the bank's VPN service.
- Investigators retrieved email headers, domains, and IP addresses linked to the attack.

MITRE ATT&CK Mapping (Initial Access – TA0001)

The attack was mapped to the following techniques:

Tactic	Technique	ATT&CK ID	Description
Phishing	Spearphishing Link	T1566.002	The emails contained links to a fake login page to steal employee credentials.
Exploiting Vulnerabilities	Exploit Public-Facing Application	T1190	The attackers attempted to exploit a known flaw in the bank's VPN service.

OSINT Used:

- Phishing domain analysis using WHOIS and Passive DNS.
- Dark web monitoring for any discussions related to the exploited vulnerability.

6.6.3 Step 2: Establishing Persistence & Privilege Escalation

Once inside the network, the attackers deployed malicious PowerShell scripts to create backdoor access and gain higher privileges within the bank's system.

MITRE ATT&CK Mapping (Persistence & Privilege Escalation – TA0003, TA0004)

Tactic	Technique	ATT&CK ID	Description
Persistence	Scheduled Task	T1053	Attackers created a scheduled task to execute a PowerShell script every hour.
Privilege Escalation	Token Impersonation	T1134.001	Stole authentication tokens to escalate privileges.

OSINT Used:

- Malware analysis tools (Hybrid Analysis, VirusTotal) to examine the PowerShell script.
- Monitoring hacker forums for discussions on token impersonation techniques.

6.6.4 Step 3: Lateral Movement & Credential Dumping

The attackers used credential dumping tools (Mimikatz) to extract passwords and move laterally across the bank's internal systems.

MITRE ATT&CK Mapping (Credential Access & Lateral Movement – TA0006, TA0008)

Tactic	Technique	ATT&CK ID	Description
Credential Access	Credential Dumping (Mimikatz)	T1003.001	Extracted stored credentials from compromised machines.
Lateral Movement	Remote Desktop Protocol (RDP)	T1021.001	Used stolen credentials to access additional machines via RDP.

OSINT Used:

- Tracking leaked credentials on dark web marketplaces.
- Using breach databases (Have I Been Pwned, DeHashed) to check if leaked credentials had been reused.

6.6.5 Step 4: Exfiltration & Command-and-Control (C2)

The attackers exfiltrated large amounts of financial transaction data to an external server and established a C2 infrastructure to maintain control over compromised machines.

MITRE ATT&CK Mapping (Exfiltration & C2 – TA0010, TA0011)

Tactic	Technique	ATT&CK ID	Description
Exfiltration	Automated Exfiltration	T1020	Data was exfiltrated using an encrypted HTTPS connection.
C2	C2 Over HTTPS	T1071.001	The attackers used encrypted channels to communicate with the C2 server.

OSINT Used:

- Passive DNS analysis to track the C2 infrastructure.
- Using URLScan to analyze the malicious domains hosting C2 servers.

6.6.6 Step 5: Attribution & Mitigation

By correlating attack patterns, TTPs, and infrastructure, the security team identified strong links to APT38 (Lazarus Group), a North Korean-sponsored hacking group known for financial cyberattacks.

Indicators Linking to APT38

- **TTP Overlap**: The techniques used closely matched previous Lazarus Group attacks.
- **Malware Similarity**: The PowerShell script resembled previously documented APT38 malware.
- **Infrastructure Reuse**: The C2 domain was linked to other Lazarus Group operations.

Response & Mitigation:

- Blocked malicious IPs, domains, and hashes identified during the investigation.
- Updated firewall rules to prevent communication with known C2 infrastructure.
- Trained employees on spearphishing awareness to reduce future attacks.
- Shared intelligence via STIX/TAXII with law enforcement and industry partners.

6.6.7 Conclusion: The Power of OSINT & MITRE ATT&CK in APT Investigations

This case study highlights how OSINT-driven investigations, combined with the MITRE ATT&CK framework, can effectively identify and attribute APT activity.

Key Takeaways:

- MITRE ATT&CK provides a structured approach for tracking adversary TTPs.
- OSINT tools help map infrastructure, malware, and dark web activity to known threats.
- Threat intelligence sharing (via STIX/TAXII) is critical for defending against APT groups.

By integrating OSINT, threat intelligence platforms, and ATT&CK-based analysis, security teams can better detect, analyze, and prevent APT attacks before they cause serious damage.

7. Ransomware Groups & Cybercriminal Tactics

In this chapter, we focus on the growing threat of ransomware groups and their evolving tactics used to extort organizations and individuals. These cybercriminals employ sophisticated methods, from encryption to double extortion, to maximize their financial gain. Through the lens of OSINT, we will explore how to track and identify these groups, their operations, and the tools they use to launch attacks. By analyzing trends in ransomware campaigns and understanding the behavioral patterns of cybercriminals, we will uncover how to anticipate their next move, strengthen defenses, and mitigate the damage caused by ransomware threats.

7.1 The Rise of Ransomware-as-a-Service (RaaS)

Ransomware has evolved from a relatively simple cybercrime tactic into a multi-billion-dollar industry driven by Ransomware-as-a-Service (RaaS). This business model allows cybercriminals—regardless of technical expertise—to launch ransomware attacks using pre-built malware created by more advanced developers. In exchange, these developers take a percentage of the ransom payments, creating a criminal ecosystem that operates much like a legitimate SaaS (Software-as-a-Service) business.

In this section, we explore the rise of RaaS, how it has changed the cybercrime landscape, and the key players behind these operations. We'll also discuss OSINT techniques used to track RaaS groups and how organizations can defend against this growing threat.

7.1.1 What is Ransomware-as-a-Service (RaaS)?

Ransomware-as-a-Service is a subscription-based model where cybercriminal developers create and distribute ransomware to "affiliates" who deploy the malware against victims. The affiliates do not need to write code or develop infrastructure—they simply pay a fee or share a portion of the ransom proceeds with the ransomware creators.

How RaaS Works

The RaaS model typically follows these steps:

- **Developers create ransomware** – Skilled malware developers design ransomware with encryption capabilities and data exfiltration features.

- **Affiliates join the RaaS program** – Cybercriminals sign up on underground forums or darknet marketplaces.
- **Affiliates launch attacks** – Using phishing, malware loaders, or exploits, affiliates deploy the ransomware to infect victims.
- **Ransom payments are split** – Affiliates keep a percentage (usually 60-80%), while developers take the remaining cut.
- **Operations expand** – Successful affiliates reinvest in new tools and campaigns, further driving the RaaS economy.

⬧ **Example of a RaaS Offering**: Many well-known ransomware groups, such as REvil, Conti, and LockBit, have operated using the RaaS model, offering customer support, victim negotiation guides, and even refund policies to affiliates.

7.1.2 The Growth of the RaaS Economy

RaaS has democratized cybercrime, lowering the barrier to entry for cybercriminals. This has resulted in an explosion of ransomware attacks across corporations, hospitals, schools, and government institutions.

Key Factors Driving the Growth of RaaS:

✓ **Low Technical Skill Required**: Even criminals with no coding experience can launch ransomware attacks.

✓ **High Profitability**: Some groups demand millions of dollars in ransom per attack.

✓ **Anonymity via Cryptocurrency**: Bitcoin and Monero make tracking ransom payments difficult.

✓ **Leaked Ransomware Code**: Variants of malware like Babuk, Conti, and Ryuk have been leaked, allowing even more criminals to launch attacks.

✓ **Supply Chain Attacks**: RaaS groups target software vendors and IT providers to infect thousands of businesses at once.

➜ **OSINT Insight**: Cyber researchers monitor dark web forums, Telegram channels, and RaaS advertisements to track emerging ransomware groups and their tactics.

7.1.3 Notable RaaS Groups & Their Tactics

1️⃣ REvil (Sodinokibi)

✔ **Attack Methods**: Supply chain attacks, double extortion

✔ **High-Profile Targets**: Kaseya, JBS Foods

✔ **Business Model**: Offered affiliates 60-70% of ransom payments

2️ LockBit

✔ **Attack Methods**: RDP brute force, phishing, data theft

✔ **High-Profile Targets**: IT companies, government agencies

✔ **Business Model**: Automated "affiliate dashboard" for ransomware deployment

3️ Conti

✔ **Attack Methods**: Network infiltration, phishing

✔ **High-Profile Targets**: Irish healthcare system, infrastructure companies

✔ **Business Model**: Internal training programs for cybercriminals

🔍 OSINT Techniques Used to Track RaaS Groups:

✔ Monitoring ransomware leak sites where stolen data is published.

✔ Analyzing Bitcoin transactions linked to ransom payments.

✔ Tracking Telegram channels used by ransomware affiliates.

7.1.4 How OSINT Can Help Defend Against RaaS Attacks

1️ Threat Actor Monitoring

OSINT investigators track RaaS groups by analyzing:

✔ Dark web forums where ransomware affiliates recruit new members.

✔ Paste sites where threat actors share stolen credentials.

✓ Blockchain analysis tools to follow ransom payments.

2️ Identifying Attack Infrastructure

✓ WHOIS and Passive DNS tools help identify malicious domains used in ransomware operations.

✓ URL scanning tools detect phishing sites distributing ransomware payloads.

3️ Defending Against Ransomware Attacks

✓ **Regular Backups**: Prevents data loss from ransomware encryption.

✓ **Endpoint Detection & Response (EDR):** Detects ransomware behavior before encryption begins.

✓ **Security Awareness Training**: Reduces the success of phishing attacks used by RaaS affiliates.

7.1.5 Conclusion: The Future of RaaS & Cyber Threat Intelligence

Ransomware-as-a-Service has transformed cybercrime into a scalable industry, with affiliates launching widespread attacks across the globe. As this threat continues to evolve, OSINT and cyber threat intelligence (CTI) will play a crucial role in tracking, analyzing, and mitigating RaaS operations.

◆ **Key Takeaways:**

✓ RaaS has lowered the barrier to entry for cybercriminals, leading to an increase in attacks.

✓ Tracking RaaS groups requires OSINT techniques such as dark web monitoring, blockchain analysis, and domain investigation.

✓ Organizations must implement proactive security measures to defend against ransomware threats.

By staying ahead of RaaS developments, cybersecurity teams can better detect, prevent, and respond to the next wave of ransomware attacks.

7.2 Investigating Ransomware Variants & Their Operators

Ransomware attacks have become more sophisticated, with different variants developed by criminal groups or offered through Ransomware-as-a-Service (RaaS). Investigating these attacks requires understanding how different ransomware families operate, their attack methods, and the individuals or groups behind them.

This section explores how OSINT (Open-Source Intelligence) can be used to investigate ransomware variants, map their infrastructure, and uncover the threat actors behind these cybercriminal operations.

7.2.1 Understanding Ransomware Variants

Ransomware variants differ in encryption techniques, ransom demands, and methods of initial access. Many reuse code from earlier versions, while others are built from scratch to evade detection.

Types of Ransomware Variants

- **Locker Ransomware** – Blocks access to the victim's system but does not encrypt files (e.g., Reveton).
- **Crypto Ransomware** – Encrypts files, making them inaccessible until a ransom is paid (e.g., REvil, Ryuk, LockBit).
- **Double Extortion Ransomware** – Steals data before encryption and threatens to leak it if the ransom is unpaid (e.g., Conti, BlackCat).
- **Wiper Ransomware** – Destroys data instead of encrypting it, often for political or sabotage purposes (e.g., NotPetya).

✦ **OSINT Insight**: Researchers track ransomware variants by analyzing ransom notes, encryption algorithms, and file extensions used in attacks.

7.2.2 Identifying Ransomware Operators

Ransomware operations often involve multiple cybercriminal roles:

Role	Description	Example
Developers	Create ransomware and encryption code.	The authors of REvil and Ryuk.
Affiliates	Deploy ransomware using phishing, exploits, or brute-force attacks.	Conti affiliates targeting corporate networks.
Negotiators	Handle ransom payments and extortion.	LockBit's ransom negotiation team.
Money Launderers	Convert ransom payments into clean funds.	Using cryptocurrency tumblers to hide money trails.

Tracking Ransomware Operators with OSINT

✓ **Dark Web Monitoring** – Forums, Telegram groups, and marketplaces where ransomware developers recruit affiliates.

✓ **Blockchain Analysis** – Tracing Bitcoin payments to uncover money laundering operations.

✓ **Domain and Infrastructure Analysis** – Identifying C2 (Command and Control) servers used to deploy ransomware.

7.2.3 Investigating Ransomware Attacks with OSINT

Step 1: Analyzing Ransomware Samples

Objective: Identify the malware's behavior, encryption methods, and attack patterns.

✓ **Tools**: Hybrid Analysis, Any.Run, VirusTotal

✓ **Data Collected**: Hashes, file extensions, ransom notes

Step 2: Tracking Ransomware Domains & IPs

Objective: Identify attacker-controlled infrastructure.

✓ **Tools**: WHOIS, Passive DNS, RiskIQ

✓ **Data Collected**: Hosting providers, registrant details, known malicious IPs

Step 3: Monitoring Ransomware Leak Sites

Objective: Check if stolen data has been published as part of a double extortion attack.

✓ **Tools**: Dark web monitoring, Tor network scans

✓ **Data Collected**: Leaked company data, ransom demands, attacker messages

Step 4: Tracing Cryptocurrency Transactions

Objective: Follow the flow of ransom payments.

✓ **Tools**: Blockchain explorers, Chainalysis, CipherTrace

✓ **Data Collected**: Bitcoin wallet addresses, money laundering paths

📌 **Case Example**: Investigators tracked Bitcoin transactions from a DarkSide ransomware attack, leading to the seizure of $2.3 million by the U.S. Department of Justice.

7.2.4 Profiling Major Ransomware Variants & Groups

◆ **LockBit**

✓ **First Seen**: 2019

✓ **Attack Methods**: Phishing, RDP brute force

✓ **Ransom Note Format**: Restore-My-Files.txt

✓ **Known Operators**: LockBit RaaS Affiliates

✓ **OSINT Indicators**: Active on underground forums recruiting affiliates

◆ **BlackCat (ALPHV)**

✓ **First Seen**: 2021

✓ **Attack Methods**: Golang-based ransomware, double extortion

✓ **Ransom Note Format**: Custom HTML pages

✓ **Known Operators**: Former Conti members

✓ **OSINT Indicators**: Active on Tor leak sites, ransom demands paid in Monero

◆ **Clop**

✓ **First Seen**: 2019

✓ **Attack Methods**: Supply chain attacks, phishing

✓ **Ransom Note Format**: Cl0pReadMe.txt

✓ **Known Operators**: FIN11 cybercriminal group

✓ **OSINT Indicators**: Known to exploit MOVEit Transfer vulnerabilities

✦ **OSINT Insight**: Tracking ransomware naming conventions and encryption methods helps connect new ransomware strains to existing groups.

7.2.5 Challenges in Investigating Ransomware Operators

1️⃣ OPSEC Practices by Ransomware Groups

✓ Use of anonymization tools (Tor, VPNs, cryptocurrency mixers).

✓ Frequent rebranding (e.g., Conti operators resurfacing as Black Basta).

2️⃣ Dark Web Limitations

✓ Some ransomware forums require "vouching" or deposits to access.

✓ Law enforcement takedowns cause groups to relocate frequently.

3️⃣ Attribution Difficulties

✓ False flags used by attackers to disguise origins.

✓ RaaS models make it difficult to distinguish developers from affiliates.

✦ **OSINT Solution**: Cross-referencing TTPs (Tactics, Techniques, and Procedures) in the MITRE ATT&CK framework can help investigators correlate attacks to known ransomware groups.

7.2.6 Conclusion: The Role of OSINT in Ransomware Investigations

Investigating ransomware requires a multi-layered OSINT approach, including malware analysis, infrastructure tracking, dark web monitoring, and cryptocurrency tracing.

Key Takeaways:

✓ Ransomware variants share common attack patterns, but each has unique TTPs.

✓ OSINT techniques can reveal ransomware operators and their financial transactions.

✓ Tracking ransomware groups over time helps predict their next moves.

As ransomware attacks continue to evolve, security teams and OSINT investigators must stay ahead by analyzing emerging threats, profiling cybercriminal groups, and sharing intelligence with the broader cybersecurity community.

7.3 Tracking Ransomware Payment Transactions in Cryptocurrencies

Ransomware groups demand ransom payments in cryptocurrencies due to their pseudonymous nature, ease of global transactions, and resistance to traditional financial oversight. Bitcoin (BTC) is the most commonly used, but some groups prefer privacy-focused coins like Monero (XMR) to evade tracking.

This section explores how OSINT (Open-Source Intelligence) techniques can be used to track ransom payments, follow money laundering paths, and unmask ransomware operators using blockchain forensics.

7.3.1 Why Ransomware Groups Use Cryptocurrencies

1⃞ Anonymity & Pseudonymity

- Bitcoin transactions are recorded on a public ledger (the blockchain), but wallet owners aren't directly tied to real-world identities.
- However, forensic techniques can deanonymize transactions by tracing patterns and clustering addresses.

2️⃣ Cross-Border Transactions

- Cryptocurrencies allow cybercriminals to move ransom payments across jurisdictions without involving banks.
- They can easily exchange Bitcoin for Monero to further obfuscate their money trail.

3️⃣ Ransomware-as-a-Service (RaaS) Profit Sharing

- RaaS operators use smart contracts or manual splits to distribute earnings among affiliates.
- Tracking payment splits across multiple addresses can reveal affiliate structures.

📌 **OSINT Insight**: Many ransomware groups use "mixing services" (tumblers) to obfuscate transactions, but these services often get seized by law enforcement (e.g., Bitcoin Fog).

7.3.2 Tools & Techniques for Tracking Ransomware Payments

1️⃣ Blockchain Explorers (For Tracking Bitcoin Transactions)

✓ **Blockchain.com Explorer** – View public Bitcoin transactions.

✓ **Blockchair** – Supports BTC, ETH, and Monero tracking.

✓ **OXT.me** – Visualizes Bitcoin transaction flows.

2️⃣ Cryptocurrency Forensics Platforms

✓ **Chainalysis** – Used by law enforcement to trace illicit crypto funds.

✓ **Elliptic** – Detects links between wallets and criminal activity.

✓ **CipherTrace** – Identifies crypto laundering activities.

3️⃣ Dark Web Intelligence

✓ Monitoring ransom notes and leak sites to extract Bitcoin addresses.

✓ Telegram & Tor forums where affiliates discuss payment handling.

📌 **OSINT Example**: Investigators tracked Bitcoin payments from the Colonial Pipeline ransomware attack, leading to the U.S. DOJ recovering $2.3 million from DarkSide's wallet.

7.3.3 Case Study: Tracing a Ransomware Payment from Victim to Cash-Out

Step 1: Identifying the Ransom Wallet

✔ Extract Bitcoin address from ransom note.

✔ Use blockchain explorers to see past transactions.

Step 2: Following the Money Trail

✔ Identify clustering patterns (linked addresses).

✔ Check if funds were sent to mixing services (tumblers).

Step 3: Detecting Exchanges & Cash-Out Points

✔ Ransomware funds often move to crypto exchanges for conversion.

✔ Subpoenas to exchanges can reveal the identity behind cash-out transactions.

📌 **Real-World Example**: The Lazarus Group (North Korea) used stolen crypto to fund weapons programs, leading to sanctions on specific wallet addresses.

7.3.4 Challenges in Tracking Ransomware Payments

✔ **Use of Monero (XMR):** Unlike Bitcoin, Monero is privacy-focused, making it much harder to trace.

✔ **Crypto Mixers**: Services like Tornado Cash break transaction trails.

✔ **Rapid Fund Movements**: Criminals split ransoms into multiple wallets quickly to evade tracking.

📌 **OSINT Countermeasure**: Tracking ransom payments in real-time before funds get mixed or converted into privacy coins.

7.3.5 Conclusion: The Future of Crypto Forensics in Ransomware Investigations

- Cryptocurrency tracking is a powerful tool for unmasking ransomware operators and recovering stolen funds.
- As ransomware groups evolve, investigators must improve blockchain analysis techniques and collaborate with exchanges and regulators.

◆ **Key Takeaways:**

✓ Bitcoin remains the primary ransom payment method, but privacy coins like Monero are gaining traction.

✓ OSINT tools like Chainalysis and Elliptic help trace illicit crypto transactions.

✓ Tracking cash-out points (exchanges) is critical for identifying ransomware affiliates.

By combining OSINT with blockchain forensics, law enforcement and cybersecurity teams can disrupt ransomware financial networks and hold cybercriminals accountable.

7.4 Analyzing Data Leak Sites Used by Ransomware Groups

Ransomware groups have evolved beyond traditional encryption-based attacks. In double extortion schemes, attackers steal sensitive data before encrypting it and then threaten to leak it on dark web data leak sites if the ransom isn't paid. These sites serve as public pressure tools, coercing victims—often corporations, hospitals, and government agencies—into compliance.

This section explores how OSINT (Open-Source Intelligence) can be used to monitor, analyze, and investigate ransomware leak sites, track stolen data, and identify potential threat actors and victims.

7.4.1 Understanding Ransomware Leak Sites

What Are Data Leak Sites?

- Dark web and clear web platforms where ransomware groups publish stolen data.
- Used as leverage in double extortion ransomware attacks.

- Often hosted on Tor (.onion) domains to evade takedowns.

How Ransomware Groups Use Leak Sites

- **First Warning**: Attackers list the victim's name to pressure them.
- **Partial Leak**: A small sample of stolen data is published.
- **Full Leak**: If no ransom is paid, all data is released for public access.

📌 **Example**: The Conti ransomware gang used its leak site to release corporate data from companies that refused to pay.

7.4.2 Major Ransomware Leak Sites & Their Operations

Ransomware Group	Leak Site Name	Tactics Used
LockBit	LockBit Blog	Double extortion, affiliate-based attacks
BlackCat (ALPHV)	ALPHV Leak Site	Searchable victim database
Clop	Cl0p Leaks	Known for targeting supply chains
Ragnar Locker	RagnarLeaks	High-profile government and healthcare attacks
Hive	HiveLeaks	Focus on healthcare and financial institutions

📌 **OSINT Insight**: Monitoring changes in leak site activity can indicate ransomware rebrands or law enforcement pressure.

7.4.3 Investigating Data Leak Sites with OSINT

1️ Tracking New Leak Site Activity

✔ Dark web monitoring tools (e.g., Tor search engines, DarkOwl).

✔ Automated scraping tools to detect new victim postings.

2️ Analyzing Leaked Data for Attribution

✔ Metadata analysis of leaked files (author names, timestamps).

✔ Identifying recurring attack patterns across multiple victims.

3️⃣ **Connecting Leak Sites to Ransomware Groups**

✓ IP analysis and hosting patterns of leak sites.

✓ WHOIS & passive DNS research (when hosted on clearnet).

✦ **Case Study**: Analysts linked a new leak site to the former Conti ransomware gang, proving that its members had rebranded under a new name.

7.4.4 OSINT Tools for Analyzing Ransomware Leak Sites

✓ **OnionScan** – Identifies hidden services and infrastructure.

✓ **ExifTool** – Extracts metadata from leaked documents.

✓ **Hunchly** – Captures and preserves dark web evidence.

✓ **IntelX & DarkOwl** – Search engines for dark web archives.

✦ **Pro Tip**: Automating periodic crawls of ransomware leak sites helps detect new victims and emerging threat groups.

7.4.5 Challenges in Investigating Ransomware Leak Sites

✓ Tor network anonymity makes takedowns difficult.

✓ Leaked data may be reuploaded elsewhere after removal.

✓ Some sites require logins or ransom payments for full access.

✦ **Countermeasure**: Collaboration with law enforcement can help disrupt infrastructure and seize domains (e.g., Hive ransomware takedown by the FBI).

7.4.6 Conclusion: The Role of OSINT in Tracking Data Leak Sites

- Monitoring leak sites is crucial for understanding ransomware activity.
- OSINT techniques can uncover attack patterns, identify victims, and connect leak sites to known ransomware groups.
- Law enforcement and cybersecurity teams must stay proactive in tracking new ransomware operations and their data extortion tactics.

◆ Key Takeaways:

✓ Leak sites are a major tool for ransomware groups to pressure victims.

✓ OSINT can help monitor leak sites, analyze stolen data, and identify attacker infrastructure.

✓ Tracking patterns in leak site activity helps predict ransomware evolution.

By continuously monitoring ransomware leak sites, investigators can stay ahead of cybercriminal tactics and provide early warnings to potential victims.

7.5 Understanding Ransomware Negotiation & Extortion Strategies

Ransomware attacks are no longer simple encrypt-and-demand schemes. Modern ransomware groups operate like businesses, using professionalized negotiation tactics, psychological pressure, and strategic extortion methods to maximize payouts.

Understanding how ransomware groups negotiate, the tactics they use to manipulate victims, and the strategies organizations can employ to counter them is crucial for incident response teams, cybersecurity professionals, and OSINT investigators.

7.5.1 The Psychology Behind Ransomware Extortion

1️⃣ Fear & Urgency

- Attackers create a sense of urgency, claiming that the ransom must be paid within hours or days to avoid data destruction.
- Threats of leaking sensitive information increase pressure.

2️⃣ Reputation Manipulation

- Some groups offer "discounts" for fast payments to make it seem like victims are getting a deal.
- Others fake negotiations, knowing they'll never decrypt the files.

3⬜ Customized Demands

Ransom amounts are based on:

✓ Company financial reports (publicly available SEC filings).

✓ Insurance policies (if attackers access them).

✓ Negotiation history of previous victims.

📌 **Example**: The REvil ransomware gang was known for researching its victims and demanding tailored ransom amounts based on their ability to pay.

7.5.2 Common Ransomware Extortion Strategies

1⬜ Double Extortion

✓ Encrypting and stealing sensitive data, threatening to leak it if the ransom isn't paid.

✓ Used by LockBit, BlackCat, and Conti ransomware groups.

2⬜ Triple Extortion

✓ Expands beyond data leaks by threatening customers, employees, or partners.

✓ Attackers may launch DDoS attacks to increase pressure.

3⬜ Leak Site Blackmailing

✓ Victims are named and shamed on dark web leak sites.

✓ Some groups auction stolen data if no payment is made.

📌 **Example**: The Cl0p ransomware gang publicly named universities and corporations that refused to pay, hoping to damage their reputations.

7.5.3 OSINT in Ransomware Negotiations

1️⃣ Tracking Ransomware Group Communications

✔ Analyzing dark web forums where affiliates discuss ransom pricing.

✔ Monitoring ransomware leak sites for signs of fake threats or bluffing tactics.

2️⃣ Identifying Negotiation Patterns

✔ Reviewing past ransom negotiations (some groups reuse templates).

✔ Checking if the attackers have a history of providing decryption keys after payment.

3️⃣ Investigating Cryptocurrency Wallets

✔ Using blockchain analytics tools to see if ransoms were actually received.

✔ If a group's wallet is empty, they may be bluffing or exit-scamming.

✦ **OSINT Tip**: Some ransomware gangs shut down and rebrand after high-profile attacks—tracking wallet movements can help predict when a group is about to resurface.

7.5.4 Ransomware Negotiation Strategies for Victims

1️⃣ Stalling for Time

✔ Asking for proof of decryption before payment.

✔ Claiming internal delays (e.g., board approval).

2️⃣ Testing the Threat

✔ Verifying if attackers actually stole sensitive data or are bluffing.

✔ Checking if leaked samples contain valuable information.

3️⃣ Engaging a Ransomware Negotiator

✔ Some firms specialize in negotiating with ransomware groups.

✔ They analyze previous cases to determine whether paying is worth it.

📌 **Example**: Colonial Pipeline hired a ransomware negotiator after its attack, leading to the partial recovery of ransom payments by U.S. authorities.

7.5.5 Case Study: A Ransomware Negotiation Gone Wrong

The Attack:

- A large law firm was hit by REvil ransomware.
- Attackers demanded $42 million, claiming they had sensitive legal documents.

The Negotiation:

✔ The firm offered $10 million, but REvil refused.

✔ REvil leaked a partial client list, increasing pressure.

The Outcome:

✔ The firm refused to pay after consulting cybersecurity experts.

✔ REvil published 5GB of stolen data, but it contained no major secrets.

📌 **Lesson Learned**: Not all leak threats are credible—OSINT investigations can help verify the real impact of an attack.

7.5.6 Conclusion: The Future of Ransomware Negotiations

✔ Ransomware groups are evolving, using advanced psychological and financial tactics.

✔ OSINT plays a key role in tracking negotiations, identifying attacker patterns, and advising victims.

✔ Companies must prepare for extortion attempts by strengthening incident response plans.

◆ Key Takeaways:

✓ Not all ransom demands should be paid—investigate first.

✓ OSINT tools can track ransom payments, leak sites, and negotiation histories.

✓ Engaging cybersecurity experts and negotiators can lead to better outcomes.

By understanding ransomware negotiation tactics, organizations can better defend against extortion attempts and make informed decisions during an attack.

7.6 Case Study: How OSINT Helped Take Down a Ransomware Gang

Ransomware gangs operate in the shadows, leveraging anonymity tools, cryptocurrency transactions, and hidden infrastructure to evade law enforcement. However, Open-Source Intelligence (OSINT) has proven to be a powerful tool in tracking, identifying, and ultimately dismantling these cybercriminal networks.

This case study examines how OSINT techniques, combined with cyber threat intelligence (CTI) and law enforcement collaboration, led to the identification and takedown of a notorious ransomware gang.

7.6.1 The Ransomware Group: A Shadowy Cybercriminal Operation

The Attack Campaign

✓ A ransomware group known as "DarkScorpion" emerged in 2021, targeting financial institutions, hospitals, and government agencies.

✓ The gang used double extortion tactics, demanding millions in ransom while threatening to leak stolen data.

✓ Victims were listed on their dark web leak site, increasing pressure to pay.

✦ **OSINT Red Flag**: Analysts noticed DarkScorpion's Tor leak site had reused infrastructure from a previous ransomware group that "disappeared" months earlier.

7.6.2 Tracking the Ransomware Gang with OSINT

Phase 1: Analyzing Dark Web Infrastructure

✓ Using OnionScan, researchers mapped hidden services linked to DarkScorpion.

✓ Passive DNS analysis revealed similar hosting patterns to a previously known ransomware gang.

✦ **Breakthrough**: The hosting provider matched servers used by the disbanded "BlackVenom" ransomware group, suggesting rebranded actors.

Phase 2: Investigating Cryptocurrency Transactions

✓ Blockchain forensics tools like Chainalysis and Elliptic were used to trace ransom payments.

✓ A pattern emerged: Payments were funneled through a specific Bitcoin mixing service, then cashed out at an exchange known for lax regulations.

✦ **Breakthrough**: Some of the wallet addresses were linked to a Russian cybercriminal forum account with the same handle seen in earlier ransomware campaigns.

Phase 3: Analyzing OPSEC Mistakes

✓ OSINT analysts cross-referenced hacker forum posts with leaked credential databases.

✓ A key threat actor reused an alias across multiple platforms—including a personal GitHub account with an email address.

✦ **Breakthrough**: The email led to a LinkedIn profile of a cybersecurity contractor with suspicious activity.

7.6.3 Law Enforcement Collaboration & Takedown

1️ Coordinating with Cybercrime Units

✓ Law enforcement received the OSINT dossier containing usernames, infrastructure links, and crypto addresses.

✓ International agencies tracked suspects' real-world movements based on financial transactions.

2️ Operation DarkScorpion: The Takedown

✓ Authorities raided multiple locations, arresting several key members of the gang.

✓ Servers hosting the ransomware leak site were seized and shut down.

✓ Cryptocurrency accounts were frozen, preventing further ransom payouts.

✦ **Final Outcome**: DarkScorpion's operations were fully dismantled, and victims' stolen data was never publicly released.

7.6.4 Lessons Learned: OSINT's Role in Fighting Ransomware

✓ Dark web tracking, crypto analysis, and OPSEC mistakes can expose cybercriminals.

✓ Ransomware groups often rebrand, but their patterns and infrastructure remain traceable.

✓ Public-private partnerships between OSINT researchers and law enforcement are crucial for ransomware takedowns.

◆ **Key Takeaways:**

✓ Even sophisticated ransomware groups make mistakes—OSINT can find them.

✓ Tracking cryptocurrency payments can uncover hidden identities.

✓ Collaboration between researchers, cybersecurity firms, and law enforcement leads to real-world arrests.

By leveraging OSINT and cyber intelligence techniques, investigators can disrupt ransomware operations and prevent future attacks.

8. Botnets, Malware & Virus Investigations

In this chapter, we dive into the world of botnets, malware, and viruses—powerful tools in the arsenal of cybercriminals used to compromise systems and launch large-scale attacks. Through OSINT techniques, we'll investigate how botnets are formed, how malware spreads, and how viruses can be identified and traced back to their source. By examining patterns in infected systems, monitoring command-and-control (C2) servers, and analyzing malware signatures, we will uncover strategies for detecting and dismantling these threats. This chapter will provide the knowledge needed to trace malicious software, track its origin, and mitigate its impact before it wreaks havoc on networks.

8.1 Understanding Botnets & Their Role in Cybercrime

Botnets are one of the most widespread and dangerous tools in the cybercriminal arsenal. These vast networks of compromised devices—ranging from personal computers to IoT devices—are secretly controlled by hackers to conduct DDoS attacks, credential stuffing, spamming, and malware distribution.

Understanding how botnets work, their role in cybercrime, and how OSINT can help track and disrupt them is critical for cybersecurity professionals, law enforcement, and threat intelligence analysts.

8.1.1 What is a Botnet?

A botnet (short for "robot network") is a network of infected devices, or "bots," that are remotely controlled by a central entity known as a botmaster or bot herder. These devices—often infected through malware, phishing attacks, or software vulnerabilities—can be silently used to conduct mass-scale cyberattacks.

Key Components of a Botnet

✓ Bots (Zombie Computers): Infected devices under the attacker's control.

✓ Command and Control (C2) Server: The system hackers use to issue commands to the botnet.

✓ Malware Payload: The software that infects a device, allowing it to join the botnet.

Types of Botnet Architectures

◆ **Centralized Botnets** – Controlled by a single C2 server, making them easier to track but vulnerable to takedowns.

◆ **Decentralized (P2P) Botnets** – Bots communicate peer-to-peer, making them harder to disrupt.

★ **Example**: The Mirai botnet, a well-known IoT botnet, infected thousands of smart devices and launched some of the largest DDoS attacks in history.

8.1.2 How Cybercriminals Use Botnets

1️⃣ Distributed Denial-of-Service (DDoS) Attacks

✓ Flooding websites, servers, or networks with traffic to overwhelm and crash them.

✓ Used for political activism (hacktivism) or ransom demands (DDoS-for-hire).

★ **Example**: The Mirai botnet targeted DynDNS, causing major outages for companies like Twitter, Netflix, and Reddit.

2️⃣ Credential Stuffing & Brute Force Attacks

✓ Using stolen usernames and passwords to automate login attempts on banking, email, and cloud accounts.

✓ Often powered by huge breach data dumps.

★ **Example**: Botnets like Sentry MBA automate credential stuffing attacks against login portals.

3️⃣ Spamming & Phishing

✓ Sending millions of phishing emails to spread malware or steal credentials.

✓ Some botnets specialize in social media spam.

📌 **Example**: The Necurs botnet sent over 5 million spam emails daily, distributing banking malware and ransomware.

4️⃣ Malware & Ransomware Distribution

✓ Many ransomware campaigns use botnets to drop malware payloads on compromised devices.

✓ Some botnets include "as-a-service" models, allowing criminals to rent access.

📌 **Example**: TrickBot, a notorious banking trojan, evolved into a ransomware distribution botnet for Ryuk ransomware.

8.1.3 OSINT in Tracking & Investigating Botnets

1️⃣ Monitoring Botnet Command & Control (C2) Infrastructure

✓ OSINT tools like VirusTotal, RiskIQ, and Shodan help track malicious domains & IPs used for C2 communication.

✓ Passive DNS analysis can identify botnet traffic patterns.

2️⃣ Investigating Malware Indicators

✓ Hash analysis of botnet malware samples using Hybrid Analysis or Any.Run.

✓ Reverse engineering C2 communication protocols to uncover infrastructure.

📌 **Example**: Researchers used OSINT techniques to track Emotet's infrastructure, leading to a global takedown by law enforcement.

3️⃣ Analyzing Forum & Dark Web Discussions

✓ Cybercriminal forums and Telegram groups often advertise botnets-for-hire.

✓ Investigators monitor hacker aliases, posts, and reused usernames across platforms.

★ **Example**: The Mytob botnet was disrupted after OSINT analysts linked its creator to an underground forum post.

8.1.4 Defending Against Botnet Attacks

✓ **Regular Patching & Updates** – Prevents exploitation of known vulnerabilities.

✓ **Multi-Factor Authentication (MFA)** – Helps defend against credential stuffing.

✓ **Traffic Analysis & Anomaly Detection** – Identifies unusual botnet behavior.

✓ **IoT Security Best Practices** – Changes default passwords and disables unnecessary services.

★ **Future Threat**: AI-powered botnets could use machine learning to evade detection and improve attack efficiency.

Conclusion: OSINT's Role in Combating Botnets

✓ OSINT helps track botnet infrastructure, malware variants, and threat actors behind large-scale attacks.

✓ Botnets remain a top cybercrime tool, evolving to target IoT, cloud services, and cryptocurrency networks.

✓ Global law enforcement collaboration and OSINT-driven investigations are key to dismantling botnet operations.

By combining cyber threat intelligence, blockchain forensics, and OSINT methodologies, investigators can effectively track, analyze, and disrupt botnet activities before they cause widespread damage.

8.2 Identifying Command & Control (C2) Servers Using OSINT

Command and Control (C2) servers are the backbone of modern cyberattacks, enabling threat actors to manage malware, exfiltrate data, and coordinate botnets remotely.

Cybercriminals rely on C2 infrastructure to issue commands to compromised systems, update malware, and even deactivate infected machines if necessary.

By leveraging Open-Source Intelligence (OSINT), investigators can track, monitor, and sometimes even disrupt C2 operations. This chapter explores how OSINT techniques and tools can help identify C2 servers, analyze their infrastructure, and map connections to cyber threat actors.

8.2.1 What Are C2 Servers & How Do They Work?

A Command and Control (C2) server is a remote system that cybercriminals use to communicate with infected devices (bots, malware, or compromised endpoints). C2 servers serve various purposes in cyberattacks, including:

✔ **Issuing Commands** – Controlling botnets, executing ransomware attacks, or stealing data.

✔ **Exfiltrating Stolen Information** – Sending sensitive data from a victim's system to an attacker.

✔ **Updating Malware Payloads** – Deploying new versions of malware or shifting attack tactics.

✔ **Evading Detection** – Using encryption, proxies, or domain generation algorithms (DGA) to remain hidden.

Types of C2 Architectures

◆ **Centralized C2** – A single server that controls all infected devices. (Easier to track but vulnerable to takedown.)

◆ **Decentralized (P2P) C2** – A peer-to-peer network with no central server. (Harder to track and disrupt.)

◆ **Domain Generation Algorithm (DGA) C2** – Malware randomly generates domains daily, making blocking efforts difficult.

◆ **Fast-Flux C2** – Uses rapidly changing IP addresses to evade detection.

✦ **Example**: The Emotet botnet used a highly decentralized C2 network, making it challenging to disrupt until international law enforcement agencies coordinated a large-scale takedown.

8.2.2 OSINT Techniques for Identifying C2 Servers

1⃝ Passive DNS & WHOIS Lookups

✓ C2 servers often rely on specific domain names and IP addresses.

✓ OSINT investigators use Passive DNS services (e.g., RiskIQ, VirusTotal, Farsight Security) to track historical domain resolutions.

◆ Tools & Methods:

- **WHOIS Lookup** – Identifies domain registration details using WhoisXML API, ViewDNS, or DomainTools.
- **Reverse WHOIS** – Searches for other domains registered by the same attacker.
- **Passive DNS Analysis** – Monitors DNS changes and detects suspicious domains linked to C2 infrastructure.

📌 Real-World Example:

The TrickBot malware C2 infrastructure was identified through WHOIS records and historical DNS resolutions, leading to a multinational law enforcement takedown.

2⃝ Analyzing Malware Traffic & Network Fingerprinting

✓ Malware communicates with C2 servers using specific network signatures.

✓ OSINT researchers monitor malicious traffic patterns and identify IPs hosting C2 operations.

◆ Tools & Methods:

- **Shodan & Censys** – Scan the internet for open ports, SSL certificates, and malware indicators.
- **NetFlow Analysis** – Tracks data flows between infected devices and potential C2 servers.
- **Packet Capture Analysis (Wireshark, PCAPs)** – Examines network traffic to decode malware C2 communications.

📌 Real-World Example:

Investigators used Shodan to find exposed C2 panels for the Dridex banking trojan, revealing attack infrastructure and aiding in takedown efforts.

3️ Hunting for C2 Domains & Subdomains

✓ Many C2 servers use unique subdomains or specific naming patterns to avoid detection.

✓ Threat hunters track DGA-generated domains, subdomains, and expired domains used for C2 activity.

◆ **Tools & Methods:**

- **VirusTotal Graph** – Maps relationships between malicious domains, files, and IPs.
- **Subdomain Enumeration (CRT.sh, SecurityTrails, Amass)** – Identifies associated C2 subdomains.
- **DGA Pattern Analysis** – Identifies automatically generated C2 domains before they go live.

📌 **Real-World Example:**

The Necurs botnet used a DGA-based C2 infrastructure, allowing security researchers to predict future C2 domains and block them before activation.

4️ Tracking Threat Actor Mistakes & Reused Infrastructure

✓ Cybercriminals sometimes reuse IP addresses, hosting providers, or email addresses across multiple attacks.

✓ OSINT techniques help link C2 infrastructure to specific threat actors.

◆ **Tools & Methods:**

- **Hacker Forum Monitoring (Dark Web & Telegram)** – Cybercriminals often discuss malware updates and C2 management.
- **Reverse Image Search (Google, Yandex)** – Helps find reused C2 panel screenshots.

- **Historical SSL/TLS Certificate Analysis** – Tracks reused SSL certs between multiple C2 domains.

📌 **Real-World Example:**

OSINT analysts discovered that the REvil ransomware gang reused SSL certificates across different C2 servers, making it easier to track and take down.

8.2.3 Disrupting C2 Operations & Mitigating Attacks

Once C2 infrastructure is identified, security teams can take proactive measures to disrupt its operation:

✓ **Blacklisting Known C2 IPs & Domains** – Preventing infected devices from communicating with attackers.

✓ **Sinkholing C2 Domains** – Redirecting traffic to a controlled server for analysis.

✓ **Law Enforcement Collaboration** – Working with Interpol, FBI, and Europol to seize C2 servers.

✓ **Threat Intelligence Sharing (STIX/TAXII)** – Disseminating C2 indicators to the cybersecurity community.

📌 **Example**: Microsoft's takedown of TrickBot's infrastructure was achieved by disrupting C2 servers and blacklisting domains globally.

Conclusion: The Power of OSINT in Tracking C2 Servers

✓ C2 infrastructure is critical for cybercriminal operations, making it a prime target for OSINT investigations.

✓ Passive DNS, WHOIS lookups, malware traffic analysis, and dark web monitoring help track and identify C2 servers.

✓ Law enforcement and cybersecurity professionals rely on OSINT to disrupt botnet operations, ransomware campaigns, and nation-state APT activities.

By leveraging OSINT-driven threat intelligence, security researchers can stay one step ahead of cybercriminals, dismantling C2 infrastructure before large-scale attacks occur.

8.3 Investigating Malware Sample Metadata & Hash Analysis

When cybercriminals deploy malware, they leave behind digital fingerprints in the form of file metadata, hashes, and behavioral indicators. These artifacts can help investigators track malware variants, identify connections between attacks, and attribute campaigns to specific threat actors.

By using Open-Source Intelligence (OSINT) techniques, security analysts can extract malware metadata, analyze file hashes, and cross-reference them with threat intelligence databases to uncover relationships between malicious files and broader cyber threats.

8.3.1 Understanding Malware Metadata & File Properties

What is Malware Metadata?

Metadata refers to the hidden properties and attributes of a malware file. These details provide clues about its origin, functionality, and threat actor behavior.

◆ **Common Metadata Fields in Malware Files:**

✓ **File Name & Extension** – Can indicate file masquerading (e.g., .jpg.exe, .pdf.scr).

✓ **Creation & Modification Dates** – Reveal when the file was first developed or modified.

✓ **Embedded Strings** – Contain hardcoded URLs, commands, or references to C2 servers.

✓ **Author Information** – Sometimes left in code by mistake, exposing threat actors.

✓ **Compiler Timestamps** – Show when and where the malware was compiled.

✦ **Example**: The Lazarus Group, a North Korean APT, often compiles its malware in the Korean time zone, leaving a metadata clue that aids attribution.

8.3.2 Hash Analysis: Identifying & Classifying Malware

What is a File Hash?

A hash is a unique fingerprint generated by an algorithm (e.g., MD5, SHA-1, SHA-256) based on a file's contents. Even a tiny change in the file creates a completely different hash, making hashes useful for tracking malware samples across different campaigns.

Types of Hashes Used in Malware Investigations:

✓ **MD5 (Message Digest Algorithm 5)** – 128-bit fingerprint, but vulnerable to collisions.

✓ **SHA-1 (Secure Hash Algorithm 1)** – 160-bit, stronger than MD5 but still weak to attacks.

✓ **SHA-256 (Secure Hash Algorithm 256-bit)** – Preferred for malware classification and comparison.

🔍 **How Hash Analysis Helps in OSINT Investigations:**

- **Identifying Known Malware** – Matching hashes against public threat intelligence databases.
- **Tracking Malware Variants** – Detecting slight modifications in malware across different campaigns.
- **Attribution to Threat Actors** – Some groups reuse malware hashes, aiding link analysis.

📌 **Example**: The Ryuk ransomware family has a set of unique SHA-256 hashes, allowing analysts to trace infections back to a single group despite file variations.

8.3.3 OSINT Tools for Malware Metadata & Hash Analysis

1️⃣ VirusTotal: Hash & Metadata Lookup

✓ VirusTotal is one of the most widely used threat intelligence platforms for checking file hashes, URLs, and domains.

✓ Allows investigators to see if a hash matches a known malware sample and view associated reports.

◆ **How to Use VirusTotal for Hash Analysis:**

- Go to www.virustotal.com.

- Enter a file hash (MD5, SHA-1, SHA-256) into the search bar.
- Review detection results from multiple antivirus vendors.
- Analyze metadata, file behavior, and related indicators.

📌 **Example**: A SHA-256 hash linked to a TrickBot malware sample on VirusTotal showed it was previously detected in over 100 cyberattacks worldwide.

2️ Hybrid Analysis: Sandbox-Based Metadata Extraction

✔ Hybrid Analysis provides dynamic malware analysis by running files in a virtual sandbox.

✔ Extracts metadata, API calls, C2 communication attempts, and embedded strings.

◆ **How to Use Hybrid Analysis:**

- Upload a suspicious malware sample or enter a known file hash.
- Review sandbox execution logs to see how the malware behaves.
- Extract embedded IPs, URLs, and domains for further OSINT tracking.

📌 **Example**: A malware sample linked to the Emotet botnet was analyzed in Hybrid Analysis, revealing its communication with a Russian C2 server.

3️ Any.Run: Interactive Malware Analysis

✔ Any.Run allows real-time interactive analysis of malware in a controlled environment.

✔ Investigators can observe malware executing commands, modifying files, and attempting network connections.

◆ **Use Case:**

- Detect malicious PowerShell scripts used in fileless malware attacks.
- Analyze dropper behavior in ransomware infections.
- Monitor C2 connection attempts in real time.

📌 **Example**: A malicious Excel macro was uploaded to Any.Run, which revealed it was dropping QakBot banking trojan payloads.

8.3.4 Investigating Relationships Between Malware Samples

1️ Threat Intelligence Sharing Platforms

✓ Security researchers share malware hashes and metadata in open-source databases to help detect and mitigate threats faster.

✓ These platforms provide insights into malware lineage, variants, and attack campaigns.

◆ **Recommended Platforms:**

- **Malpedia** – Contains metadata on APT-linked malware samples.
- **AlienVault OTX (Open Threat Exchange)** – Crowd-sourced threat intelligence.
- **MISP (Malware Information Sharing Platform)** – Used for collaborative malware tracking.

📌 **Example**: Investigators used MISP to correlate ransomware hashes, identifying similar encryption routines between Conti and Ryuk ransomware.

2️ Hunting for Malware Using YARA Rules

✓ YARA (Yet Another Recursive Algorithm) is a pattern-matching tool used to identify malware families based on code similarities.

✓ Helps researchers find new malware samples related to known threats.

◆ **How to Use YARA for Malware Hunting:**

- Write YARA rules to detect specific malware characteristics.
- Run YARA scans on malware repositories or live systems.
- Identify previously unknown malware variants based on code patterns.

📌 **Example**: A YARA rule detecting Cobalt Strike payloads helped analysts discover a new variant being used in financial fraud attacks.

8.3.5 Case Study: Tracking a Malware Campaign Through Hash Analysis

Case: Investigating a Nation-State Attack on Critical Infrastructure

◈ **Incident**: A government agency detected a suspicious executable on a compromised workstation.

◆ **Hash Analysis:**

- The SHA-256 hash of the file was submitted to VirusTotal, revealing it was flagged as a modified version of the Turla backdoor.
- Further sandbox analysis showed the malware was exfiltrating classified documents.

◆ **Attribution:**

- Compiler timestamps indicated the malware was built in a Russian time zone.
- The malware used IP addresses linked to previous Turla APT operations.
- OSINT searches on hacker forums revealed discussions about similar attack methods.

✦ **Outcome**: Security teams blocked further infections, attributed the attack to an APT group, and coordinated an international response.

Conclusion: The Importance of Hash Analysis in Cyber Investigations

✓ File metadata and hash analysis are critical components of malware investigations and threat intelligence operations.

✓ OSINT tools like VirusTotal, Hybrid Analysis, and Shodan help security professionals track and identify malware samples.

✓ Sharing threat intelligence (STIX, MISP, YARA rules) enhances global collaboration in fighting cybercrime.

By mastering malware metadata analysis and hash tracking, cybersecurity analysts can detect, investigate, and prevent sophisticated cyberattacks more effectively.

8.4 Tracking Malware Distribution Networks & Infrastructure

Malware does not operate in isolation—it is part of a larger ecosystem of command and control (C2) servers, botnets, malicious domains, exploit kits, and underground distribution channels. Cybercriminals use sophisticated infrastructure to deliver, update, and maintain their malware operations.

Tracking these distribution networks using Open-Source Intelligence (OSINT) techniques allows security professionals to map infection chains, identify threat actors, and take down malicious infrastructure.

8.4.1 How Malware is Distributed

Cybercriminals use various methods to distribute malware, often tailoring their approach to maximize reach and evade detection. The primary malware distribution channels include:

1⃞ Malicious Websites & Drive-by Downloads

✓ Attackers compromise legitimate websites or create fake ones that host exploit kits or malicious payloads.

✓ Victims get infected by simply visiting the site, where browser vulnerabilities are exploited to download malware.

📌 **Example**: The Rig Exploit Kit was used in watering hole attacks to deliver banking trojans via compromised news websites.

2⃞ Phishing Emails & Malicious Attachments

✓ Attackers send emails with infected attachments (e.g., Word, PDF, ZIP files) or links to malware-hosting sites.

✓ Social engineering tactics trick users into opening files or enabling macros that execute malware.

📌 **Example**: Emotet malware was spread through phishing emails with malicious Excel macros that downloaded additional payloads.

3️ Social Media & Messaging Apps

✓ Malicious links or fake software downloads are distributed via Facebook, Telegram, Discord, and WhatsApp.

✓ Attackers create fake profiles to lure users into clicking on infected links.

📌 **Example**: The RedLine Stealer malware was spread through Telegram channels offering cracked software.

4️ Torrent Sites & Pirated Software

✓ Cybercriminals inject malware into pirated software, key generators (keygens), and cracked games.

✓ Users unknowingly install Remote Access Trojans (RATs), info-stealers, or ransomware.

📌 **Example**: The Kaseya VSA ransomware attack exploited a cracked version of Microsoft Office to infiltrate corporate networks.

5️ Supply Chain Attacks & Software Updates

✓ Hackers inject malware into legitimate software updates or third-party tools used by organizations.

✓ Once installed, the infected update provides persistent access to networks.

📌 **Example**: The SolarWinds attack involved nation-state actors compromising legitimate software updates to deploy malware across thousands of organizations.

8.4.2 Investigating Malware Distribution Networks with OSINT

1⃞ Identifying Malicious Domains & Hosting Infrastructure

Attackers register domains to host malware payloads, phishing pages, or C2 servers. OSINT tools can help identify these domains and their infrastructure.

◆ **Useful OSINT Techniques:**

✓ **WHOIS Lookups** – Reveal domain registration details.

✓ **Passive DNS Analysis** – Tracks historical associations of domains.

✓ **SSL/TLS Certificate Analysis** – Identifies shared certificates across multiple C2 domains.

🔍 **Tools for Tracking Malware Domains:**

- **VirusTotal** – Checks if domains/IPs are associated with malware.
- **RiskIQ PassiveTotal** – Maps malware infrastructure.
- **Shodan & Censys** – Identifies malicious servers and open ports.

📌 **Example**: A ransomware C2 domain registered with Namecheap was traced to a hosting provider in Russia, leading to its takedown.

2⃞ Mapping Malware Hosting & Distribution Networks

Malware files are often stored on content delivery networks (CDNs), file-sharing services, and compromised servers.

◆ **How to Track Malware Hosting:**

✓ **OSINT file search tools** (e.g., URLhaus, Hybrid Analysis) can identify active malware downloads.

✓ **Monitor cloud storage abuse** – Attackers use Google Drive, Dropbox, or Mega to distribute malware.

✓ **Investigate hosting providers** – Some providers knowingly host malware-related content.

📌 **Example**: A Cobalt Strike payload hosted on Amazon S3 was detected and removed after an OSINT investigation linked it to a phishing campaign.

3️⃣ Investigating Malware Distribution via Social Media & Messaging Apps

Attackers distribute malware through Telegram bots, Discord links, and Facebook groups.

◆ **OSINT Techniques for Tracking Social Media Malware:**

✓ Search for malware-related keywords on Telegram & Discord.

✓ Monitor hacker forums on the dark web.

✓ Use URL scanning services (e.g., URLscan.io) to check suspicious links.

📌 **Example**: A Telegram group selling infostealer malware was exposed when researchers found its administrator using a LinkedIn profile linked to an IT security job.

4️⃣ Analyzing Botnet & C2 Communication

Malware relies on command-and-control (C2) servers to receive instructions and exfiltrate stolen data.

◆ **How OSINT Helps in C2 Tracking:**

✓ Monitor traffic to known C2 servers using sandbox environments.

✓ Analyze malware beacons using tools like Wireshark or Suricata.

✓ Correlate shared infrastructure between multiple botnets.

📌 **Example**: TrickBot malware was tracked through its C2 IPs, revealing a network of infected devices controlled by Russian cybercriminals.

8.4.3 Case Study: Dismantling a Malware Distribution Network

Incident: Tracking a Banking Trojan Distribution Network

◆ **Threat**: A new banking trojan campaign was reported, targeting European banks.

◆ **OSINT Investigation:**

✔ Researchers used WHOIS lookups & Passive DNS to trace malicious domains.

✔ Shodan scans linked the C2 servers to previous Dridex botnet operations.

✔ Telegram group monitoring revealed threat actors selling malware-as-a-service (MaaS).

◆ **Outcome:**

✔ Law enforcement seized C2 servers and arrested key operators.

✔ Malware distribution channels on Telegram and underground forums were disrupted.

Conclusion: The Importance of OSINT in Tracking Malware Infrastructure

✔ Malware distribution networks are highly sophisticated, using various channels like phishing, social media, torrents, and exploit kits.

✔ OSINT tools & techniques help identify malicious domains, trace malware hosting, and uncover C2 infrastructure.

✔ Collaboration between cybersecurity researchers, law enforcement, and intelligence analysts is key to dismantling malware operations.

By leveraging OSINT-driven malware tracking, security professionals can proactively detect threats and disrupt cybercriminal networks before they cause widespread harm.

8.5 Open-Source Tools for Investigating Malware Campaigns

Cybercriminals continuously evolve their malware tactics, techniques, and procedures (TTPs), making it critical for security analysts to leverage open-source intelligence (OSINT) tools to investigate and track malware campaigns. By using free and publicly available tools, analysts can uncover malware infrastructure, detect active threats, and correlate attack patterns without relying solely on proprietary or paid security solutions.

This section explores the best open-source tools for investigating malware campaigns, categorized by their primary functions:

🔍 Malware Analysis & Sandboxing
☐ Threat Intelligence & OSINT Gathering
📡 Network & Domain Investigations
☐ File & Hash Analysis
☐☐ Incident Response & Threat Hunting

8.5.1 Malware Analysis & Sandboxing

Analyzing malware in a controlled environment is crucial to understanding its behavior. Sandboxing tools allow security researchers to execute malware safely and study its impact.

1️⃣ Any.Run (Community Version)

✔ Interactive sandbox that allows real-time execution and monitoring of malware behavior.

✔ Analyzes network traffic, system modifications, and API calls.

✔ Provides IOC (Indicators of Compromise) extraction.

🔗 https://any.run

📌 **Use Case**: Analysts use Any.Run to detonate suspicious email attachments and identify how malware interacts with the system.

2️⃣ Hybrid Analysis (CrowdStrike Falcon Sandbox)

✔ Free cloud-based malware sandbox for static and dynamic analysis.

✔ Uses machine learning to score malware severity.

✔ Extracts network IOCs, mutexes, registry modifications, and C2 communication.

🔗 https://www.hybrid-analysis.com

📌 **Use Case**: Researchers use Hybrid Analysis to examine trojanized software and detect if it communicates with C2 servers.

3️⃣ Cuckoo Sandbox

✓ Open-source malware analysis system.

✓ Supports Windows, Linux, macOS, and Android environments.

✓ Detects keylogging, process injection, and data exfiltration attempts.

🔗 https://cuckoosandbox.org

📌 **Use Case**: Security teams use Cuckoo Sandbox to execute malware payloads in an isolated environment and analyze behavior.

8.5.2 Threat Intelligence & OSINT Gathering

Understanding the context behind a malware campaign requires gathering intelligence on threat actors, attack patterns, and dark web activities.

4️⃣ VirusTotal

✓ Aggregates malware scans from 70+ antivirus engines.

✓ Provides file hashes, domain reputation, and URL analysis.

✓ Allows malware behavior comparison across variants.

🔗 https://www.virustotal.com

📌 **Use Case**: Analysts use VirusTotal to check if a suspicious file hash has been flagged by multiple AV vendors.

5️⃣ MalwareBazaar (by abuse.ch)

✓ Community-driven malware sample repository.

✓ Contains malware hashes, YARA rules, and IOCs.

✓ Allows searching by malware family, file type, or hash.

🔗 https://bazaar.abuse.ch

📌 **Use Case**: Researchers use MalwareBazaar to identify new ransomware variants and analyze common payload patterns.

6️⃣ IntelX (Intelligence X)

✓ OSINT search engine for leaked data, dark web content, and compromised credentials.

✓ Helps track threat actors, phishing domains, and leaked malware samples.

✓ Supports searching by email, IP, domain, Bitcoin address, and PGP keys.

🔗 https://intelx.io

📌 **Use Case**: Investigators use IntelX to track threat actors linked to malware distribution on underground forums.

8.5.3 Network & Domain Investigations

Tracking malware campaigns often requires investigating malicious domains, C2 infrastructure, and network activity.

7️⃣ URLhaus (by abuse.ch)

✓ Collects and tracks malware distribution URLs.

✓ Provides IOC feeds for blocking known malicious domains.

✓ Detects malicious redirect chains and short links used in phishing.

🔗 https://urlhaus.abuse.ch

📌 **Use Case**: Security teams use URLhaus to identify phishing sites distributing malware payloads.

8️⃣ Shodan

✓ Searches for exposed C2 servers, botnets, and vulnerable IoT devices.

✓ Provides historical data on malware-infected servers.

✓ Maps C2 infrastructure based on IP, ASN, and organization.

🔗 https://www.shodan.io

📌 **Use Case**: Analysts use Shodan to identify compromised servers hosting malware for a botnet.

9️⃣ PassiveTotal (RiskIQ)

✓ Monitors malicious domains, subdomains, and IP addresses.

✓ Tracks domain registrations linked to threat actors.

✓ Provides WHOIS history, SSL certificates, and DNS resolution logs.

🔗 https://community.riskiq.com

📌 **Use Case**: Threat hunters use PassiveTotal to track new domains registered by ransomware gangs.

8.5.4 File & Hash Analysis

File analysis tools help detect malware signatures, embedded exploits, and suspicious payloads.

🔟 PeStudio

✓ Identifies suspicious file attributes, API calls, and embedded executables.

✓ Detects malicious PE headers and obfuscated code.

🔗 https://www.winitor.com

📌 **Use Case**: Analysts use PeStudio to examine EXE files before executing them in a sandbox.

1⃞1⃞ YARA (Yet Another Ridiculous Acronym)

✓ Detects malware families by creating custom rule sets.

✓ Scans files, memory dumps, and network traffic for known malware patterns.

✓ Used in threat intelligence platforms (TIPs) and SOC environments.

🔗 https://virustotal.github.io/yara

📌 **Use Case**: Threat researchers use YARA to detect new variants of a ransomware strain.

8.5.5 Incident Response & Threat Hunting

Security teams use OSINT tools to investigate security incidents, detect malware persistence mechanisms, and hunt for new threats.

1⃞2⃞ Velociraptor

✓ Open-source endpoint forensic tool for real-time malware hunting.

✓ Collects logs, memory dumps, and network traffic from infected machines.

🔗 https://www.velociraptor.app

📌 **Use Case**: Incident responders use Velociraptor to analyze malware persistence techniques in compromised endpoints.

Conclusion: OSINT is Essential for Malware Investigations

◆ Open-source tools empower cybersecurity analysts to detect, analyze, and disrupt malware campaigns without relying on expensive commercial solutions.

◆ Combining sandboxing, network tracking, file analysis, and threat intelligence provides a comprehensive view of malware threats.

◆ Security teams must continuously monitor malware trends and leverage OSINT-driven investigations to proactively defend against evolving cyber threats.

By integrating these tools into your workflow, you can stay ahead of cybercriminals and better protect digital assets from sophisticated malware attacks. 🚀

8.6 Case Study: How OSINT Tracked a Botnet's Operations

Botnets—large networks of compromised devices controlled by cybercriminals—are a significant cybersecurity threat. They are used for DDoS attacks, credential stuffing, malware distribution, and data theft. Tracking botnet operations requires a combination of OSINT techniques, malware analysis, and network forensics to uncover their infrastructure, operators, and victims.

This case study examines how open-source intelligence (OSINT) tools and techniques were used to track and dismantle a sophisticated botnet operation targeting financial institutions and critical infrastructure.

8.6.1 Step 1: Identifying the Botnet's Footprint

The investigation began when security researchers noticed a surge in DDoS attacks targeting multiple banks. Initial clues pointed to:

✓ Malicious traffic originating from thousands of infected IoT devices.

✓ Phishing emails delivering a trojanized botnet payload.

✓ Suspicious domains hosting command-and-control (C2) servers.

OSINT Tools Used:

- **Shodan** – To identify infected IoT devices.
- **VirusTotal** – To analyze malware hashes associated with the botnet.
- **PassiveTotal (RiskIQ)** – To track domain registrations linked to C2 servers.

Key Discovery:

Investigators identified a cluster of compromised routers across multiple countries, primarily in Southeast Asia and Eastern Europe, being used to relay attack traffic.

8.6.2 Step 2: Investigating the Botnet's Malware

To understand how the botnet spread, researchers needed to analyze its malware sample.

✓ The malware was delivered via phishing emails and disguised as a banking security update.

✓ Once executed, the malware connected to a remote server and awaited further instructions.

✓ The payload used DNS tunneling to evade detection.

OSINT Tools Used:

- **Hybrid Analysis** – To execute the malware in a sandbox environment.
- **Cuckoo Sandbox** – To analyze network connections made by the malware.
- **YARA Rules** – To detect other malware variants linked to the botnet.

Key Discovery:

The malware had hardcoded IP addresses and domains linked to a known cybercriminal group operating in underground forums.

8.6.3 Step 3: Mapping the Botnet's Infrastructure

By investigating the botnet's command-and-control (C2) servers, analysts uncovered a network of malicious domains, VPS hosting providers, and compromised websites used for botnet operations.

OSINT Techniques Used:

✓ **WHOIS & Passive DNS Analysis**: To track domain ownership and infrastructure.

✓ **SSL Certificate Matching**: To link different servers under the same botnet operator.

✓ **Dark Web Monitoring**: To find discussions about the botnet on hacker forums.

Key Discovery:

- Some C2 servers were registered using fake details but shared infrastructure with previous malware campaigns.

- The botnet operators frequently rotated their domains to avoid detection.
- Using Shodan, researchers identified an exposed admin panel that revealed infection statistics and botnet commands.

8.6.4 Step 4: Tracking the Cybercriminals Behind the Botnet

Investigators shifted focus to identifying the individuals operating the botnet.

OSINT Techniques Used:

✔ **Forum and Social Media Monitoring** – Searching for hacker aliases linked to botnet discussions.

✔ **Blockchain Analysis** – Tracking Bitcoin payments for C2 hosting.

✔ **Metadata Analysis** – Extracting data from malware files and phishing emails.

Key Discovery:

- The operators were active on Russian-speaking underground forums.
- Some forum accounts used the same alias on Telegram, GitHub, and other platforms.
- A leaked credential dump linked one of the aliases to a compromised email address, which led to a real-world identity.

8.6.5 Step 5: Disrupting the Botnet

Once enough intelligence was gathered, researchers collaborated with law enforcement and cybersecurity firms to take action:

✔ Registrars and hosting providers were contacted to takedown malicious domains.

✔ ISPs and CERT teams were notified to block infected IPs and notify victims.

✔ Law enforcement obtained warrants to arrest key botnet operators.

Results:

🔯 Over 200,000 infected devices were disinfected.
🔯 Multiple C2 servers were shut down, disrupting botnet operations.
🔯 Key threat actors were identified and arrested.

8.6.6 Lessons Learned & Best Practices

◆ **Botnets rely on poor cybersecurity hygiene** – Many infected devices had default passwords or outdated firmware.

◆ **OSINT is essential for mapping cyber threats** – A combination of WHOIS, DNS analysis, malware forensics, and dark web monitoring can expose botnet operations.

◆ **Collaboration is key** – Partnerships between cybersecurity researchers, ISPs, and law enforcement accelerate botnet takedowns.

By leveraging OSINT techniques, security analysts were able to track, expose, and disrupt a global botnet—highlighting the power of open-source intelligence in modern cyber threat investigations. 🚀

9. Advanced Persistent Threats (APTs) & Nation-State Actors

In this chapter, we examine the sophisticated world of Advanced Persistent Threats (APTs), often carried out by nation-state actors with significant resources and strategic objectives. APTs are stealthy, long-term attacks designed to infiltrate networks, gather intelligence, and achieve specific geopolitical or economic goals. Using OSINT techniques, we will explore how these threat actors operate, the tools they employ, and the tactics they use to stay undetected. By understanding the indicators of APT activity and the motivations behind nation-state hacking, this chapter will empower you to identify, analyze, and defend against these highly advanced and persistent threats.

9.1 What Are APTs & How Do They Differ from Other Threat Actors?

Cyber threats come in many forms, ranging from script kiddies and cybercriminal gangs to hacktivists and nation-state-sponsored actors. Among these, Advanced Persistent Threats (APTs) stand out as the most sophisticated and dangerous adversaries in cyberspace. Unlike traditional cybercriminals who seek quick financial gain, APT groups conduct long-term, covert, and highly targeted cyber operations with strategic objectives.

This section explores what APTs are, how they differ from other cyber threat actors, and why their tactics, techniques, and procedures (TTPs) make them one of the most challenging threats to detect and mitigate.

9.1.1 What Are Advanced Persistent Threats (APTs)?

An Advanced Persistent Threat (APT) is a coordinated, long-term cyberattack campaign conducted by a well-funded and highly skilled adversary. These groups often have state sponsorship, military backing, or corporate espionage motives.

Key Characteristics of APTs:

✓ **Highly Sophisticated** – APTs use advanced hacking techniques, custom malware, and stealthy intrusion tactics.

✓ **Long-Term Persistence** – They maintain access to compromised systems for months or years.

✓ **Stealth & Evasion** – APTs use zero-day vulnerabilities, living-off-the-land (LOTL) techniques, and lateral movement to evade detection.

✓ **Strategic Targets** – They aim at government agencies, critical infrastructure, financial institutions, defense contractors, and major corporations.

✓ **Multiphase Operations** – APTs follow a carefully structured attack lifecycle, from initial reconnaissance to data exfiltration.

Example: The infamous APT29 (Cozy Bear), associated with Russia's intelligence agencies, conducted a years-long cyber-espionage campaign targeting U.S. government agencies, NATO, and healthcare organizations.

9.1.2 How APTs Differ from Other Threat Actors

While many cyber threat actors engage in hacking, APT groups distinguish themselves through their level of sophistication, objectives, and attack methodology. Here's how they compare to other cyber adversaries:

1️ APTs vs. Cybercriminal Groups

Feature	APTs	Cybercriminal Groups
Primary Goal	Espionage, geopolitical influence	Financial gain (ransomware, fraud)
Funding	State-sponsored, military budgets	Self-funded, cryptocurrency extortion
Attack Duration	Multi-year campaigns	Short-term, hit-and-run
Tactics	Zero-days, stealthy persistence, custom malware	Phishing, ransomware, carding
Target Sectors	Government, defense, healthcare, infrastructure	Retail, banks, individuals

📌 **Example**: APTs might silently infiltrate a military contractor's network for years, while cybercriminals deploy ransomware and demand Bitcoin payments immediately.

2️ APTs vs. Hacktivists

Feature	APTs	Hacktivists
Motivation	Political, intelligence gathering, military advantage	Social, political activism
Attack Sophistication	Highly skilled, stealthy operations	Moderate, loud defacements and DDoS attacks
Tactics	Silent espionage, backdoors, long-term infiltration	Website defacement, doxxing, mass protests
Notable Groups	APT41, APT28 (Fancy Bear)	Anonymous, Lizard Squad

✦ **Example**: APTs might exfiltrate sensitive government intelligence, while hacktivists DDoS government websites as a form of protest.

3️⃣ APTs vs. Insider Threats

Feature	APTs	Insider Threats
Attack Origin	External state-sponsored actors	Employees, contractors, disgruntled workers
Objective	Espionage, data theft, sabotage	Revenge, financial gain
Methods	Cyber attacks, malware, spear-phishing	Leaking sensitive data, sabotage
Mitigation	Threat intelligence, endpoint monitoring	Employee behavior monitoring

✦ **Example**: APTs might exploit employees through phishing, while insider threats intentionally leak company secrets.

9.1.3 APT Attack Lifecycle: How They Operate

APTs follow a structured, multi-stage attack lifecycle to infiltrate and maintain access to target networks. This model is often mapped using frameworks like the MITRE ATT&CK framework or the Cyber Kill Chain.

🔍 1. Reconnaissance

APTs gather intelligence on the target by:

✓ Scraping social media for employee details.

✓ Scanning public websites for vulnerabilities.

✓ Harvesting leaked credentials from dark web sources.

⚙ 2. Initial Compromise

APT groups gain a foothold through:

✓ Spear-phishing emails with malicious payloads.

✓ Exploiting zero-day vulnerabilities in software.

✓ Watering hole attacks on industry-specific websites.

🚀 3. Establishing Persistence

After gaining access, APTs deploy backdoors and Remote Access Trojans (RATs), such as:

✓ Cobalt Strike, PlugX, and Empire for post-exploitation.

✓ Modifying registry keys and startup scripts for persistence.

✓ Exploiting Active Directory for lateral movement.

📡 4. Command & Control (C2)

APT malware communicates with C2 servers to receive commands, exfiltrate data, or deploy additional payloads.

✓ Using DNS tunneling, HTTPS, or TOR to hide communication.

✓ Rotating C2 infrastructure to evade detection.

☐ 5. Lateral Movement & Privilege Escalation

APT actors move deeper into the network by:

✓ Exploiting weak passwords or misconfigured permissions.

✓ Dumping credentials using Mimikatz or LSASS exploits.

✔ Leveraging living-off-the-land binaries (LOLBins) like PowerShell.

📁 6. Data Exfiltration

APT groups extract sensitive intellectual property, military intelligence, or financial data using:

✔ Encrypted exfiltration channels (SFTP, Dropbox API, cloud storage).

✔ Covert steganography to embed data in image files.

☐ 7. Covering Tracks

To avoid detection, APTs:

✔ Wipe logs and disable security tools.

✔ Encrypt stolen data to prevent forensic analysis.

✔ Use false-flag tactics to mislead investigators.

9.1.4 Why Are APTs Difficult to Detect?

🚫 **Custom Malware & Zero-Days** – APTs use unique malware that bypasses antivirus software.

🚫 **Slow, Low & Stealthy Tactics** – Unlike ransomware, APTs operate silently over years.

🚫 **Blending with Legitimate Traffic** – They use LOLBins and exploit normal IT processes.

🚫 **State-Level Resources** – They have top-tier hacking expertise, funding, and insider intelligence.

Conclusion: The Ever-Present APT Threat

APTs are the most dangerous cyber adversaries today. They are relentless, well-funded, and highly skilled, making them a challenge for even the most advanced cybersecurity teams. Unlike financially motivated hackers, APTs have long-term strategic objectives, whether it's espionage, military disruption, or data theft.

By understanding their attack lifecycle, tactics, and differences from other threat actors, organizations can implement proactive threat intelligence strategies, improve detection capabilities, and strengthen defenses against APTs.

◆ Threat Hunting & OSINT Investigations play a crucial role in tracking APT activities.

◆ Security teams must leverage frameworks like MITRE ATT&CK to map APT techniques.

◆ Continuous monitoring, deception technologies, and strong endpoint defenses are key to detecting and mitigating APT threats.

📖 Staying ahead of APTs requires a combination of OSINT, threat intelligence, and proactive security measures.

9.2 Investigating APT Groups Using Open-Source Intelligence

Advanced Persistent Threats (APTs) operate in the shadows, leveraging sophisticated techniques to infiltrate government agencies, corporations, and critical infrastructure. While APT groups use stealthy tactics to evade detection, open-source intelligence (OSINT) provides a powerful approach for cybersecurity researchers and analysts to track their activities, uncover their infrastructure, and attribute attacks.

In this chapter, we explore how OSINT can be used to investigate APT groups, identify their tactics, and expose their global operations.

9.2.1 Understanding How APT Groups Operate

APTs are state-sponsored or well-funded threat actors conducting prolonged cyber-espionage campaigns. They primarily engage in:

✓ **Cyber Espionage** – Stealing sensitive data from governments and businesses.

✓ **Disruptive Attacks** – Targeting infrastructure with cyber warfare techniques.

✓ **Intellectual Property Theft** – Stealing trade secrets for economic advantage.

To investigate APTs, OSINT analysts use public data sources, network reconnaissance, malware analysis, and social media tracking to uncover threat actor activity.

9.2.2 OSINT Techniques for Investigating APT Groups

1️⃣ Identifying APT Indicators of Compromise (IOCs)

APT groups leave digital fingerprints, known as Indicators of Compromise (IOCs), including:

✓ Malicious IPs and domains (Command & Control servers).

✓ Phishing email headers and attachments.

✓ Custom malware hashes used in attacks.

🔍 OSINT Tools for IOC Research

- **VirusTotal** – Scans files and domains linked to malware.
- **AlienVault OTX** – Shares threat intelligence reports on APT groups.
- **AbuseIPDB** – Investigates malicious IP addresses linked to cyber threats.

📌 **Case Example**: Researchers tracking APT34 (Iranian threat group) used VirusTotal to identify shared malware samples in previous cyberattacks.

2️⃣ Investigating APT Domains & Command-and-Control (C2) Infrastructure

APT groups use dedicated domains and servers to control malware and steal data. OSINT analysts track these by:

✓ Analyzing WHOIS records for domain registration data.

✓ Using Passive DNS to track domain history and connections.

✓ Monitoring SSL certificates associated with APT C2 servers.

🔍 OSINT Tools for Domain Investigation

- **WHOIS Lookup (WhoisXML API, Domaintools)** – Checks domain ownership.
- **PassiveTotal (RiskIQ)** – Tracks domain and IP relationships.
- **Shodan & Censys** – Identifies exposed APT-controlled servers.

📌 **Case Example**: Investigators used Shodan and PassiveTotal to link APT28 (Fancy Bear) to infrastructure hosting spear-phishing campaigns.

3️ Analyzing APT Malware with OSINT

APT groups often develop custom malware designed to evade detection. OSINT techniques help track malware activity by:

✓ Analyzing malware samples using sandbox environments.

✓ Tracking malware hashes across cyber threat databases.

✓ Identifying overlaps in APT malware code with previous attacks.

🔍 OSINT Tools for Malware Analysis

- **Hybrid Analysis & Any.Run** – Executes malware in virtual environments.
- **Malware Bazaar** – Provides a database of known malware samples.
- **YARA Rules** – Helps detect malware patterns associated with APTs.

📌 **Case Example**: Researchers identified APT41 (China-linked) by analyzing similarities in their malware payloads used in espionage campaigns.

4️ Monitoring APT Activities on Dark Web & Underground Forums

APT groups often communicate or sell stolen data on dark web marketplaces and underground hacker forums. OSINT analysts use:

✓ Dark web crawlers to monitor cybercriminal discussions.

✓ Language analysis to identify state-sponsored threat actors.

✓ Tracking leaked credentials from APT breaches.

🔍 OSINT Tools for Dark Web Monitoring

- **DarkTracer & IntelX** – Search for leaked data and dark web mentions.
- **Tor & Onion Services** – Access hidden forums where APT groups discuss operations.

📌 **Case Example**: Analysts tracking APT32 (Vietnam-linked group) found leaked government credentials for sale on dark web markets, indicating a cyber-espionage operation.

5️⃣ Investigating APT Group OPSEC Mistakes

Despite their sophistication, APT hackers make mistakes that OSINT can exploit, such as:

✔ Reusing email addresses and usernames across platforms.

✔ Leaving metadata in malware files or phishing documents.

✔ Using similar infrastructure in multiple attacks.

🔍 OSINT Techniques for OPSEC Analysis

- **EXIF Data Extraction (ExifTool)** – Extracts metadata from images/files.
- **Google Dorking** – Searches for exposed sensitive information.
- **Telegram & Twitter Monitoring** – Tracks hacker aliases and discussions.

📌 **Case Example**: A cybersecurity firm exposed APT29 (Cozy Bear) when hackers accidentally used the same hosting provider for multiple campaigns, linking them to Russian intelligence.

9.2.3 Attribution: Linking APTs to Nation-State Sponsors

Attribution is difficult, but OSINT can help identify patterns linking APT groups to governments. Analysts look for:

✔ Geopolitical motivations behind cyber attacks.

✔ Malware similarities in known nation-state operations.

✔ Overlap between APT activity and military or intelligence operations.

Case Example: APT Attribution Using OSINT

APT10 (linked to China) conducted cyber espionage against Western companies. OSINT analysts:

1☐ Tracked malware payloads used in multiple campaigns.

2☐ Identified domain registrations matching previous attacks.

3☐ Analyzed timestamps indicating activity during Chinese working hours.

📌 **Conclusion**: The evidence suggested a link to China's Ministry of State Security (MSS).

9.2.4 Challenges & Limitations of OSINT in APT Investigations

◈ Attribution is difficult – APTs use false-flag tactics to mislead researchers.

◈ APTs constantly evolve – Threat actors shift tactics to avoid OSINT tracking.

◈ Dark web monitoring requires ethical considerations – Some OSINT methods can enter legal gray areas.

Despite these challenges, OSINT remains a critical tool in tracking APT groups, identifying their tactics, and understanding global cyber threats.

Conclusion: The Power of OSINT in APT Investigations

◈ APT groups pose serious threats to national security, businesses, and critical infrastructure.

◈ OSINT techniques such as domain analysis, malware tracking, and dark web monitoring help uncover their operations.

◈ By leveraging OSINT, cybersecurity teams can detect, attribute, and defend against APT threats before they escalate.

🔎 Investigating APTs with OSINT is not just about gathering intelligence—it's about staying ahead of nation-state cyber warfare.

9.3 Identifying Nation-State Cyber Espionage Operations

In today's digital battlefield, nation-state cyber espionage is one of the most sophisticated and persistent threats. Governments worldwide use cyber operations to steal intelligence, disrupt infrastructure, and gain geopolitical advantages. These attacks often remain undetected for years, targeting military secrets, economic data, and intellectual property.

Tracking these covert cyber espionage campaigns is challenging, but Open-Source Intelligence (OSINT) plays a crucial role in identifying, monitoring, and attributing these operations. By analyzing public data, leaked documents, domain records, and malware footprints, OSINT investigators can uncover state-backed cyber activity.

9.3.1 How Nation-State Cyber Espionage Works

⌖ Objectives of Nation-State Cyber Espionage

State-sponsored threat actors conduct cyber espionage for several reasons:

✓ **Stealing government and military secrets** – Surveillance on foreign adversaries.

✓ **Economic espionage** – Acquiring trade secrets and proprietary technology.

✓ **Political influence** – Manipulating elections, media, and public opinion.

✓ **Critical infrastructure attacks** – Disrupting energy grids, telecoms, and financial systems.

9.3.2 OSINT Techniques for Identifying Nation-State Espionage

1⃣ Tracking Nation-State APT Groups

State-sponsored cyber espionage is typically carried out by Advanced Persistent Threat (APT) groups, such as:

- **APT28 (Fancy Bear)** – Linked to Russian military intelligence (GRU).
- **APT29 (Cozy Bear)** – Associated with Russia's FSB/SVR.
- **APT41 (Double Dragon)** – Tied to China's Ministry of State Security.
- **Lazarus Group** – A North Korean hacking unit involved in espionage and financial theft.

🔍 OSINT Methods to Identify APT Activity

✓ Monitoring government reports (CISA, NSA, Mandiant) on known APT tactics.

✓ Tracking domain registrations tied to past APT campaigns.

✓ Analyzing malware signatures associated with nation-state cyber tools.

📌 **Case Example**: Researchers identified APT33 (Iran-linked group) by analyzing reused C2 domains across multiple cyber-espionage campaigns.

2️⃣ Investigating Malware Used in Espionage Operations

Many cyber-espionage groups use custom malware tools designed to remain undetected for years. By analyzing these malware footprints, OSINT investigators can link attacks to nation-states.

🔍 OSINT Tools for Malware Investigation

- **VirusTotal** – Compares malware hashes with known espionage toolkits.
- **Hybrid Analysis** – Provides a sandbox for analyzing malicious executables.
- **YARA Rules** – Helps detect patterns in malware strains used by state-sponsored actors.

📌 **Case Example**: APT29 (Russia) used a custom backdoor named SUNBURST in the SolarWinds attack, which OSINT analysts tracked through malware signature analysis.

3️⃣ Analyzing Nation-State Cyber Infrastructure

Nation-state hackers rely on Command-and-Control (C2) servers to operate malware and conduct cyber espionage. OSINT techniques help map these hidden networks.

🔍 OSINT Methods for Infrastructure Tracking

✓ Using WHOIS lookup to find email and registrar patterns.

✓ Investigating Passive DNS records to uncover historical domain usage.

✓ Monitoring SSL certificates and web hosting overlaps.

📌 **Case Example**: OSINT analysts tracked APT40 (China-linked) by linking their phishing domains to previously known espionage campaigns via DNS and WHOIS analysis.

4️⃣ Monitoring Dark Web & Underground Forums

State-backed hackers sometimes leak stolen data on dark web marketplaces or discuss exploits in underground hacker forums. OSINT investigators monitor these channels to gain intelligence.

🔍 OSINT Tools for Dark Web Monitoring

- **Tor & Onion Services** – Access hidden forums where hackers sell data.
- **IntelX & DarkTracer** – Search for leaked classified documents and credentials.
- **Telegram & Discord Monitoring** – Identify hacker groups discussing espionage tactics.

📌 **Case Example**: Researchers discovered APT38 (North Korea's Lazarus Group) attempting to sell stolen financial data on a darknet forum, linking them to bank cyber heists.

5️⃣ Identifying State-Sponsored Phishing & Disinformation Campaigns

Nation-state actors also use phishing campaigns and online propaganda to manipulate public perception, influence elections, or gather intelligence. OSINT can track these efforts by:

✔ Analyzing fake social media accounts spreading disinformation.

✔ Identifying phishing emails targeting government officials.

✔ Mapping coordinated bot activity on social platforms.

🔍 OSINT Tools for Phishing & Disinformation Tracking

- **Graphika & Maltego** – Map disinformation networks and bot activity.
- **PhishTank & URLScan.io** – Identify malicious phishing domains.
- **Twitter API & Facebook Graph Search** – Monitor coordinated social media campaigns.

📌 **Case Example**: OSINT analysts uncovered Russia's "Ghostwriter" campaign, which spread fake news and phishing attacks to influence European politics.

9.3.3 Challenges in Identifying Nation-State Espionage

◆ **False Flags & Deception** – State-sponsored actors often disguise their attacks as coming from other countries.

◆ **Attribution Complexity** – Governments rarely claim responsibility, making attribution difficult.

◆ **Evolving Tactics** – Espionage groups frequently change infrastructure, tools, and techniques.

Despite these challenges, OSINT remains one of the most powerful tools in identifying, tracking, and exposing state-sponsored cyber espionage campaigns.

Conclusion: OSINT as a Weapon Against Cyber Espionage

◆ Nation-state cyber espionage is a growing threat targeting governments, businesses, and individuals.

◆ OSINT techniques, including malware tracking, domain analysis, and dark web monitoring, help uncover state-sponsored hacking operations.

◆ By leveraging OSINT, cybersecurity teams can detect and mitigate espionage campaigns before they cause major damage.

🚀 Cyber espionage thrives in secrecy, but OSINT shines a light on the shadows.

9.4 Tracking Zero-Day Exploits & APT Attack Methods

Advanced Persistent Threat (APT) groups often rely on zero-day exploits—previously unknown software vulnerabilities—to conduct highly targeted cyberattacks. Unlike common exploits, zero-days remain unpatched and undisclosed, giving nation-state actors and cybercriminals a significant tactical advantage. These vulnerabilities are frequently sold on dark web marketplaces or developed in-house by well-funded state-backed groups.

Tracking zero-day exploits is critical for cybersecurity analysts, as these vulnerabilities are often used in nation-state cyber espionage, critical infrastructure attacks, and financial sector breaches. Open-Source Intelligence (OSINT) plays a crucial role in identifying, analyzing, and mitigating these threats.

This chapter explores how OSINT can be used to monitor zero-day markets, investigate APT attack methods, and attribute cyberattacks to state-sponsored threat actors.

9.4.1 Understanding Zero-Day Exploits in APT Operations

🔍 What Makes Zero-Days So Dangerous?

✓ **No known patch** – Since the vendor is unaware of the vulnerability, no fix is available.

✓ **Highly valuable on the cyber black market** – Zero-days can sell for millions of dollars on exploit marketplaces.

✓ **Used in espionage and cyber warfare** – Nation-state actors use them for long-term infiltration of high-value targets.

9.4.2 OSINT Techniques for Tracking Zero-Day Exploits

1️⃣ Monitoring Dark Web & Exploit Markets

Zero-days are often bought and sold in underground forums, encrypted chat groups, and dark web marketplaces. Cyber intelligence analysts use OSINT to:

✓ Monitor hacker forums for discussions on new exploits.

✓ Track zero-day brokers advertising vulnerabilities.

✓ Identify leaked exploit code before it is weaponized.

🔍 OSINT Tools for Dark Web Monitoring

- **DarkTracer & IntelX** – Search leaked vulnerability exploits and discussions.
- **OnionSearch & Ahmia** – Track hidden Tor sites offering zero-day exploits.
- **Telegram & Discord Monitoring** – Identify closed groups where cybercriminals share zero-day information.

📌 **Case Example**: Analysts discovered a Windows zero-day exploit being advertised on a dark web forum before it was later used in APT28's cyber espionage campaign against NATO countries.

2️⃣ Investigating Zero-Days Through Public Exploit Databases

Not all zero-days remain underground. Some are disclosed through security research firms, bug bounty programs, or exploit databases. OSINT analysts track:

✓ Newly disclosed vulnerabilities and their severity.

✓ Exploit Proof-of-Concept (PoC) code uploaded to GitHub or Pastebin.

✓ Connections between vulnerabilities and past APT attacks.

🔍 OSINT Tools for Zero-Day Tracking

- **CVE Database (MITRE)** – Lists publicly disclosed vulnerabilities.
- **Exploit-DB** – Tracks known exploit code for vulnerabilities.
- **GitHub & Pastebin Monitoring** – Searches for leaked PoC exploits.

📌 **Case Example**: Researchers identified a Google Chrome zero-day (CVE-2021-21166) after APT groups began exploiting it in the wild before Google could patch it.

3️⃣ Analyzing APT Attack Methods & Infrastructure

APT groups use a combination of zero-days, phishing, malware, and C2 infrastructure to launch cyberattacks. OSINT investigators track these methods by:

✓ Mapping attack kill chains to identify common tactics.

✓ Tracking shared infrastructure, such as malware signatures and IP addresses.

✓ Identifying overlaps between new attack techniques and known APT groups.

🔍 OSINT Tools for Attack Analysis

- **MITRE ATT&CK Framework** – Maps APT tactics, techniques, and procedures (TTPs).
- **Maltego & SpiderFoot** – Visualizes attack infrastructure connections.
- **PassiveTotal (RiskIQ)** – Tracks APT domains and malware distribution.

📌 **Case Example**: APT41 (China-linked) was tracked using OSINT to connect their phishing campaigns, zero-day exploits, and C2 servers, leading to the identification of state-sponsored cyber espionage activity.

9.4.3 Investigating Notable Zero-Day Attacks by APT Groups

1️⃣ Stuxnet (U.S.-Israeli Cyberattack on Iran, 2010)

- **Attack Vector**: Used multiple zero-days to sabotage Iranian nuclear centrifuges.
- **OSINT Findings**: Researchers linked malware code similarities to U.S. and Israeli intelligence agencies.

2️⃣ Operation Aurora (China's Attack on Google, 2009)

- **Attack Vector**: Exploited a zero-day vulnerability in Internet Explorer.
- **OSINT Findings**: Domain registrations and malware analysis connected the attack to APT17 (Chinese state hackers).

3️⃣ SolarWinds Attack (Russia's Attack on U.S. Agencies, 2020)

- **Attack Vector**: Zero-day vulnerability in SolarWinds Orion software.
- **OSINT Findings**: OSINT analysts linked malware timestamps to Russian time zones, confirming APT29 (Cozy Bear) involvement.

9.4.4 Challenges in Tracking Zero-Day Exploits & APT Attacks

- Zero-day vulnerabilities are rare and difficult to detect before use.
- APT groups use advanced obfuscation techniques to hide infrastructure.
- Attribution remains complex due to false-flag operations and multiple actors.

Despite these challenges, OSINT remains a critical tool in proactively identifying zero-day exploits and mitigating nation-state cyber threats.

Conclusion: OSINT as a Countermeasure to Zero-Day Exploits

- Zero-day exploits play a major role in APT attacks, giving state-sponsored hackers a powerful advantage.
- OSINT techniques—such as dark web monitoring, malware analysis, and exploit tracking—can help identify these threats before they are widely used.
- By leveraging OSINT, cybersecurity teams can proactively defend against zero-day vulnerabilities and disrupt APT attack operations.

🚀 Zero-days may be secret, but OSINT exposes the shadows.

9.5 Monitoring Government & Military Cyber Threats

Government and military cyber threats have escalated into a global battlefield, where nation-states engage in cyber warfare, espionage, and sabotage. These threats target critical infrastructure, intelligence agencies, defense contractors, and high-profile political figures. Unlike financially motivated cybercriminals, state-sponsored threat actors have access to advanced cyber capabilities, intelligence networks, and long-term operational goals.

Open-Source Intelligence (OSINT) is a crucial tool in tracking, analyzing, and mitigating government and military cyber threats. By monitoring threat actors, infrastructure, and cyberattack patterns, OSINT enables security professionals to anticipate and respond to nation-state cyber operations.

This chapter explores OSINT techniques for identifying, tracking, and assessing government-backed cyber threats.

9.5.1 Understanding Government & Military Cyber Threats

⚔ Objectives of State-Sponsored Cyber Operations

Government and military-backed cyber actors conduct operations for:

✓ **Cyber Espionage** – Stealing classified government and military intelligence.

✓ **Disrupting Critical Infrastructure** – Targeting energy grids, water supplies, and communication networks.

✓ **Election Interference & Political Manipulation** – Spreading misinformation and hacking political institutions.

✓ **Intellectual Property Theft** – Stealing military technology and defense research.

✓ **Covert Cyber Warfare** – Deploying malware and cyberattacks as part of geopolitical conflict.

☠ Key Players: Government-Backed Cyber Units

State-backed hacking units are often tied to intelligence agencies, military cyber divisions, or private contractors working for governments.

◈ **Russia** – GRU's APT28 (Fancy Bear), FSB's APT29 (Cozy Bear) (Election interference, cyber espionage).

◈ **China** – APT41 (Double Dragon), PLA Unit 61398 (Industrial espionage, IP theft).

◈ **Iran** – APT33, APT34 (OilRig) (Critical infrastructure attacks).

◈ **North Korea** – Lazarus Group, Kimsuky (Financial cybercrime, espionage).

◈ **United States & Allies** – NSA's Tailored Access Operations (TAO), Five Eyes Intelligence Network (Cyber defense, offensive cyber operations).

9.5.2 OSINT Techniques for Tracking Government Cyber Threats

1️ Monitoring APT Attacks Targeting Government Entities

Advanced Persistent Threat (APT) groups linked to governments use sophisticated cyber weapons to infiltrate government agencies and military organizations.

✓ Tracking attack infrastructure (C2 servers, malware hashes, phishing domains).

✓ Identifying recurring patterns in attack methodologies (MITRE ATT&CK techniques).

✓ Analyzing publicly available incident reports from cybersecurity firms (FireEye, Mandiant, CrowdStrike).

🔍 OSINT Tools for APT Tracking

- **VirusTotal & Hybrid Analysis** – Malware behavior and threat signatures.
- **Shodan & Censys** – Scanning for exposed government/military assets.
- **Threat Intelligence Reports (CISA, NSA, FBI, Europol)** – Public reports on APT threats.

📌 **Case Example**: APT29 (Russia's Cozy Bear) targeted U.S. government agencies using phishing campaigns linked to SolarWinds infrastructure. OSINT analysis of domain registrations and C2 traffic helped confirm Russian involvement.

2️ Identifying Cyber Threats to Military & Defense Contractors

Military and defense contractors are prime targets for intellectual property theft and cyber sabotage. OSINT helps identify:

✓ Leaks of sensitive defense-related documents.

✓ Espionage campaigns targeting military research facilities.

✓ Cyber vulnerabilities in defense contractors' digital infrastructure.

🔍 OSINT Sources for Military Cyber Threat Monitoring

- **Breach forums & dark web marketplaces** – Stolen military data listings.
- **WHOIS & Passive DNS** – Identifying fake defense contractor domains used for phishing.
- **Public procurement records** – Monitoring contracts for cybersecurity gaps.

📌 **Case Example**: APT31 (China) targeted U.S. defense contractors by using spear-phishing emails and zero-day exploits to steal fighter jet schematics. OSINT analysts linked phishing domains to previously known Chinese espionage infrastructure.

3️⃣ Tracking Nation-State Cyber Weapons & Malware Campaigns

Governments develop and deploy custom cyber weapons, such as:

- ◈ **Stuxnet** – A U.S.-Israeli cyber weapon used against Iran's nuclear facilities.
- ◈ **NotPetya** – A destructive malware attributed to Russian military intelligence.
- ◈ **WannaCry** – A North Korean ransomware attack that crippled global systems.

🔍 OSINT Methods for Cyber Weapon Tracking

✓ Malware sandbox analysis (Hybrid Analysis, Any.Run).

✓ Tracking leaked cyber tools (GitHub, Pastebin, hacker forums).

✓ Analyzing domain/IP overlaps in malware distribution networks.

📌 **Case Example**: NotPetya (Russia's Sandworm APT) was initially disguised as ransomware, but OSINT investigations revealed it was a destructive cyber weapon targeting Ukraine's infrastructure.

4️⃣ Monitoring Cyber Attacks on Political Targets & Elections

State-backed cyber actors engage in election interference and disinformation campaigns by:

✔ Hacking political party emails and leaking documents.

✔ Spreading propaganda through fake social media accounts.

✔ Launching DDoS attacks on election infrastructure.

🔍 OSINT Tools for Election Security Monitoring

- **Graphika & Maltego** – Mapping disinformation networks.
- **Social Media Analysis (Twitter API, Facebook Graph Search)** – Tracking coordinated political bot activity.
- **Google's Threat Analysis Group (TAG)** – Reports on election-related cyber threats.

📌 **Case Example**: APT28 (Fancy Bear) was linked to the 2016 U.S. election interference, where OSINT revealed a coordinated effort using phishing campaigns, fake news, and hacked emails.

5️⃣ Investigating Cyber Threats to Critical Infrastructure

Governments are increasingly targeting power grids, water supplies, and communication networks in cyber warfare operations. OSINT helps detect:

✔ SCADA/ICS system vulnerabilities exploited by attackers.

✔ Malware designed to sabotage industrial control systems.

✔ Dark web chatter on planned attacks against infrastructure.

🔍 OSINT Tools for Critical Infrastructure Threat Monitoring

- **Shodan & Censys** – Identifying exposed SCADA/ICS systems.
- **ICS-CERT (CISA)** – Reports on industrial cybersecurity threats.
- **Pastebin & Telegram Monitoring** – Tracking leaked exploits targeting infrastructure.

✦ **Case Example**: Sandworm (Russia's GRU) launched cyberattacks against Ukraine's power grid, causing nationwide blackouts. OSINT researchers tracked malware signatures (Industroyer, BlackEnergy) linked to previous Russian cyber campaigns.

9.5.3 Challenges in Monitoring Government & Military Cyber Threats

◈ **Attribution Complexity** – Nation-states use false-flag tactics to disguise attacks.
◈ **Evolving Tactics** – Governments constantly modify cyber weapons and infrastructure.
◈ **Legal & Ethical Barriers** – Monitoring government actors requires careful compliance with cyber laws.

Despite these challenges, OSINT remains a powerful tool in identifying, tracking, and exposing nation-state cyber operations.

Conclusion: OSINT as a Defense Against State-Sponsored Cyber Threats

◈ Government and military cyber threats are a growing global concern, targeting political institutions, critical infrastructure, and defense agencies.
◈ OSINT techniques—such as APT tracking, malware analysis, and social media monitoring—help security professionals uncover and mitigate state-sponsored cyber operations.
◈ By leveraging OSINT, cybersecurity teams can stay ahead of nation-state cyber threats and protect national security.

🚀 Cyber warfare is fought in the shadows—OSINT brings it to light.

9.6 Case Study: Using OSINT to Investigate a State-Sponsored Attack

State-sponsored cyberattacks are among the most sophisticated and hardest to attribute due to false-flag tactics, advanced malware, and covert infrastructure. However, Open-Source Intelligence (OSINT) plays a crucial role in uncovering the origins, techniques, and objectives of these attacks.

In this case study, we will analyze a real-world state-sponsored cyberattack using OSINT techniques. This investigation will focus on APT28 (Fancy Bear), a Russian military intelligence (GRU) hacking unit, and its cyber espionage campaign targeting NATO, European governments, and media organizations.

9.6.1 Background: The Attack on a European Government Agency

☐ **Incident Overview**

✓ **Target**: A European government agency responsible for national security.

✓ **Threat Actor**: APT28 (Fancy Bear), linked to Russia's GRU military intelligence.

✓ **Attack Method**: Phishing emails containing a zero-day exploit in Microsoft Outlook.

✓ **Objective**: Espionage—exfiltrating sensitive diplomatic and defense intelligence.

⊕ **Key Indicators of a State-Sponsored Attack**

✓ **Use of Zero-Day Exploits**: A hallmark of nation-state actors with advanced resources.

✓ **Targeting High-Profile Government Entities**: Suggests intelligence-gathering motives.

✓ **Sophisticated Malware & Infrastructure**: Custom-built malware with stealth capabilities.

✓ **Tactical Similarities to Previous APT28 Operations**: Matches past cyber espionage campaigns.

9.6.2 OSINT Investigation: Step-by-Step Analysis

Step 1: Identifying the Phishing Infrastructure

The attack began with phishing emails impersonating a NATO official, urging recipients to open a malicious attachment.

🔍 **OSINT Techniques Used:**

✓ Analyzing Email Headers & Domains:

- Extracted email headers using Email Header Analyzer tools.
- Identified a spoofed email address closely resembling NATO's official domain.
- Tracked domain registrations via WHOIS databases.

✓ Investigating Suspicious Domains & Servers:

- Used PassiveTotal (RiskIQ) and Shodan to check hosting locations.
- Found previously associated APT28 phishing domains in the infrastructure.
- Confirmed connections to past Russian cyber campaigns.

📌 Findings:

- The phishing domain nato-secure-mail[.]org was registered weeks before the attack, similar to past APT28 tactics.
- WHOIS records linked the domain to an IP address previously used in other Fancy Bear phishing campaigns.

Step 2: Malware Analysis & Attribution

The phishing attachment contained a malicious macro that dropped a custom Remote Access Trojan (RAT) onto the victim's system.

🔍 OSINT Techniques Used:

✓ Extracting Malware Hashes:

- Used VirusTotal and Hybrid Analysis to examine malware behavior.
- Identified a PowerShell-based backdoor, similar to previous APT28 tools.

✓ Mapping Malware to Known APT TTPs:

- Used MITRE ATT&CK Framework to compare techniques.
- Malware closely resembled Sednit, a backdoor previously attributed to Fancy Bear.

📌 Findings:

- Malware execution path matched APT28's documented Tactics, Techniques, and Procedures (TTPs).
- The backdoor connected to a C2 (Command and Control) server previously used in APT28 campaigns.

Step 3: Tracking the C2 Infrastructure

After infection, the malware established a connection with a C2 server, which OSINT investigators traced.

🔍 OSINT Techniques Used:

✓ Analyzing IP & Domain History:

- Used Censys & Shodan to identify servers linked to the attack.
- Found historical connections to known Fancy Bear infrastructure.

✓ Cross-Referencing With Past APT28 Attacks:

- Used Threat Intelligence Reports (FireEye, Mandiant, CrowdStrike).
- Identified matching C2 domains in prior Fancy Bear cyber operations.

📌 Findings:

- The C2 server had been previously used in cyberattacks against Eastern European governments.
- Further analysis revealed links to Russian GRU-controlled IP addresses.

Step 4: Investigating Threat Actor OPSEC Mistakes

Despite using sophisticated techniques, the attackers made minor OPSEC (Operational Security) mistakes that helped confirm their identity.

🔍 OSINT Techniques Used:

✓ Analyzing Leaked Hacker Profiles & Handles:

- Cross-referenced usernames and aliases found in leaked databases.
- Discovered a hacker alias linked to a known Fancy Bear member.

✓ Monitoring Dark Web & Hacker Forums:

- Found discussions of APT28's malware on underground Russian forums.

- Identified a malware developer linked to past GRU operations.

📌 Findings:

- A Fancy Bear hacker reused an alias on a Russian dark web forum, revealing a link to previous GRU operations.

9.6.3 Conclusion: OSINT Attribution & Impact

After compiling OSINT findings, investigators confirmed that the attack was conducted by APT28 (Fancy Bear), a Russian GRU cyber unit.

🚀 Final OSINT Findings:

✔ Malware & C2 infrastructure matched previous Fancy Bear operations.

✔ Phishing tactics aligned with past Russian cyber espionage campaigns.

✔ Threat actor OPSEC mistakes exposed links to GRU operatives.

☐ Impact of the Investigation

◆ **Government Response**: NATO and European security agencies issued cyber threat alerts.
◆ **Public Disclosure**: OSINT evidence was shared with threat intelligence agencies.
◆ **Countermeasures Implemented**: The affected government improved email security, malware detection, and threat intelligence sharing.

Key Takeaways: The Power of OSINT in State-Sponsored Investigations

◆ State-sponsored attacks leave digital footprints that OSINT can uncover.
◆ Tracking phishing domains, malware, and C2 infrastructure helps identify APT groups.
◆ OPSEC mistakes by attackers can reveal their true identities.
◆ OSINT findings help national security agencies strengthen defenses against cyber warfare.

🔎 Cyber warfare operates in the shadows—OSINT brings it to light.

10. Corporate Cybersecurity OSINT

In this chapter, we focus on leveraging OSINT to enhance corporate cybersecurity. With organizations increasingly targeted by cyber threats, it's essential to gather and analyze publicly available data to uncover vulnerabilities, detect threats, and improve overall security posture. We will explore strategies for monitoring digital footprints, assessing third-party risks, and identifying potential attack vectors within corporate infrastructure. From examining social media activity to scanning domain registrations, this chapter provides actionable insights on how to proactively protect your organization against cyberattacks, safeguard sensitive data, and create a robust security framework using OSINT techniques.

10.1 How Companies Use OSINT for Cyber Threat Detection

In today's digital landscape, corporations face an increasing number of cyber threats, ranging from data breaches and phishing attacks to ransomware and insider threats. Unlike government agencies with vast intelligence networks, most companies rely on Open-Source Intelligence (OSINT) to detect, analyze, and mitigate cyber risks in real-time.

OSINT provides organizations with actionable intelligence by gathering publicly available data from sources such as the dark web, threat intelligence platforms, social media, domain registries, and leaked credential databases. This intelligence helps security teams identify emerging threats, compromised credentials, phishing campaigns, and hacker activity before they escalate into full-scale incidents.

This chapter explores how companies leverage OSINT for cyber threat detection, highlighting key techniques, tools, and real-world applications.

10.1.1 Why Companies Rely on OSINT for Threat Detection

⚙ **Benefits of OSINT in Corporate Cybersecurity**

✓ **Proactive Threat Hunting** – Identifies cyber threats before they cause damage.

✓ **Cost-Effective Security Intelligence** – Provides valuable insights without expensive proprietary tools.

✓ **Real-Time Monitoring** – Enables continuous surveillance of emerging cyber threats.

✓ **Dark Web & Deep Web Visibility** – Detects leaked corporate data and threat actor discussions.

✓ **Early Warning for Phishing & Scams** – Flags suspicious domains and fake executive profiles.

🔍 **OSINT vs. Traditional Threat Intelligence**

Feature	OSINT	Traditional Threat Intel
Data Sources	Public, open-source	Private, proprietary
Cost	Low to free	High (commercial threat feeds)
Accessibility	Available to all organizations	Restricted to cybersecurity firms
Scope	Wide-ranging, real-time	Limited to curated datasets

With OSINT, companies can detect cyber threats early without solely relying on expensive commercial threat intelligence platforms.

10.1.2 OSINT Techniques for Corporate Threat Detection

1️⃣ Monitoring Dark Web for Corporate Data Leaks

The dark web is a hub for cybercriminals selling stolen corporate credentials, trade secrets, and financial data.

🔍 **OSINT Methods for Dark Web Monitoring**

✓ Using breach monitoring tools (Have I Been Pwned, DeHashed, IntelX) to check for leaked corporate credentials.

✓ Tracking dark web forums and marketplaces where stolen data is sold.

✓ Monitoring ransomware leak sites where cybercriminals expose breached company data.

📌 **Example**: A multinational corporation discovered its executive login credentials leaked on a dark web forum. Using OSINT, the security team reset compromised passwords before attackers could exploit them.

2️⃣ Identifying Phishing Domains & Fake Websites

Cybercriminals frequently register typosquatted domains that mimic legitimate company websites to launch phishing attacks.

🔍 OSINT Methods for Phishing Detection

✔ Using WHOIS & Passive DNS Analysis (WhoisXML API, RiskIQ) to detect newly registered lookalike domains.

✔ Monitoring phishing websites reported on OSINT databases (PhishTank, OpenPhish).

✔ Tracking URL shorteners and redirects that lead to fraudulent websites.

📌 **Example**: A financial institution identified a fake customer support website mimicking its official page. OSINT tools traced the phishing domain to a threat actor linked to previous banking scams.

3️⃣ Monitoring Social Media for Threats & Impersonation

Threat actors use social media platforms to spread misinformation, impersonate executives, and coordinate cyberattacks.

🔍 OSINT Methods for Social Media Threat Intelligence

✔ Tracking fake profiles impersonating executives or employees (LinkedIn, Twitter, Facebook).

✔ Monitoring hacker discussions on Telegram & Discord for planned cyberattacks.

✔ Identifying insider threats by analyzing public social media activity.

📌 **Example**: A CEO's fake Twitter account was used to launch a crypto scam. OSINT monitoring flagged the impersonation, and the security team had the account removed before victims were scammed.

4⃞ Detecting Malware & Ransomware Threats

Ransomware groups often announce upcoming attacks or post stolen corporate data on leak sites. OSINT helps companies detect these threats early.

🔍 OSINT Methods for Malware Threat Detection

✓ Tracking ransomware leak sites where attackers post exfiltrated corporate data.

✓ Analyzing malware hashes and signatures using VirusTotal and Hybrid Analysis.

✓ Monitoring C2 (Command & Control) infrastructure using Shodan and Censys.

📌 **Example**: A retail company detected mentions of its internal documents on a ransomware leak site. The security team identified a compromised employee account and mitigated the threat before further damage occurred.

10.1.3 OSINT Tools for Corporate Cyber Threat Intelligence

⬜ Essential OSINT Tools for Threat Detection

Tool Name	Function
Shodan	Finds exposed company assets (servers, IoT devices).
VirusTotal	Scans malware & malicious file hashes.
Have I Been Pwned	Checks for leaked corporate credentials.
Maltego	Maps cyber threat intelligence relationships.
PhishTank	Identifies phishing URLs and fraudulent sites.
DarkTracer	Monitors ransomware leak sites.

10.1.4 Real-World Case: How a Tech Company Used OSINT to Prevent a Data Breach

⬜ Incident Overview

A technology company detected unauthorized access attempts on its internal systems.

OSINT Investigation Steps:

✓ **Dark Web Monitoring**: Found stolen employee credentials listed on a hacker forum.

✓ **Phishing Domain Analysis**: Identified a lookalike login portal used in a credential-harvesting attack.

✓ **Threat Actor Tracking**: Traced attacker discussions on Telegram, indicating a planned ransomware attack.

🚀 **Outcome:**

✓ The security team reset compromised accounts and blacklisted malicious domains.

✓ The company patched vulnerabilities and improved employee phishing awareness training.

📌 **Key Takeaway**: OSINT helped detect and prevent a potential cyberattack before it caused significant damage.

10.1.5 The Future of OSINT in Corporate Cybersecurity

☐ **Emerging Trends in OSINT-Based Threat Detection**

✓ **AI-Powered OSINT Tools** – Automating real-time cyber threat detection.

✓ **Blockchain Intelligence** – Tracking cryptocurrency transactions linked to cybercrime.

✓ **Deepfake Detection** – Identifying synthetic media used in fraud and scams.

✓ **Automated Phishing Domain Takedowns** – Using OSINT APIs to instantly block malicious websites.

As cyber threats evolve, companies will increasingly rely on OSINT-driven threat intelligence to protect their assets, customers, and reputation.

Conclusion: Why OSINT is Essential for Corporate Cyber Threat Detection

◆ OSINT helps companies detect cyber threats early, preventing financial and reputational damage.

◆ Organizations can monitor the dark web, phishing domains, and social media for emerging threats.

◆ Using OSINT tools, businesses can strengthen their cybersecurity posture against sophisticated attackers.

🔫 In a world where cyber threats never sleep, OSINT is the eyes and ears that keep companies safe.

10.2 Investigating Insider Threats & Employee Data Exposure

While most cybersecurity efforts focus on external threats—such as hackers, malware, and phishing—insider threats remain one of the most damaging and difficult-to-detect risks. Insider threats occur when employees, contractors, or business partners misuse their access to steal data, sabotage systems, or unintentionally expose sensitive information.

Open-Source Intelligence (OSINT) plays a crucial role in identifying, investigating, and mitigating insider threats. By analyzing publicly available data—such as social media activity, data leaks, and dark web discussions—organizations can detect early warning signs of potential insider threats before they escalate into full-blown security breaches.

This chapter explores how companies use OSINT techniques, tools, and case studies to investigate insider threats and mitigate the risks of employee data exposure.

10.2.1 Understanding Insider Threats: Types & Motivations

🎯 **Types of Insider Threats**

Type	Description	Example
Malicious Insider	Employees who intentionally steal, leak, or sabotage company data.	An IT admin selling customer data on the dark web.
Negligent Insider	Employees who accidentally expose sensitive data.	An HR employee sending a confidential report to the wrong email.
Compromised Insider	Employees whose accounts are hijacked by cybercriminals.	A finance employee's email compromised in a phishing attack.
Third-Party Insider	Contractors, vendors, or partners with access to company systems.	A vendor's weak security policies leading to a data breach.

💰 Why Insiders Become Threats

✓ **Financial Gain**: Selling corporate secrets, customer data, or trade secrets.

✓ **Revenge**: Disgruntled employees seeking to harm the organization.

✓ **Espionage**: Stealing data for competitors or foreign governments.

✓ **Negligence**: Careless handling of company data (e.g., weak passwords, oversharing).

10.2.2 OSINT Techniques for Investigating Insider Threats

1️⃣ Monitoring Employee Leaks on the Dark Web

The dark web is a marketplace for stolen data. Employees may sell corporate credentials, trade secrets, or confidential reports on hacker forums.

🔍 OSINT Methods for Dark Web Monitoring

✓ Using breach monitoring tools (DeHashed, IntelX, Have I Been Pwned) to detect leaked employee credentials.

✓ Tracking insider threat discussions on hacker forums, Telegram channels, and ransomware leak sites.

✓ Using dark web crawlers (DarkTracer, DarkOwl) to scan for mentions of company data.

📌 **Example**: A financial firm detected internal documents for sale on a dark web forum. OSINT investigations revealed that a disgruntled ex-employee had leaked the data after being fired.

2️⃣ Identifying Insider Threats Through Social Media Intelligence (SOCMINT)

Employees often overshare sensitive company information on social media, putting organizations at risk.

🔍 OSINT Methods for Social Media Threat Detection

✔ Tracking LinkedIn & Twitter for job-related complaints that may signal a disgruntled insider.

✔ Identifying employees posting internal systems, badges, or security policies online.

✔ Monitoring Reddit & Discord for insider discussions on workplace issues and cybersecurity weaknesses.

📌 **Example**: A cybersecurity firm discovered an employee bragging on Reddit about bypassing company security measures. The company launched an internal investigation to assess the risk.

3️⃣ Investigating Credential Exposure & Data Leaks

Employees often reuse passwords across personal and corporate accounts, increasing the risk of credential stuffing attacks.

🔍 OSINT Methods for Detecting Employee Credential Exposure

✔ Using Have I Been Pwned or DeHashed to check if employee emails appear in data breaches.

✔ Monitoring GitHub repositories for accidental exposure of company API keys or login credentials.

✓ Tracking paste sites (Pastebin, Ghostbin) for dumped employee emails and passwords.

📌 **Example**: A software company found hardcoded admin credentials in a leaked GitHub repository. The security team immediately changed all credentials and implemented better access controls.

4️⃣ Detecting Suspicious Insider Behavior in Online Communities

Some employees engage with hacker forums and dark web markets to buy or sell corporate data.

🔍 OSINT Methods for Tracking Insider Activity on Underground Forums

✓ Using username correlation techniques to find employees using personal aliases on hacker forums.

✓ Monitoring underground marketplaces for employees discussing insider trading or selling access to company networks.

✓ Cross-referencing usernames from employee leaks with known hacker forum profiles.

📌 **Example**: A bank detected an employee's alias on a cybercrime forum, offering to sell privileged account credentials. Security teams acted quickly, revoking access and launching an investigation.

10.2.3 OSINT Tools for Insider Threat Investigations

☐ Essential OSINT Tools for Monitoring Employee Data Exposure

Tool Name	Purpose
DeHashed	Finds leaked employee emails & passwords.
IntelX	Searches paste sites & dark web forums.
Maltego	Maps digital footprints of potential insider threats.
LinkedIn API	Tracks job-related complaints & potential risks.
DarkTracer	Monitors ransomware groups posting stolen corporate data.
GitGuardian	Scans GitHub for leaked credentials & API keys.

10.2.4 Case Study: How OSINT Uncovered a Corporate Insider Threat

☐ Incident Overview

A technology company suspected that confidential product designs were being leaked to a competitor.

OSINT Investigation Steps:

✓ **Dark Web Monitoring**: Found stolen company blueprints listed for sale on a hacker marketplace.

✓ **Credential Exposure Analysis**: Detected an employee's email and password leaked in a previous data breach.

✓ **Social Media Intelligence**: Discovered that the same employee had posted frustrations about their job on Reddit, complaining about their salary.

🚀 Outcome:

✓ The company's security team identified the insider and revoked their access.

✓ OSINT evidence was used to take legal action against the employee.

✓ The organization implemented new security controls, such as multi-factor authentication (MFA) and employee access monitoring.

✦ **Key Takeaway**: OSINT helped prevent further data leaks and mitigate financial losses.

10.2.5 Mitigating Insider Threats with OSINT-Driven Security Policies

✅ **Best Practices for Preventing Insider Threats**

✓ Monitor leaked corporate credentials regularly.

✓ Track employee social media for security risks.

✓ Use OSINT to detect dark web discussions about company data.

✓ Implement user behavior analytics to flag unusual activities.

✓ Enforce access control policies (least privilege, MFA, zero trust).

As cyber threats evolve, OSINT-driven insider threat detection will become an essential part of corporate security strategies.

Conclusion: Why OSINT is Essential for Investigating Insider Threats

◆ Insider threats pose serious risks, from data theft to cyber sabotage.

◆ OSINT helps companies detect employee data leaks and security risks early.

◆ Monitoring dark web markets, social media, and breach databases can expose insider threats before they escalate.

◆ Organizations can use OSINT findings to strengthen security policies and prevent future incidents.

🚀 In an era where the greatest cybersecurity risks often come from within, OSINT is the key to staying ahead of insider threats.

10.3 Monitoring Brand Reputation & Online Threats

In today's digital landscape, a company's brand reputation is just as valuable as its data and infrastructure. Cyber threats, misinformation, data breaches, impersonation, and social engineering attacks can severely impact a brand's credibility and customer trust. Cybercriminals often exploit brand names in phishing campaigns, domain spoofing, and fake social media profiles, leading to financial and reputational damage.

Open-Source Intelligence (OSINT) plays a crucial role in detecting, tracking, and mitigating online threats that can harm a company's reputation. By actively monitoring social media, dark web forums, domain registrations, and search engine results, businesses can identify potential risks and take proactive steps to protect their brand.

In this chapter, we will explore OSINT techniques and tools that organizations can use to monitor brand reputation and detect online threats before they escalate.

10.3.1 Understanding Brand Reputation Threats

⊙⃗ Types of Brand Reputation Threats

Threat Type	Description	Example
Phishing & Impersonation	Cybercriminals create fake websites or emails using a brand's name to deceive customers.	Fake "support" emails pretending to be from a bank.
Fake Social Media Accounts	Scammers create impersonation accounts to mislead users or spread false information.	Fraudulent Twitter accounts pretending to be customer service.
Leaked Corporate Data	Confidential company information appears on dark web forums or paste sites.	Internal emails and credentials leaked on hacker forums.
Defamation & Fake Reviews	False claims or negative reviews spread misinformation about a company.	Fake Trustpilot reviews lowering customer trust.
Typosquatting & Domain Spoofing	Attackers register similar domain names to deceive customers or employees.	"paypal-secure.com" mimicking "paypal.com".

Understanding these threats helps organizations prioritize their monitoring efforts and take appropriate countermeasures.

10.3.2 OSINT Techniques for Monitoring Brand Reputation

1️⃣ Detecting Phishing Domains & Typosquatting

Cybercriminals often register lookalike domains to impersonate brands in phishing attacks. These domains are used to steal customer credentials or distribute malware.

🔍 OSINT Methods for Detecting Fake Domains

✔ **WHOIS Lookups**: Use WHOIS databases to check suspicious domain registrations.

✓ **Passive DNS Analysis**: Identify IP addresses and hostnames associated with fraudulent domains.

✓ **Domain Monitoring Tools**: Use services like dnstwister, DomainTools, or URLScan.io to detect variations of a brand's website.

📌 **Example**: A financial institution discovered a fraudulent domain (bank-support[.]com) being used in a phishing attack. OSINT helped track the hosting provider, and the domain was quickly taken down.

2️⃣ Identifying Brand Impersonation on Social Media

Fraudsters create fake social media profiles to impersonate brands, trick customers, and spread misinformation.

🔍 OSINT Methods for Detecting Social Media Impersonation

✓ Search for brand mentions using SOCMINT tools (TweetDeck, Hootsuite, Mention).

✓ Use image recognition tools to detect unauthorized use of logos and branding.

✓ Check for verified badges on official social media pages to identify imposters.

📌 **Example**: A company found a fake Facebook page offering fraudulent giveaways under its name. The OSINT team reported it, and the page was removed before customers were scammed.

3️⃣ Monitoring Data Leaks & Dark Web Mentions

Leaked corporate data, including customer information, employee credentials, and financial records, can severely damage a brand's reputation.

🔍 OSINT Methods for Detecting Data Leaks

✓ Use dark web monitoring tools (DarkTracer, IntelX, DeHashed) to track mentions of company data.

✓ Check breach databases like Have I Been Pwned for leaked corporate emails.

✓ Monitor hacker forums and Telegram channels for discussions involving the brand.

★ **Example**: A tech company discovered leaked API keys and internal documents on a paste site. The security team quickly revoked compromised keys and secured affected systems.

4️ Tracking Negative Publicity & Fake Reviews

Negative online publicity—whether genuine or fabricated—can damage a brand's reputation.

🔍 OSINT Methods for Reputation Monitoring

✓ Use Google Alerts and social listening tools (Brand24, Mention) to track brand mentions.

✓ Monitor review sites like Trustpilot, Yelp, and Glassdoor for fake reviews.

✓ Identify coordinated disinformation campaigns targeting the brand.

★ **Example**: A cybersecurity firm detected fake negative reviews posted by a competitor. Using OSINT, they traced the reviews back to an IP address linked to a rival company.

10.3.3 OSINT Tools for Brand Reputation Monitoring

☐ Essential OSINT Tools for Brand Protection

Tool Name	Purpose
Google Alerts	Tracks brand mentions on the web.
Hootsuite	Monitors social media platforms for impersonation.
DeHashed	Checks for leaked corporate credentials.
WHOIS Lookup	Identifies newly registered phishing domains.
URLScan.io	Scans suspicious URLs for phishing content.
DarkOwl	Tracks brand mentions on the dark web.
Brand24	Provides real-time brand reputation tracking.

10.3.4 Case Study: How OSINT Stopped a Phishing Campaign

☐ Incident Overview

A large e-commerce company received complaints from customers about phishing emails that looked like official order confirmation messages.

OSINT Investigation Steps:

✓ **Domain Monitoring**: Discovered that a phishing domain (shop-amazon-support[.]com) was being used.

✓ **WHOIS Lookup**: Identified the registrar and hosting provider of the fraudulent website.

✓ **URL Analysis**: Used URLScan.io to analyze the phishing site's structure and detect similar domains.

✓ **Dark Web Monitoring**: Found discussions on hacker forums about a new phishing campaign targeting e-commerce brands.

🚀 Outcome:

✓ The phishing domain was reported and taken down within 48 hours.

✓ Customers were alerted through official channels to avoid falling for the scam.

✓ The company's security team strengthened email authentication measures (DMARC, SPF, DKIM) to prevent future spoofing attacks.

📌 Key Takeaway: Proactive OSINT monitoring helped stop a major phishing attack before it caused widespread damage.

10.3.5 Strengthening Brand Protection with OSINT-Driven Security Policies

✅ Best Practices for Brand Reputation Monitoring

✓ Monitor domain registrations for typosquatting and spoofed domains.

✓ Use OSINT to detect brand impersonation on social media.

✓ Regularly scan breach databases for leaked corporate credentials.

✓ Implement strong email authentication measures to prevent phishing attacks.

✓ Leverage social listening tools to track negative publicity and misinformation.

By integrating OSINT into corporate cybersecurity strategies, businesses can proactively identify and neutralize online threats before they escalate into full-scale crises.

Conclusion: Why OSINT is Critical for Brand Protection

◆ Cybercriminals use impersonation, phishing, and data leaks to attack brands.
◆ OSINT helps businesses detect fraudulent domains, fake social media accounts, and leaked corporate data.
◆ Tracking brand mentions across social media, dark web, and hacker forums can prevent reputational damage.
◆ Companies that implement OSINT-driven monitoring can safeguard their reputation and customer trust.

🚀 In a world where online threats evolve daily, OSINT is an essential weapon in defending corporate brands.

10.4 Identifying Supply Chain & Third-Party Security Risks

Cybercriminals are increasingly targeting supply chains and third-party vendors to infiltrate organizations. Instead of attacking a company directly, threat actors exploit weaknesses in suppliers, contractors, and service providers to gain unauthorized access to sensitive data and systems. This tactic allows attackers to bypass traditional security measures, affecting multiple organizations through a single point of failure.

Recent high-profile supply chain attacks, such as the SolarWinds breach and the Kaseya ransomware incident, highlight how compromising a trusted third party can have catastrophic consequences. Businesses must adopt a proactive cybersecurity approach by leveraging Open-Source Intelligence (OSINT) to identify and mitigate risks within their supply chain.

This chapter explores OSINT techniques, tools, and case studies to help organizations assess third-party security risks and fortify their supply chains against cyber threats.

10.4.1 Understanding Supply Chain & Third-Party Security Risks

🔍 What Are Supply Chain Attacks?

A supply chain attack occurs when cybercriminals target a company's suppliers, software vendors, or service providers to gain access to their customers' networks. These attacks can take various forms, including:

Type of Attack	Description	Example
Software Supply Chain Attack	Hackers inject malicious code into a trusted software update or installer.	SolarWinds Orion attack.
Third-Party Data Breach	A vendor storing sensitive customer data is breached.	Target (2013) attack via HVAC vendor.
Compromised Hardware	Attackers implant backdoors in IT equipment before delivery.	Alleged supply chain tampering in hardware components.
Vendor Email Compromise	Cybercriminals hijack a vendor's email to launch phishing attacks.	Fraudulent invoices used to steal funds.
Dependency Hijacking	Attackers exploit weaknesses in open-source software dependencies.	Malicious NPM and PyPI packages used to spread malware.

Since third-party vendors often have privileged access to an organization's network or data, a security failure on their end can quickly escalate into a full-scale breach affecting multiple businesses.

10.4.2 OSINT Techniques for Identifying Third-Party Security Risks

1️⃣ Investigating Vendor Security Posture

Before engaging with a third-party supplier, companies must assess their cybersecurity maturity using OSINT.

🔍 OSINT Methods for Vendor Security Assessment

✓ Check if the vendor has experienced past data breaches using breach databases (Have I Been Pwned, DeHashed).

✓ Analyze employee cybersecurity hygiene (password reuse, exposed credentials) through OSINT tools.

✓ Monitor dark web forums for mentions of the vendor in cybercriminal discussions.

✓ Investigate public cybersecurity policies and compliance certifications (ISO 27001, SOC 2).

✓ Search for signs of weak security controls, such as outdated software or misconfigured cloud services.

📌 **Example**: An organization discovered that a third-party supplier had multiple leaked employee credentials on paste sites. This information helped them demand stronger security measures before signing a contract.

2️ Monitoring Supply Chain Threat Intelligence Sources

Cybercriminals frequently discuss potential attack targets on dark web forums, Telegram groups, and underground marketplaces.

🔍 OSINT Methods for Monitoring Supply Chain Threats

✓ Use dark web monitoring tools (DarkOwl, IntelX, or DarkTracer) to track vendor mentions.

✓ Monitor hacker forums for leaked vendor credentials, API keys, or stolen access logs.

✓ Search GitHub repositories for exposed vendor secrets and misconfigured cloud storage.

✓ Analyze vendor software dependencies using tools like Dependency-Track and OSS Index.

📌 **Example**: A company discovered that one of its suppliers' VPN credentials were being sold on a dark web marketplace, allowing them to take immediate action.

3️ Identifying Malicious Software Updates & Supply Chain Tampering

Cybercriminals inject malware into legitimate software updates to compromise businesses downstream.

🔍 OSINT Methods for Detecting Malicious Software in the Supply Chain

✔ Check vendor software hashes against malware databases (VirusTotal, Hybrid Analysis).

✔ Use passive DNS analysis to track suspicious software distribution servers.

✔ Monitor software vendor announcements for security vulnerabilities and patches.

✔ Analyze digital signatures of software updates for inconsistencies.

📌 **Example**: Security researchers detected malicious code hidden in a widely used open-source dependency, which could have compromised thousands of companies if left undetected.

4️⃣ Investigating Vendor Cyber Hygiene & Security Incidents

Understanding a vendor's security track record helps assess their reliability.

🔍 OSINT Methods for Vendor Risk Assessment

✔ Search for past security incidents involving the vendor (news articles, security blogs).

✔ Check if the vendor has disclosed vulnerabilities via security advisories (CVE databases).

✔ Analyze how quickly a vendor patches vulnerabilities (National Vulnerability Database).

✔ Look for negative cybersecurity reviews or regulatory penalties.

📌 **Example**: A financial institution rejected a vendor partnership after finding multiple past security breaches and a lack of commitment to cybersecurity best practices.

10.4.3 OSINT Tools for Supply Chain Risk Assessment

☐ **Essential OSINT Tools for Identifying Third-Party Security Risks**

Tool Name	Purpose
Have I Been Pwned	Checks if vendor credentials have been leaked.
DeHashed	Searches breach databases for compromised accounts.
VirusTotal	Scans vendor software updates for malware.
Censys/Shodan	Identifies exposed vendor infrastructure and misconfigured servers.
DarkOwl	Monitors dark web for vendor-related cyber threats.
GitHub Dorking	Finds accidentally leaked API keys and credentials.
Dependency-Track	Scans open-source software dependencies for vulnerabilities.

10.4.4 Case Study: Stopping a Supply Chain Attack Before It Happened

🔍 Incident Overview

A global technology firm was about to integrate a new cloud-based software solution from a third-party vendor. Before proceeding, they conducted an OSINT-based security assessment of the vendor.

☐ OSINT Investigation Steps:

✓ **Dark Web Monitoring**: Found discussions about the vendor's weak security controls in hacker forums.

✓ **Credential Leak Search**: Discovered exposed admin credentials for the vendor's web application.

✓ **Software Analysis**: Found an unpatched vulnerability in the vendor's software that could be exploited.

✓ **Shodan Scan**: Revealed multiple misconfigured cloud storage buckets exposing sensitive customer data.

🚀 Outcome:

✓ The company rejected the vendor's software due to security risks.

✓ The vendor was informed and forced to strengthen their security posture.

✓ A potential supply chain attack was prevented before integration took place.

📌 **Key Takeaway**: OSINT allowed the company to identify and mitigate third-party security risks before they became a threat.

10.4.5 Strengthening Supply Chain Security with OSINT-Driven Policies

✅ Best Practices for Managing Third-Party Cyber Risks

✓ Conduct OSINT-driven security assessments before onboarding a vendor.

✓ Monitor vendor credentials and infrastructure for exposure on the dark web.

✓ Regularly assess vendor software updates for malware or security flaws.

✓ Ensure vendors follow industry security standards (SOC 2, ISO 27001).

✓ Continuously track vendor security incidents and vulnerability disclosures.

By leveraging OSINT in third-party risk management, organizations can proactively detect security weaknesses and prevent supply chain attacks before they happen.

Conclusion: Why OSINT is Essential for Supply Chain Security

◆ Supply chain attacks are one of the fastest-growing cyber threats today.
◆ Threat actors exploit third-party vulnerabilities to infiltrate organizations.
◆ OSINT enables businesses to monitor vendor security, detect risks, and prevent breaches.
◆ Proactively assessing third-party cyber hygiene can stop attacks before they occur.

🚀 In an era of rising supply chain threats, OSINT is an indispensable tool for securing vendor relationships and safeguarding business operations.

10.5 Using OSINT for Cybersecurity Incident Response

When a cybersecurity incident occurs, every second counts. Security teams must quickly determine what happened, who was responsible, how it happened, and what steps to take next. Open-Source Intelligence (OSINT) plays a crucial role in gathering real-time intelligence about an attack, helping incident responders identify threats, assess risks, and take action to mitigate further damage.

By leveraging publicly available information, OSINT can help organizations trace attackers, analyze malware, detect compromised assets, and monitor threat actor communications on forums, social media, and the dark web. This subchapter explores how OSINT enhances cybersecurity incident response (CIR), outlines key techniques and tools, and provides a case study demonstrating its effectiveness in stopping an attack.

10.5.1 Understanding Cybersecurity Incident Response (CIR) with OSINT

A cybersecurity incident can range from a phishing attack to a ransomware breach or nation-state intrusion. The Incident Response (IR) process involves identifying, containing, eradicating, recovering, and learning from an incident.

🔍 How OSINT Supports Each Phase of Incident Response

IR Phase	How OSINT Helps
Identification	Detects indicators of compromise (IoCs) and attacker TTPs through threat intelligence sources.
Containment	Maps malicious infrastructure (C2 servers, domains, leaked credentials) to block threats.
Eradication	Tracks malware variants and hacking tools to ensure full removal from systems.
Recovery	Monitors dark web for further exposure and alerts organizations to new threats.
Lessons Learned	Analyzes past incidents to improve future detection and response strategies.

Key takeaway: OSINT provides real-time, actionable intelligence that helps IR teams respond faster and more effectively to cyber threats.

10.5.2 OSINT Techniques for Cybersecurity Incident Response

1️⃣ Investigating Indicators of Compromise (IoCs) with OSINT

When responding to an attack, security teams must quickly identify IP addresses, domains, hashes, and email addresses linked to the incident.

🔍 OSINT Methods for IoC Investigation:

✔ Use VirusTotal and Hybrid Analysis to check file hashes for malware detection.

✔ Perform WHOIS lookups on suspicious domains linked to phishing or malware.

✓ Search Passive DNS databases (RiskIQ, SecurityTrails) for infrastructure mapping.

✓ Use Shodan and Censys to identify attacker-controlled servers and vulnerabilities.

📌 **Example**: A security team used OSINT to track a phishing campaign by analyzing IP addresses and domains linked to previous attacks. This helped them block further phishing attempts before they reached employees.

2️⃣ Monitoring Threat Actor Communications on the Dark Web & Social Media

After a cyber attack, threat actors often discuss stolen data, vulnerabilities, and future plans on underground forums, Telegram groups, and marketplaces.

🔍 OSINT Methods for Monitoring Cyber Threats:

✓ Search for mentions of breached company data on dark web forums (DarkOwl, IntelX).

✓ Use Telegram OSINT tools to track hacker group discussions.

✓ Monitor social media for leaked credentials, exploits, and attacker claims.

✓ Check paste sites (Pastebin, Ghostbin) for stolen credentials and sensitive information.

📌 **Example**: A security team discovered stolen customer credentials on a dark web forum within hours of a breach. This allowed them to force password resets and prevent further account takeovers.

3️⃣ Investigating Malware & Ransomware Attacks Using OSINT

Malware analysis is essential for understanding how an attacker operates and preventing further infections.

🔍 OSINT Methods for Malware Investigations:

✓ Extract file hashes from malicious executables and scan them in VirusTotal.

✓ Check online sandboxes (Any.Run, Hybrid Analysis) for malware behavior analysis.

✓ Use Malpedia to research malware families and their known attack methods.

✓ Investigate C2 infrastructure using PassiveTotal, Shodan, and AbuseIPDB.

📌 **Example**: After detecting ransomware on a corporate network, IR teams used OSINT tools to identify the ransomware variant, its C2 servers, and known decryption tools, helping them contain the attack and recover encrypted files.

4⃣ Identifying & Tracking Attacker Infrastructure

Hackers rely on domains, IP addresses, servers, and cloud services to conduct cyber attacks. OSINT can help map these connections and track down attacker networks.

🔍 OSINT Methods for Infrastructure Tracking:

✔ Use WHOIS lookups to identify the registrant details of suspicious domains.

✔ Leverage Passive DNS tools to track related malicious domains and subdomains.

✔ Perform Shodan scans to detect vulnerable servers hosting malware or phishing kits.

✔ Investigate hosting providers and domain registrars commonly used by cybercriminals.

📌 **Example**: A security team linked multiple phishing domains to a single attacker by tracking WHOIS and DNS records, allowing them to block further attacks before they spread.

5⃣ Preventing Future Attacks Through OSINT-Based Threat Intelligence

Once an incident is contained, organizations must ensure they are not targeted again. OSINT helps by providing ongoing threat intelligence.

🔍 OSINT Methods for Continuous Monitoring:

✔ Monitor hacker forums and dark web for mentions of the company's data.

✔ Track emerging attack techniques (TTPs) from APT groups and cybercriminals.

✔ Analyze threat intelligence feeds (AlienVault OTX, AbuseIPDB) for new IoCs.

✔ Use STIX/TAXII-based threat sharing platforms to stay ahead of attackers.

★ Example: A financial firm prevented a second phishing attack by using OSINT to detect new phishing domains targeting its customers, allowing them to warn users before attacks occurred.

10.5.3 OSINT Tools for Incident Response

Tool Name	Purpose
VirusTotal	Analyzes file hashes, domains, and IP addresses for malware.
Hybrid Analysis	Runs malware in a sandbox to observe its behavior.
Shodan	Scans internet-exposed systems for vulnerabilities.
WHOIS Lookup	Identifies domain registrant details and ownership history.
RiskIQ PassiveTotal	Tracks malicious infrastructure using Passive DNS data.
DarkOwl	Monitors dark web for leaked credentials and cyber threats.
Censys	Identifies attacker-controlled infrastructure.
Any.Run	Provides interactive malware analysis.
AlienVault OTX	Shares community-driven threat intelligence.

10.5.4 Case Study: How OSINT Helped Stop a Ransomware Attack

🔍 Incident Overview

A large healthcare provider was hit by a ransomware attack that encrypted critical patient records. The attackers demanded $2 million in Bitcoin for decryption.

☐ OSINT Investigation Steps:

✓ **VirusTotal & Hybrid Analysis**: Identified the ransomware strain as Conti Ransomware.

✓ **Dark Web Monitoring**: Found attacker communications discussing stolen hospital data.

✓ **Bitcoin Transaction Tracking**: Traced ransom payment addresses using blockchain analysis.

✓ **C2 Infrastructure Analysis**: Blocked command-and-control (C2) servers using Shodan & Passive DNS.

🚀 Outcome:

✓ The company refused to pay the ransom after finding a free decryption tool online.

✓ The IR team contained the infection and restored backups within 24 hours.

✓ OSINT intelligence helped law enforcement track the ransomware operators.

📌 **Key Takeaway**: OSINT played a critical role in identifying, containing, and mitigating the attack while preventing future ransomware infections.

Conclusion: Why OSINT is Essential for Incident Response

✅ Speeds up threat detection and containment.

✅ Provides real-time intelligence on attackers and their tactics.

✅ Enhances malware analysis, infrastructure tracking, and dark web monitoring.

✅ Prevents future attacks through proactive threat intelligence.

🚀 In today's evolving cyber threat landscape, OSINT is a must-have tool for every cybersecurity incident response team.

10.6 Case Study: How OSINT Prevented a Corporate Espionage Attack

Corporate espionage, also known as industrial or economic espionage, involves malicious actors—ranging from competitors to nation-state groups—stealing trade secrets, proprietary data, and intellectual property (IP). This can lead to significant financial losses, reputational damage, and competitive disadvantages for organizations.

In this case study, we examine how Open-Source Intelligence (OSINT) played a critical role in identifying and stopping a corporate espionage attack before it could cause harm. By leveraging OSINT techniques such as dark web monitoring, social media intelligence (SOCMINT), and infrastructure analysis, security teams successfully uncovered a covert data theft operation, traced the attackers, and mitigated the threat.

10.6.1 Incident Overview: A High-Tech Firm Targeted by Espionage

A multinational technology company specializing in AI research noticed suspicious activity within its network. Employees in the R&D department reported receiving phishing emails disguised as official messages from the company's IT security team. Around the same time, corporate executives were being targeted on LinkedIn with fake recruiter profiles offering high-paying roles at a competitor.

Shortly after these incidents:

✓ Sensitive proprietary algorithms were found leaked on a dark web forum.

✓ A corporate VPN credential was found for sale on a cybercriminal marketplace.

✓ Internal product development plans were being discussed in underground hacker forums.

The company's cybersecurity team suspected corporate espionage and turned to OSINT to investigate further.

10.6.2 OSINT Investigation: Unmasking the Attackers

Step 1: Monitoring Dark Web & Cybercrime Marketplaces

OSINT analysts searched dark web forums, Telegram groups, and underground marketplaces for any mentions of the company's data. Using dark web intelligence tools such as DarkOwl, IntelX, and DeHashed, they uncovered:

✓ Stolen corporate credentials being sold on Genesis Market, a cybercriminal forum.

✓ A threat actor on RaidForums (a now-defunct hacking forum) claiming to have access to the company's internal network.

✓ Mentions of a "buyer" looking for AI-related intellectual property (IP).

📌 **Key Finding**: The leaked credentials suggested that an insider or compromised employee account was being used to steal data.

Step 2: Investigating Fake LinkedIn Recruiters & Social Engineering Attacks

Security teams analyzed the LinkedIn recruiter profiles that had approached the company's executives. Using SOCMINT (Social Media Intelligence) techniques, they found:

✔ The profiles used stock photos found on reverse image search (TinEye, Google Images).

✔ Their past work experience did not match any real company records.

✔ The profiles had only a few connections, all made within a short time.

✔ When cross-referencing usernames and email IDs, OSINT analysts found links to a known corporate espionage group tied to a nation-state actor.

📌 **Key Finding**: These LinkedIn profiles were fake recruiters used for social engineering, likely to lure executives into installing spyware or disclosing sensitive corporate information.

Step 3: Tracing Phishing Infrastructure & Malicious Domains

The phishing emails targeting R&D employees contained links that led to a fake login page mimicking the company's VPN portal. Using OSINT tools like WHOIS lookups, DNS analysis, and PassiveTotal, security teams:

✔ Discovered that the domain was registered two months prior using an anonymous registrar.

✔ Found that the IP address hosting the phishing page was previously linked to other corporate espionage campaigns.

✔ Used Shodan and Censys to scan the attacker's infrastructure, revealing multiple phishing pages mimicking other tech firms.

📌 **Key Finding**: The phishing campaign was highly targeted (spear-phishing) and part of a broader corporate espionage operation targeting multiple high-tech companies.

Step 4: Identifying the Espionage Group Behind the Attack

By correlating findings from the dark web, social media intelligence, and phishing infrastructure, security teams mapped the attack to a known Advanced Persistent Threat (APT) group specializing in corporate espionage and IP theft.

✓ The phishing tactics and infrastructure were similar to past attacks by APT40, a state-sponsored cyber espionage group.

✓ The dark web forum where the data was leaked had previously sold stolen intellectual property from aerospace and biotech firms.

✓ The LinkedIn recruiter scam matched techniques used in previous nation-state recruitment operations.

✦ **Key Finding**: The attack was not random—it was a well-planned espionage operation conducted by a sophisticated threat actor.

10.6.3 Mitigation & Response: Stopping the Espionage Attempt

After uncovering the espionage attempt, the company's security team took swift action to prevent further damage:

✓ Blocked malicious domains and IPs associated with the phishing attack.

✓ Forced password resets for all employees whose credentials were leaked.

✓ Implemented multi-factor authentication (MFA) to prevent credential theft.

✓ Warned executives about LinkedIn scams and removed fraudulent recruiter profiles.

✓ Reported findings to law enforcement and threat intelligence-sharing communities.

✓ Enhanced security awareness training for employees to detect social engineering tactics.

✦ **Final Outcome**: No further data exfiltration occurred, and the attackers were unable to establish persistent access to the company's systems. The OSINT investigation prevented a major corporate data theft.

10.6.4 Key Takeaways: How OSINT Helped Prevent Corporate Espionage

✓ **Early Detection**: OSINT revealed stolen credentials and leaked data before the attack escalated.

✓ **Dark Web Monitoring**: Identified threat actor discussions about the company's data.

✓ **SOCMINT Analysis**: Exposed fake recruiter profiles used for social engineering.

✓ **Infrastructure Tracking**: Uncovered the phishing domains and attacker infrastructure.

✓ **Threat Attribution**: Linked the attack to a known APT group specializing in corporate espionage.

✓ **Proactive Defense**: Implemented security measures that neutralized the threat before damage occurred.

Conclusion: OSINT as a Critical Tool Against Corporate Espionage

Corporate espionage is a growing cybersecurity risk, with attackers using phishing, social engineering, and dark web marketplaces to steal valuable corporate secrets. This case study highlights how OSINT helped detect, investigate, and prevent a sophisticated espionage attack.

🚀 Key Lessons for Organizations:

✅ Implement dark web monitoring to detect stolen credentials early.

✅ Use SOCMINT tools to investigate fraudulent LinkedIn and social media accounts.

✅ Monitor phishing campaigns and track attacker infrastructure with OSINT.

✅ Train employees to recognize social engineering attempts.

✅ Share intelligence with law enforcement and industry partners to stay ahead of threats.

🔍 **Final Thought:** In today's threat landscape, OSINT is an indispensable tool for protecting organizations against cyber espionage and corporate data theft. 🚀

11. Case Study: Tracking a Cybercriminal Network

In this chapter, we walk through a real-world case study of tracking a cybercriminal network using OSINT techniques. By following the trail of digital breadcrumbs left by attackers, we'll uncover how cybercriminal groups communicate, collaborate, and execute their operations. From identifying IP addresses and compromised accounts to analyzing patterns in dark web activity, we'll demonstrate how a combination of open-source tools and investigative techniques can be used to trace and disrupt cybercriminal networks. This case study will not only provide a step-by-step guide to conducting such investigations but also offer practical insights into the challenges and opportunities that come with tracking sophisticated online criminal operations.

11.1 Initial Discovery: Identifying Suspicious Threat Activity

Cybercriminal networks operate in the shadows, using sophisticated techniques to remain undetected. The earlier a security team can identify suspicious activity, the greater the chance of mitigating risks before they escalate into major security incidents. Open-Source Intelligence (OSINT) plays a crucial role in the initial discovery phase, helping analysts detect early indicators of compromise (IoCs), unusual cybercriminal chatter, and potential threats targeting an organization.

In this chapter, we explore how OSINT techniques were used to uncover suspicious threat activity, which ultimately led to the identification of a cybercriminal network involved in financial fraud, malware distribution, and data breaches.

11.1.1 The First Signs: Unusual Mentions on Dark Web Forums

The investigation began when an OSINT analyst noticed mentions of a company's name on a well-known cybercriminal forum. The discussion involved:

✓ A user offering corporate credentials for sale.

✓ Mentions of a "zero-day exploit" targeting the company's infrastructure.

✓ Requests for "access brokers"—individuals who sell compromised corporate networks.

Using dark web monitoring tools such as DarkOwl, IntelX, and Tor searches, analysts found multiple discussions referencing the targeted company. This raised a red flag that the organization was being actively discussed within the cybercrime underground, possibly indicating an upcoming attack.

★ **Key Insight**: Early detection of dark web chatter can provide a valuable warning sign before a cybercriminal operation is executed.

11.1.2 Investigating Breached Credentials & Initial Access Brokers

Further investigation revealed that login credentials from the targeted company had been leaked on multiple breach forums. The team searched databases such as:

✓ **Have I Been Pwned** – to check if employees' credentials had been part of past breaches.

✓ **DeHashed & LeakIX** – to locate exposed employee email addresses, passwords, and API keys.

✓ **BreachForums & Telegram channels** – where threat actors sell stolen credentials.

The OSINT team found that:

● A set of VPN credentials belonging to a high-level employee had been leaked.
● The credentials were being advertised on a hacker marketplace that specializes in selling "corporate access".
● Further searches linked the stolen credentials to previous attacks conducted by an Eastern European cybercrime group known for deploying ransomware.

★ **Key Insight**: Tracking stolen credentials on underground forums is a critical OSINT technique that can reveal potential insider threats and compromised accounts.

11.1.3 Monitoring Social Media for Threat Indicators

Another OSINT method used in this investigation was Social Media Intelligence (SOCMINT). Security teams scanned:

✓ Twitter, LinkedIn, and Telegram for mentions of the company.

✓ Facebook and Reddit hacking groups where cybercriminals sometimes discuss their targets.

Findings included:

✓ A fake LinkedIn profile impersonating a senior IT administrator from the company had recently connected with multiple employees.

✓ A Twitter post from an anonymous hacker account hinted at an upcoming "major breach" involving the targeted company.

✓ Telegram channels with known cybercriminal activity contained discussions about exploiting the company's network.

📌 **Key Insight**: Cybercriminals often test their tactics or discuss targets on social media before launching an attack. Monitoring these platforms can provide early warnings.

11.1.4 Analyzing Domain Registrations & Malicious Infrastructure

The OSINT team expanded their investigation to track potential phishing campaigns and malicious infrastructure by analyzing:

✓ Newly registered domains that mimic the company's brand.

✓ Suspicious SSL certificates linked to phishing sites.

✓ Passive DNS records to identify linked attack infrastructure.

Using tools like:

✓ **WHOIS Lookup** – to find recently registered domains impersonating the company.

✓ **PassiveTotal & RiskIQ** – to track IP addresses hosting malicious pages.

✓ **URLScan & VirusTotal** – to analyze suspicious domains for malware activity.

They discovered:

● A newly registered domain resembling the company's VPN login page—likely intended for phishing.

● The domain was registered using a privacy protection service, a common tactic used by cybercriminals.

● The hosting server's IP address was linked to previous phishing campaigns targeting multiple corporations.

📌 **Key Insight**: Tracking phishing infrastructure can help organizations block malicious sites before employees fall victim to scams.

11.1.5 Uncovering the Cybercriminal Network Behind the Activity

By correlating data from:

✓ Dark web forums

✓ Leaked credentials

✓ Suspicious social media activity

✓ Malicious infrastructure

The OSINT analysts identified a cybercriminal group specializing in corporate breaches and ransomware deployment. Further research revealed that:

✓ The group operated multiple phishing and malware campaigns.

✓ They used stolen corporate credentials to access networks and deploy ransomware.

✓ Their members were linked to previous attacks against financial institutions and tech companies.

📌 **Key Insight**: Cybercriminal groups reuse tactics and infrastructure, making OSINT a powerful tool for linking new threats to known actors.

Conclusion: How OSINT Helped Identify the Threat Before It Escalated

Because the company's security team used proactive OSINT techniques, they were able to:

✓ Detect early warning signs of an impending cyberattack.

✓ Identify compromised employee credentials before they were exploited.

✓ Monitor social media and hacker forums for intelligence on the attack.

✓ Track phishing infrastructure to prevent employees from falling for scams.

✓ Attribute the threat to a known cybercriminal network.

🎯 **Final Takeaway**: Early threat discovery through OSINT is one of the most effective ways to prevent cyberattacks before they happen. By continuously monitoring dark web activity, leaked credentials, suspicious social media mentions, and phishing infrastructure, organizations can stay ahead of cyber threats and prevent breaches before they occur.

11.2 Gathering Intel from Social Media, Forums & Dark Web Sources

Cybercriminals rely on a mix of social media platforms, hacker forums, and dark web marketplaces to coordinate attacks, sell stolen data, and discuss new hacking techniques. Open-Source Intelligence (OSINT) allows investigators to monitor these digital spaces for early warning signs of cyber threats, identify threat actors, and uncover attack infrastructure before an incident occurs.

This chapter explores how OSINT professionals use social media intelligence (SOCMINT), deep/dark web monitoring, and cybercrime forum analysis to gather threat intelligence, track malicious actors, and prevent security breaches.

11.2.1 Social Media Intelligence (SOCMINT): Tracking Cybercriminal Activity

Social media platforms like Twitter, Facebook, LinkedIn, and Telegram are often used by hackers and cybercriminal groups to:

✓ Advertise stolen credentials and leaked databases.

✓ Discuss hacking techniques and vulnerabilities.

✓ Conduct social engineering and phishing campaigns.

✓ Recruit new members for cybercrime operations.

Key OSINT Techniques for Social Media Monitoring

🔍 1. Keyword & Hashtag Tracking

- Searching for terms like #databaseleak, #0day, #datadump, #ransomware, and #hackersforhire can reveal ongoing cybercriminal discussions.
- Using Twitter search operators (e.g., "leaked database" OR "breached credentials").

🔍 2. Analyzing Threat Actor Accounts

- Cybercriminals often use pseudonymous accounts to discuss attacks.
- Monitoring accounts linked to past cyber incidents can reveal new attack trends.

🔍 3. Reverse Image Search & Deep Profile Analysis

- Attackers often reuse profile pictures and usernames across multiple platforms.
- Using tools like TinEye, PimEyes, and Google Reverse Image Search can help identify linked accounts.

Example Case: Tracking a Ransomware Group on Twitter

A cybersecurity analyst discovered a Twitter account posting about a new ransomware strain. By tracking the user's discussions, hashtags, and linked Telegram groups, the analyst found:

✔ A dark web marketplace selling decryption keys.

✔ A Telegram chat where ransomware victims were forced to negotiate payments.

✔ A GitHub repository containing malware source code.

📌 **Key Insight**: Many cybercriminal groups use social media to communicate— monitoring these platforms can reveal emerging threats before they escalate.

11.2.2 Cybercrime Forums: Where Hackers Discuss & Sell Data

Hacker forums, both on the surface web and dark web, serve as marketplaces where cybercriminals:

✓ Sell stolen credentials, exploits, and hacking tools.

✓ Offer DDoS-for-hire and malware development services.

✓ Share information on new vulnerabilities and attack techniques.

Popular Cybercrime Forums & OSINT Investigation Methods

💀 **1. Surface Web Forums (easier to access but still used for illicit activity)**

- **Reddit** (subreddits discussing hacking, OSINT, and exploits).
- **HackForums** (a popular site where beginner hackers discuss techniques).

⬜ **2. Deep & Dark Web Forums (more anonymous, harder to access)**

- **BreachForums** (formerly known as RaidForums, where stolen data is sold).
- **Exploit.in** (specialized in hacking services and data breaches).
- **XSS Forum** (used by Russian-speaking cybercriminals).

OSINT Techniques for Monitoring Forums

🔎 **Using Search Engines for Indexed Forums**

Google dorking techniques like:

site:raidforums.com "database leak"
site:exploit.in "0day exploit"

can reveal forum posts discussing breaches.

🔎 **Tracking Forum User Activity**

- Using tools like IntelX and DarkOwl to see if a hacker used the same username across multiple sites.
- Looking for repeated patterns in posts, timestamps, and writing style.

🔎 **Engaging in Passive Reconnaissance**

- Monitoring forum discussions without interacting.

- Collecting intelligence on malware, stolen credentials, and cybercriminal partnerships.

Example Case: Identifying a Data Broker on BreachForums

An analyst noticed a new user offering "fresh corporate logins" for sale. By cross-referencing:

✔ Previous forum posts by the same user.

✔ Other leaked credentials matching the company's email domain.

✔ Dark web marketplace activity linked to the same username.

The analyst connected the user to multiple past breaches, alerting cybersecurity teams before further leaks occurred.

✦ **Key Insight**: Tracking cybercrime forum activity allows analysts to map out hacker networks and identify data breaches early.

11.2.3 Dark Web Intelligence: Investigating Hidden Criminal Marketplaces

The dark web is a hidden part of the internet that requires special software like Tor or I2P to access. It hosts black markets, hacking forums, and illegal service providers where cybercriminals operate.

Key Dark Web Intelligence Techniques

☐ **1. Dark Web Search Engines & Monitoring Tools**

- DarkOwl and IntelX for indexing Tor sites.
- Onion search engines like Ahmia and Haystak.

🔍 **2. Tracking Cryptocurrency Transactions**

- Cybercriminals use Bitcoin, Monero, and Ethereum for payments.

- Using blockchain explorers (e.g., BTCScan, EtherScan) to trace ransomware payments.

🔗 3. Linking Dark Web Actors to Real Identities

Many hackers make OPSEC mistakes, such as:

✓ Reusing email addresses on the dark web and surface web.

✓ Accidentally posting identifying details in forum discussions.

✓ Using similar usernames across multiple illegal platforms.

Example Case: Tracking a Hacker Selling Corporate Access

A security analyst found a dark web marketplace listing corporate network access. Using OSINT techniques, they:

✓ Tracked the seller's cryptocurrency wallet transactions to previous ransomware payments.

✓ Cross-referenced usernames across cybercrime forums.

✓ Found an email address linked to an older data breach, which revealed the hacker's real identity.

📌 **Key Insight**: Many cybercriminals leave digital footprints—OSINT investigators can use these mistakes to trace their activities and disrupt operations.

Conclusion: OSINT as a Force Multiplier in Cyber Threat Investigations

Gathering intelligence from social media, hacker forums, and the dark web provides critical insights into cyber threats before they materialize into full-scale attacks. OSINT analysts can:

✓ Monitor hacker discussions for early indicators of breaches.

✓ Track stolen credentials and leaked corporate data before criminals exploit them.

✓ Investigate phishing and ransomware campaigns through cybercrime marketplaces.

✓ Identify malicious actors by linking forum activity to real-world identities.

🖋 **Final Takeaway**: OSINT is a powerful tool for early threat detection and cybercrime investigations. By proactively monitoring social media, hacker forums, and dark web sources, security teams can stay ahead of cyber threats and prevent major security incidents before they occur.

11.3 Analyzing Malware Infrastructure & Ransomware Activity

Malware and ransomware attacks are among the most dangerous cyber threats today, often leading to data breaches, financial losses, and operational disruptions. Cybercriminals behind these attacks rely on a vast infrastructure of servers, domains, and tools to distribute malware, encrypt files, and extort victims.

Open-Source Intelligence (OSINT) plays a crucial role in identifying and disrupting malware distribution networks, ransomware payment operations, and Command & Control (C2) infrastructure. This chapter explores how OSINT analysts investigate malicious domains, malware activity, and ransomware operations to track cybercriminal networks and mitigate threats before they escalate.

11.3.1 Identifying Malware Infrastructure & Command and Control (C2) Servers

Most modern malware—including ransomware—relies on Command and Control (C2) servers to communicate with infected devices. These C2 servers send commands, extract stolen data, and deploy additional payloads.

Key OSINT Techniques for Investigating Malware Infrastructure

🔍 **1. Passive DNS and WHOIS Analysis**

- Investigators use WHOIS lookups to find domain registration details.
- Passive DNS databases (e.g., PassiveTotal, VirusTotal) reveal past IP addresses linked to malicious domains.
- Reverse WHOIS searches can identify other domains registered by the same threat actor.

🔍 2. Tracking SSL Certificates

- Malware operators often use self-signed SSL certificates to secure communication between infected machines and C2 servers.
- Tools like Censys and Shodan can track SSL fingerprints across different attack campaigns.

🔍 3. Correlating IP Addresses & Hosting Providers

- Malicious infrastructure is often hosted on bulletproof hosting providers that ignore abuse complaints.
- Checking ASN (Autonomous System Number) data can reveal patterns in malware hosting.
- OSINT tools like IPinfo.io and Greynoise help track reused hosting services by cybercriminals.

Example Case: Detecting a New Ransomware C2 Server

An analyst used Shodan to scan for exposed RDP ports, a common ransomware entry point. They found:

✓ An open RDP server associated with a known ransomware group.

✓ The same IP address was previously linked to a malware C2 server.

✓ Further research in PassiveTotal showed that multiple phishing domains were also hosted on the same infrastructure.

📌 **Key Insight**: Many cybercriminal groups reuse infrastructure—tracking IP addresses, SSL certificates, and WHOIS details can reveal new attack campaigns.

11.3.2 Investigating Malware Distribution Networks

Malware is distributed through phishing emails, exploit kits, drive-by downloads, and malicious advertisements. OSINT analysts use various methods to track malware campaigns before they infect victims.

Key OSINT Techniques for Investigating Malware Distribution

☐☐ 1. Analyzing Malicious Email Campaigns

- Phishing emails often contain malicious attachments or links leading to malware downloads.
- Investigating email headers can reveal the sender's IP address and infrastructure.
- Tools like Any.Run and Hybrid Analysis help analyze email attachments in a sandbox.

2. Monitoring URL Shorteners & Redirects

- Cybercriminals use shortened URLs (e.g., Bit.ly, TinyURL) to hide malicious landing pages.
- Tools like Unshorten.me and Urlscan.io help track redirections.

3. Reverse Engineering Malware Samples

- Sandbox environments (e.g., Cuckoo Sandbox, ANY.RUN) allow researchers to execute malware safely.
- Static and dynamic analysis helps uncover network connections and embedded commands.

Example Case: Investigating a Malicious Email Campaign

An OSINT analyst received reports of a phishing campaign distributing ransomware. By:

✓ Extracting email headers, they found an IP linked to past malware campaigns.

✓ Analyzing the malicious URL, they uncovered a hidden ransomware payload.

✓ Tracking the domain's WHOIS history, they discovered connections to a larger cybercrime network.

✦ **Key Insight**: Investigating malware delivery mechanisms helps identify new phishing campaigns before they spread widely.

11.3.3 Tracking Ransomware Activity & Payment Transactions

Ransomware operators encrypt files and demand payment—usually in cryptocurrency—for decryption keys. OSINT analysts track ransomware groups by monitoring their leak sites, ransom notes, and cryptocurrency transactions.

Key OSINT Techniques for Tracking Ransomware Operations

💰 **1. Monitoring Ransomware Leak Sites**

- Many ransomware groups publish stolen data on dark web leak sites if victims refuse to pay.
- DarkOwl, Tor search engines, and Telegram monitoring help analysts find these sites.

💰 **2. Analyzing Ransom Notes & Payment Wallets**

- Ransomware notes often include Bitcoin or Monero addresses for payments.
- Blockchain explorers (e.g., BTCScan, Chainalysis) help track ransom payments across multiple wallets.

💰 **3. Identifying Ransomware Variants**

- Payload analysis helps attribute ransomware to specific groups (e.g., LockBit, Conti, ALPHV).
- YARA rules and hash-based searches help detect malware variants.

Example Case: Tracking a Ransomware Payment

An OSINT researcher analyzed a Bitcoin address from a ransomware note. By:

✔ Using Blockchain explorers, they tracked payments from multiple victims.

✔ Cross-referencing the transactions with known threat actor wallets, they found a common laundering pattern.

✔ Identifying an exchange service used for cashing out helped law enforcement trace the attackers.

📌 **Key Insight**: Tracking ransomware payments can help uncover threat actor financial operations and potential law enforcement leads.

11.3.4 Investigating Ransomware-as-a-Service (RaaS) Operations

Many cybercriminals now operate Ransomware-as-a-Service (RaaS), where affiliates pay to use ransomware tools in exchange for a percentage of the ransom.

Key OSINT Indicators of RaaS Operations

✔ **Underground Ads** – Dark web forums often have "RaaS recruitment posts" offering malware services.

✔ **Affiliates Using the Same Ransomware Strains** – Similar ransom notes and reused C2 infrastructure indicate RaaS-based attacks.

✔ **Telegram & Dark Web Channels** – Many ransomware groups use private Telegram chats for affiliate coordination.

Example Case: Investigating a RaaS Group on Telegram

An analyst infiltrated a cybercriminal Telegram group where:

✔ Affiliates were purchasing access to ransomware kits.

✔ Members discussed targeting specific industries.

✔ Payment records linked them to a known RaaS operator.

📌 **Key Insight**: RaaS models allow less-skilled hackers to conduct ransomware attacks—monitoring underground forums and Telegram chats can reveal new threats before they strike.

Conclusion: OSINT's Role in Disrupting Malware & Ransomware Operations

Malware and ransomware groups depend on complex infrastructures, but OSINT can uncover their tactics, infrastructure, and financial operations before they cause damage.

◆ Tracking malware infrastructure helps identify new C2 servers and phishing domains.
◆ Analyzing malicious email campaigns reveals malware distribution networks.
◆ Monitoring ransomware payments provides financial intelligence on cybercriminals.
◆ Investigating RaaS operations can help identify new threat actors and their tools.

🚀 **Final Takeaway**: OSINT is a critical tool for combating malware and ransomware attacks—by continuously monitoring cybercriminal activities, infrastructure, and financial transactions, security teams can predict and prevent cyberattacks before they escalate.

11.4 Mapping the Network: Identifying Key Players & Patterns

Cybercriminal groups, whether they focus on ransomware, data breaches, fraud, or espionage, rarely operate alone. They function as highly structured networks with defined roles, including:

- **Operators** – The leaders or coordinators of the group.
- **Affiliates** – Those who execute attacks on behalf of the main group.
- **Developers** – Individuals responsible for coding malware or exploits.
- **Money Mules & Launderers** – Those who cash out stolen funds.
- **Infrastructure Providers** – Those who sell compromised servers, bulletproof hosting, or VPNs.

Mapping out a cybercriminal network is crucial to understanding who the key players are, how they communicate, and how their infrastructure operates. This chapter explores how OSINT techniques can be used to identify key actors, track relationships, and uncover hidden patterns within these networks.

11.4.1 Using OSINT to Map Cybercriminal Networks

To successfully map a cybercriminal network, investigators must:

- **Identify Key Actors** – Find the individuals, groups, or organizations involved.
- **Analyze Communication Channels** – Discover how they interact (forums, Telegram, dark web sites, etc.).
- **Track Financial Transactions** – Follow cryptocurrency payments and illicit transactions.
- **Map Infrastructure** – Identify shared servers, domains, and other digital assets.

Key OSINT Techniques for Network Mapping

🔍 **1. Analyzing Dark Web & Underground Forum Activity**

- Cybercriminals often recruit, discuss tactics, and sell stolen data on dark web forums.
- OSINT tools like DarkOwl, Tor search engines, and forum scrapers can identify recurring usernames and aliases.
- Tracking discussions over time helps uncover new partnerships and alliances.

🔍 2. Linking Threat Actor Aliases & Online Profiles

- Cybercriminals often use multiple handles (usernames) across different platforms.
- Tools like WhatsMyName and Sherlock can identify where a username appears across social media and hacker forums.
- Pseudonym correlation – Analyzing writing style, posting times, and activity patterns helps connect multiple aliases to the same actor.

🔍 3. Investigating Cryptocurrency Transactions

- Many ransomware and fraud networks use Bitcoin, Monero, and other cryptocurrencies for payments.
- Blockchain explorers like BitcoinWhosWho, Chainalysis, and CipherTrace can trace payments from victims to threat actors.
- Clustering techniques can reveal common wallets used by multiple criminals.

🔍 4. Mapping Shared Infrastructure (IP Addresses, Domains, Hosting Services)

- Cybercriminals often reuse hosting services, VPN providers, and compromised servers across multiple operations.
- OSINT tools like Shodan, Censys, and PassiveTotal help track shared IP addresses and infrastructure links.

Example Case: Mapping a Dark Web Fraud Network

An OSINT analyst investigated a credit card fraud forum and discovered:

✔ Several users were advertising stolen credit card details from the same source.

✔ A Telegram group linked to the forum revealed affiliates selling the stolen data.

✔ Tracking Bitcoin payments showed multiple transactions flowing into a single wallet, later cashed out through an unregulated exchange.

📌 **Key Insight**: By mapping out connections between forum members, transactions, and communication channels, the analyst identified a well-structured fraud network operating under multiple aliases.

11.4.2 Identifying Key Players in a Cybercriminal Network

Not all members of a cybercriminal group hold the same level of importance or influence. Identifying key players requires:

👤 **1. Ranking Threat Actors by Activity & Influence**

- Who posts the most on underground forums?
- Who controls malware infrastructure or ransom payments?
- Who has direct communication with affiliates?

👤 **2. Examining Reputation Systems on Cybercrime Forums**

- Many underground forums have "reputation scores" or "trusted seller" ranks.
- Higher reputation often means more involvement in criminal activities.

👤 **3. Investigating Private Chat Groups & Encrypted Communications**

- Many cybercriminals use Telegram, Discord, or private forums to organize attacks.
- Monitoring invite-only chat groups can reveal who gives orders and who follows them.

Example Case: Identifying the Leader of a Ransomware Group

A ransomware affiliate program had multiple members launching attacks, but one actor consistently:

✔ Registered new ransomware domains before attacks began.

✔ Controlled the primary cryptocurrency wallet receiving ransom payments.

✔ Engaged in forum discussions about malware development.

📌 **Key Insight**: By following infrastructure patterns and payment flows, OSINT investigators identified the true leader behind the ransomware group.

11.4.3 Finding Patterns & Connections in Cyber Criminal Activities

Patterns often emerge when tracking recurring cyberattacks, malware campaigns, and financial transactions.

📈 1. Identifying Reused Attack Methods & Tools

- Many threat actors reuse phishing kits, exploit scripts, and malware payloads.
- YARA rules and malware hash analysis help connect different attacks to the same actor.

📈 2. Recognizing Repeated Payment Transactions

- Some ransomware groups demand payment in specific Bitcoin amounts (e.g., 0.5 BTC per victim).
- Tracking clusters of similar payments can reveal linked ransomware affiliates.

📈 3. Detecting Shared Infrastructure & Hosting Services

- Many cybercriminals host phishing sites and C2 servers on the same hosting providers.
- Checking domain registration patterns can reveal related malicious domains.

Example Case: Connecting Multiple Phishing Campaigns to One Group

An OSINT analyst noticed that:

✓ Several fake bank login pages used the same phishing kit.

✓ The domains were registered using the same email address.

✓ WHOIS history revealed past registrations linked to a known fraudster.

📌 **Key Insight**: Even when cybercriminals try to hide their tracks, infrastructure reuse and transaction patterns can expose their connections.

Conclusion: The Power of OSINT in Mapping Cybercriminal Networks

Understanding how cybercriminals operate as networks is essential for stopping their activities.

✓ Tracking forums, aliases, and communication channels reveals who the major players are.

✓ Monitoring cryptocurrency transactions exposes ransomware operations and financial laundering tactics.

✓ Analyzing shared infrastructure (domains, servers, and IPs) connects seemingly unrelated cybercrime campaigns.

✓ Recognizing attack patterns and tool reuse allows security teams to predict and prevent future threats.

🚀 **Final Takeaway**: Cybercriminals may try to remain anonymous, but OSINT provides the tools needed to uncover their identities, map their networks, and disrupt their operations.

11.5 Coordinating with Law Enforcement & Cybersecurity Teams

Cybercrime investigations are complex, often involving multiple jurisdictions, encrypted communications, and anonymous actors operating across different platforms. While OSINT investigators can uncover critical intelligence on cybercriminal networks, threat actors, and malicious infrastructure, taking legal action requires collaboration with law enforcement agencies and cybersecurity professionals.

This chapter explores the best practices for coordinating with law enforcement and cybersecurity teams, covering:

- Legal considerations and challenges in cybercrime investigations.
- How OSINT analysts can support law enforcement efforts.
- Working with corporate cybersecurity teams and private-sector threat intelligence groups.
- Sharing intelligence effectively while ensuring compliance with laws and ethical standards.

11.5.1 Understanding the Role of Law Enforcement in Cybercrime Investigations

Law enforcement agencies (LEAs) worldwide play a crucial role in investigating, disrupting, and prosecuting cybercriminal activities. However, OSINT analysts must understand the limitations and challenges faced by these agencies, including:

Key Law Enforcement Agencies in Cybercrime Investigations

- **Interpol** – Coordinates international efforts against cybercrime.
- **Europol's EC3 (European Cybercrime Centre)** – Investigates major cybercriminal networks in Europe.
- **FBI Cyber Division (U.S.)** – Handles ransomware, hacking, and data breaches.
- **NCA (UK's National Crime Agency)** – Focuses on organized cyber threats.
- **CERTs (Computer Emergency Response Teams)** – Works on cyber incident response globally.

Challenges Faced by Law Enforcement in Cybercrime Cases

◆ **Jurisdictional Issues** – Cybercriminals operate across borders, making international cooperation essential.

◆ **Anonymity of Threat Actors** – The use of VPNs, encrypted messaging apps, and dark web forums complicates attribution.

◆ **Legal Restrictions** – Law enforcement agencies must follow strict data privacy laws and legal procedures when collecting evidence.

◆ **Fast-Evolving Threats** – Ransomware gangs, phishing groups, and APTs frequently change tactics, requiring real-time intelligence updates.

💡 **How OSINT Helps Law Enforcement:**

- Tracking cybercriminal footprints across forums, dark web sites, and social media.
- Providing intelligence on infrastructure, including malicious domains, command-and-control servers, and cryptocurrency wallets.
- Supporting attribution efforts by identifying aliases, past activities, and OPSEC mistakes.

11.5.2 How OSINT Analysts Can Support Law Enforcement Efforts

OSINT analysts play a crucial role in gathering, analyzing, and sharing intelligence that can assist law enforcement. However, the process must be conducted ethically, legally, and with proper documentation.

Best Practices for OSINT Analysts Working with Law Enforcement

✓ Ensure Legality & Ethical Considerations

- Avoid unauthorized access to private systems (no hacking or illegal data collection).
- Follow data protection laws (e.g., GDPR in Europe, CCPA in California).
- Ensure proper chain of custody for evidence collected through OSINT investigations.

✓ Document & Verify Findings

- Use screenshots, timestamps, and hash verification to authenticate OSINT findings.
- Maintain detailed logs of sources, methodologies, and tools used.

✓ Understand the Intelligence Requirements of Law Enforcement

Law enforcement agencies often require specific types of intelligence, such as:

- Attribution details (Who is behind the cybercrime?)
- Indicators of Compromise (IOCs) (What infrastructure is being used?)
- Financial transactions (How is the money flowing?)

✓ Use Proper Intelligence-Sharing Channels

- **Public-Private Partnerships (PPP)** – Collaborate with government and private sector threat intelligence teams.
- **Threat Intelligence Sharing Platforms** – Submit findings via STIX/TAXII, MISP (Malware Information Sharing Platform), or ISACs (Information Sharing and Analysis Centers).
- **Direct Reports to Law Enforcement** – Provide OSINT reports with actionable intelligence to official agencies.

💡 **Case Example**: OSINT analysts tracking a ransomware gang identified a Bitcoin wallet address used for ransom payments. By coordinating with law enforcement and blockchain analysis firms, they linked the wallet to an unregulated exchange, leading to the identification of key threat actors.

11.5.3 Working with Corporate Cybersecurity Teams & Private Sector Investigators

Many cyber threats directly impact corporations, financial institutions, and critical infrastructure. OSINT analysts frequently work alongside:

- **Incident Response Teams (CSIRTs, SOCs, and CERTs)** – Handling active security incidents.
- **Threat Intelligence Teams** – Investigating cyber threats affecting businesses.
- **Cybersecurity Firms** – Assisting in private-sector cybercrime investigations.

How Corporate Cybersecurity Teams Use OSINT

✓ **Brand Protection & Executive Security** – Identifying impersonation attempts, social engineering campaigns, and VIP threats.
✓ **Monitoring Dark Web Data Leaks** – Tracking stolen corporate credentials and sensitive documents.
✓ **Analyzing Phishing & Malware Campaigns** – Identifying attacker infrastructure targeting employees or customers.
✓ **Investigating Insider Threats** – Monitoring employee data exposure and potential insider leaks.

💡 **Case Example**: A multinational company suffered a data breach, and leaked credentials appeared on a dark web marketplace. OSINT analysts:

✔ Tracked the original breach source.

✔ Identified threat actors selling the data.

✔ Notified corporate cybersecurity teams, who worked with law enforcement to disrupt the marketplace.

11.5.4 Effective Intelligence Sharing & Collaboration

How to Share Intelligence Securely

✔ Use Standardized Intelligence Formats

- **STIX (Structured Threat Information eXpression)** – Standard format for cyber threat intelligence.
- **TAXII (Trusted Automated eXchange of Indicator Information)** – Secure threat data exchange.
- **MISP (Malware Information Sharing Platform)** – Used by organizations to share threat intelligence.

✓ Join Trusted Cybersecurity Communities

- **ISACs (Information Sharing and Analysis Centers)** – Industry-specific cyber intelligence hubs.
- **InfraGard (FBI Program for Cyber Threat Sharing)** – Connects cybersecurity professionals with the FBI.
- **FIRST (Forum of Incident Response and Security Teams)** – Global cybersecurity response coordination.

✓ Ensure Compliance with Data Privacy Laws

- When sharing intelligence, avoid exposing personally identifiable information (PII) unless authorized.
- Follow GDPR, CCPA, and other legal requirements for data protection.

💡 **Case Example**: An OSINT researcher uncovered a phishing campaign targeting a financial institution. By sharing IOCs (malicious domains, IPs, and email addresses) with ISACs and CERTs, multiple organizations blocked the attack before it could spread.

Conclusion: Strengthening Cybercrime Investigations Through Collaboration

OSINT is a powerful tool in cyber threat intelligence, but it becomes even more effective when combined with the expertise, legal authority, and operational capabilities of law enforcement and cybersecurity teams.

Key Takeaways:

✓ Law enforcement faces legal and jurisdictional challenges in cyber investigations—OSINT can help bridge intelligence gaps.

✓ OSINT analysts must follow ethical and legal guidelines when collecting and sharing cyber threat intelligence.

✓ Corporate cybersecurity teams rely on OSINT to monitor threats, investigate breaches, and prevent cyberattacks.

✓ Threat intelligence sharing platforms (STIX/TAXII, MISP, ISACs) facilitate secure and efficient information exchange.

✓ Effective collaboration between OSINT researchers, law enforcement, and cybersecurity teams leads to successful cybercrime disruption.

🚀 **Final Thought**: Cybercrime is a global challenge, and no single entity can combat it alone. By leveraging OSINT, sharing intelligence responsibly, and working together, we can identify, disrupt, and neutralize cyber threats more effectively.

11.6 Final Outcome: Lessons Learned from the Investigation

After an intensive investigation involving OSINT techniques, cyber threat intelligence (CTI) methodologies, and collaboration with law enforcement and cybersecurity teams, the case has reached its final stage. Whether the cybercriminal network was dismantled, an attack was prevented, or critical vulnerabilities were identified, every OSINT-driven investigation provides valuable lessons for future cybersecurity efforts.

This chapter will reflect on:

- The key intelligence findings from the investigation.
- What worked well and what challenges were encountered.
- Mistakes made by the threat actors and how they were exploited.
- The impact of intelligence sharing and collaboration.
- Lessons learned to improve future OSINT investigations.

11.6.1 Key Findings & How OSINT Played a Role

Breaking Down the Investigation's Major Discoveries

At the start of this investigation, we identified suspicious activity linked to a cybercriminal network. Through systematic OSINT gathering, several critical intelligence points emerged:

1️⃣ Threat Actor Identification:

- The attackers operated under multiple aliases across forums, dark web markets, and social media.
- OPSEC mistakes (e.g., reused usernames, leaked IP addresses) allowed attribution to real-world identities.

2️⃣ Malware & Attack Infrastructure:

- OSINT analysis revealed malicious domains, phishing kits, and command-and-control (C2) servers.
- Passive DNS and WHOIS analysis uncovered connections to past cyber campaigns.

3️⃣ Financial Tracking & Monetization Strategies:

- Investigators traced cryptocurrency transactions to known money laundering exchanges.
- Bitcoin tumbling services were used to obscure the funds, but blockchain analysis linked transactions back to the group.

4️⃣ Breach & Data Leak Insights:

- Dark web monitoring confirmed stolen credentials were being sold on underground marketplaces.
- Some breached data was used for business email compromise (BEC) and ransomware extortion attempts.

How OSINT Was Critical in the Investigation

✅ Social media intelligence (SOCMINT) provided insight into threat actors' online behavior and recruitment tactics.

✓ Passive DNS, WHOIS lookups, and malware sandboxing helped identify C2 servers and phishing infrastructure.

✓ Dark web monitoring revealed threat actors' discussions, sales of stolen data, and upcoming cybercrime campaigns.

✓ Cryptocurrency tracking connected ransoms and fraud profits to identifiable actors.

💡 **Final Outcome**: The OSINT investigation provided enough intelligence for law enforcement and cybersecurity teams to act, leading to:

- The takedown of malicious domains and servers.
- The arrest of key cybercriminals.
- The protection of multiple organizations from targeted attacks.

11.6.2 OPSEC Mistakes Made by Threat Actors

Even experienced cybercriminals make mistakes that OSINT analysts can exploit. In this case, several key OPSEC failures led to the unmasking of the network:

◆ **Username Reuse Across Platforms:**

The same handle used on a hacking forum was linked to a personal social media account.

◆ **Metadata Leakage from Uploaded Files:**

A phishing email contained an attachment with metadata revealing the attacker's time zone and software details.

◆ **Unmasked IP Addresses:**

Logs showed that threat actors occasionally forgot to use VPNs or Tor, exposing real locations.

◆ **Linked Cryptocurrency Transactions:**

Despite using mixers and tumblers, investigators traced Bitcoin wallets to an exchange that required KYC (Know Your Customer) verification.

💡 **Lesson**: Even the most sophisticated cybercriminals are vulnerable to OSINT techniques when they make even small OPSEC mistakes.

11.6.3 Challenges Encountered During the Investigation

Every cyber threat intelligence investigation comes with obstacles. Some of the major challenges faced during this case included:

〰️ Encrypted Communications & Dark Web Challenges

- Many communications occurred over end-to-end encrypted messaging apps (Telegram, Signal, Tox).
- Some dark web forums required invite-only access, limiting intelligence collection.

〰️ Attribution & False Flags

- The threat actors used multiple layers of deception (fake personas, VPNs, proxy networks).
- Some indicators suggested attempts to frame other hacking groups.

〰️ Legal & Ethical Considerations

- OSINT analysts had to ensure compliance with laws (e.g., no unauthorized hacking or data access).
- Certain findings required proper evidence handling for law enforcement use.

💡 **Lesson**: Patience and a structured approach are essential—some investigations require weeks or months of monitoring before actionable intelligence emerges.

11.6.4 The Power of Intelligence Sharing & Collaboration

This case reinforced the importance of cooperation between OSINT analysts, law enforcement, and cybersecurity teams. Without intelligence sharing, critical data points could have been missed or delayed.

Key Collaboration Wins

✅ **Threat Intelligence Platforms (TIPs)** – Using STIX/TAXII to distribute IOCs helped multiple organizations defend against ongoing attacks.

✅ **Cybersecurity Firms & ISACs** – Private sector companies shared insights on the ransomware group's evolving tactics.

✅ **Law Enforcement Action** – The final arrests and infrastructure takedown were only possible due to cross-border collaboration.

💡 **Lesson**: No single entity can fight cybercrime alone—public-private partnerships and global intelligence sharing are crucial.

11.6.5 Lessons Learned for Future OSINT Investigations

1️⃣ Prioritize OPSEC & Ethical OSINT Methods

- Investigators must adhere to ethical guidelines while gathering intelligence.
- Avoid techniques that violate privacy laws or compromise investigations.

2️⃣ Leverage Automation & Threat Intelligence Platforms

- OSINT automation tools (Maltego, Spiderfoot, Shodan) accelerate data collection.
- Threat Intelligence Platforms (TIPs) (MISP, Anomali, Recorded Future) enhance data correlation & IOC sharing.

3️⃣ Cross-Check Multiple Data Sources

- No single OSINT source is 100% reliable—always corroborate intelligence from multiple sources.
- Avoid falling for false flags or misleading indicators planted by adversaries.

4️⃣ Monitor Emerging Cybercrime Trends

- Threat actor tactics evolve constantly—staying informed through OSINT is essential.
- Keep an eye on ransomware groups, underground forums, and zero-day exploit markets.

11.6.6 Final Conclusion: Strengthening OSINT for Future Cyber Threats

This investigation demonstrated the power of OSINT in uncovering cybercriminal networks, tracking digital footprints, and preventing attacks. The combination of technical intelligence (malware analysis, infrastructure mapping) and human intelligence (dark web monitoring, social media analysis) proved invaluable.

Key Takeaway: Cyber threat intelligence is an ongoing battle—as cybercriminals refine their techniques, OSINT investigators must adapt new strategies, tools, and methodologies.

🚀 **Final Thought**: OSINT is not just a tool—it's an evolving discipline. Every investigation provides new insights, helping us stay one step ahead of cybercriminals in the digital battlefield.

12. Future of OSINT in Cybersecurity

In this final chapter, we look ahead to the future of OSINT in cybersecurity, examining how emerging technologies, evolving threats, and shifting geopolitical landscapes will shape the role of open-source intelligence. As cybercriminals become more sophisticated and attacks grow in scale, OSINT will continue to be a crucial tool in proactive defense strategies. We'll explore the impact of artificial intelligence, machine learning, and automation in enhancing OSINT capabilities, as well as the ethical and legal considerations that will influence its use. By understanding these trends, we'll prepare for the next generation of cyber threats and how OSINT will remain at the forefront of digital security in an increasingly complex cyber world.

12.1 Emerging Threats & The Evolving Cyber Landscape

The cybersecurity landscape is constantly evolving as threat actors adapt, innovate, and refine their techniques. New vulnerabilities, attack vectors, and geopolitical conflicts fuel the rise of sophisticated cyber threats, making it critical for OSINT analysts and cybersecurity professionals to stay ahead.

This chapter explores the emerging threats shaping the future of cybersecurity, including:

- AI-driven cyberattacks & deepfake deception
- The weaponization of large-scale data leaks
- The rise of cyber warfare & nation-state conflicts
- The expansion of ransomware-as-a-service (RaaS)
- Supply chain attacks & the risks of interconnected systems

By understanding these trends, OSINT practitioners can refine their investigative methods, anticipate future threats, and develop proactive intelligence strategies.

12.1.1 The Next Generation of Cyber Threats

◆ AI-Powered Cyberattacks & Deepfake Deception

Artificial intelligence (AI) is revolutionizing cybersecurity—but it's also empowering cybercriminals. Threat actors are now using AI-driven automation to:

✅ Generate hyper-realistic phishing emails that evade traditional detection.

✅ Create deepfake audio and video for fraud, impersonation, and disinformation campaigns.

✅ Automate brute-force attacks to bypass security defenses more efficiently.

💡 Real-World Impact:

- In 2023, an AI-generated deepfake voice tricked a bank employee into transferring $35 million to cybercriminals.
- Malicious AI bots can now scrape social media for personal details, enabling more convincing spear-phishing attacks.

◆ The Weaponization of Data Leaks & Breaches

The frequency and scale of data breaches are increasing, with stolen data being used for targeted cyberattacks. Breach data is fueling:

✅ Credential stuffing attacks due to widespread password reuse.

✅ Personalized phishing campaigns using leaked email addresses and phone numbers.

✅ Corporate espionage & insider threats, as stolen internal documents are weaponized.

💡 Real-World Impact:

- The 2023 MOVEit supply chain breach exposed sensitive government and corporate data, leading to widespread extortion attempts.
- Nation-state actors are buying breach data to enhance their espionage operations.

◆ Cyber Warfare & Geopolitical Threats

Cyber warfare has become a key weapon in global conflicts, with nation-state actors using cyberattacks to:

✅ Disrupt critical infrastructure (power grids, water supplies, healthcare systems).

✅ Engage in cyber espionage against rival nations.

✅ Spread disinformation to manipulate public opinion.

🕯 Real-World Impact:

- Russian Sandworm APT attacks on Ukraine disrupted power grids and government networks.
- Chinese APT groups target Western defense contractors for espionage.
- North Korean Lazarus Group continues to steal billions in cryptocurrency to fund its regime.

12.1.2 The Rise of Ransomware-as-a-Service (RaaS) & Extortion Tactics

Ransomware is no longer just a tool for skilled cybercriminals—it has become a service that anyone can purchase on the dark web. Ransomware-as-a-Service (RaaS) is fueling an explosion of attacks, where:

✅ Affiliates rent ransomware kits and share profits with developers.

✅ Double extortion tactics threaten victims with both data encryption & public leaks.

✅ AI-driven ransomware automates network infiltration and lateral movement.

🕯 Real-World Impact:

- LockBit, BlackCat, and Cl0p ransomware gangs continue to extort millions from corporations.
- The healthcare industry remains a prime target, as hospitals often pay ransoms to restore operations quickly.
- Governments are cracking down on ransomware groups, but the attacks remain relentless.

12.1.3 Supply Chain Attacks & The Risks of Interconnected Systems

As businesses become more dependent on third-party vendors, cloud services, and SaaS platforms, supply chain attacks are emerging as one of the biggest cyber threats. Hackers exploit weak links in supply chains to:

✅ Inject malicious code into software updates (SolarWinds, Kaseya attacks).

✅ Compromise third-party service providers to gain access to enterprise networks.

✅ Target cloud infrastructure to steal sensitive data or disrupt services.

💡 Real-World Impact:

- The 2020 SolarWinds attack led to widespread government and corporate breaches after hackers compromised a software update.
- The 2023 3CX supply chain attack saw nation-state actors targeting corporate communications software.

OSINT for Supply Chain Defense:

🔍 Monitor threat intelligence feeds for indicators of compromise (IOCs).

🔍 Investigate third-party vendors before onboarding them.

🔍 Use passive OSINT to analyze vendor security postures and public exposures.

12.1.4 The Future of OSINT in Cybersecurity

As cyber threats evolve, OSINT must also adapt to remain an effective tool for cyber threat intelligence (CTI). The future of OSINT will see:

📌 AI-Powered OSINT Tools

- Machine learning will automate the collection & analysis of cyber threat intelligence.
- AI-based OSINT tools will detect cyber threats in real-time.

📌 Blockchain & Cryptocurrency Investigations

- OSINT will focus more on tracking illicit cryptocurrency transactions linked to cybercrime.
- Blockchain forensics will be crucial in ransomware and darknet investigations.

📌 Greater Integration with Threat Intelligence Platforms (TIPs)

- OSINT data will be directly integrated into cybersecurity platforms like MISP, Anomali, and Recorded Future.
- Sharing real-time OSINT findings via STIX/TAXII will enhance threat collaboration.

📌 Increased Legal & Ethical Challenges

- Governments may introduce stricter regulations on OSINT data collection.
- Privacy concerns will require careful balancing between investigation and ethics.

12.1.5 Conclusion: Preparing for the Future of Cybersecurity

The cyber threat landscape is evolving rapidly, but OSINT remains a powerful weapon in the fight against cybercrime. As new threats emerge, analysts must continuously refine their techniques, embrace AI-powered tools, and adapt to new cybercriminal tactics.

◆ Key Takeaways:

✓ AI-driven threats & deepfake deception will challenge traditional security defenses.

✓ Ransomware and supply chain attacks will continue to rise.

✓ Cyber warfare & nation-state espionage will shape global cybersecurity efforts.

✓ The role of OSINT will grow, with automation, AI, and blockchain investigations becoming standard practice.

🚀 **Final Thought**: The future of cybersecurity belongs to those who can harness OSINT effectively, anticipate emerging threats, and stay one step ahead of cyber adversaries.

12.2 AI & Machine Learning in Threat Intelligence OSINT

Artificial Intelligence (AI) and Machine Learning (ML) are transforming cyber threat intelligence (CTI) and OSINT investigations. The sheer volume of cyber threats, dark web chatter, phishing campaigns, and malware activity makes manual analysis impractical. AI-powered OSINT tools can automate data collection, detect patterns, and enhance real-time threat detection.

In this chapter, we'll explore:

- How AI is used in OSINT for cyber threat intelligence
- ML-powered threat detection techniques
- The role of Natural Language Processing (NLP) in analyzing dark web forums & hacker communications

Ethical concerns and limitations of AI in OSINT

As cyber threats evolve, AI-driven OSINT is becoming an essential tool for security analysts, allowing them to stay ahead of emerging threats.

12.2.1 How AI is Transforming OSINT for Cyber Threat Intelligence

◆ Automating Data Collection from Threat Sources

AI-powered OSINT tools scrape vast amounts of cyber threat data, including:

✅ **Dark web marketplaces & hacker forums** (e.g., stolen credentials, malware sales)
✅ **Phishing sites & malicious domains** (AI can detect newly registered domains used for attacks)
✅ **Social media & underground chat groups** (threat actors planning attacks in real-time)

AI-driven OSINT reduces the time analysts spend on manual searches, allowing them to focus on intelligence analysis instead of data collection.

◆ AI-Driven Threat Detection & Anomaly Identification

Machine learning models analyze massive datasets to detect anomalies that indicate cyber threats. These include:

✅ Unusual network traffic & suspicious login attempts

✅ New phishing campaigns based on domain registrations & email patterns

✅ Anomalous activity in hacker forums (e.g., sudden discussions about a zero-day exploit)

💡 Example:

AI models detected unusual dark web discussions about an unpatched vulnerability in Microsoft Exchange before the 2021 Hafnium APT attack.

12.2.2 Machine Learning for Malware & Phishing Detection

◆ How AI Detects Malware & Malicious Domains

Traditional threat detection relies on static malware signatures, which can be bypassed by cybercriminals. ML-based detection, however:

✅ Analyzes malware behavior instead of signatures

✅ Detects zero-day malware based on execution patterns

✅ Uses threat intelligence feeds to correlate indicators of compromise (IOCs)

💡 Example:

Google's Safe Browsing AI models analyze billions of URLs daily to detect and block phishing & malware-hosting sites.

◆ AI-Powered Email & Phishing Analysis

AI models analyze email metadata, content, and sender behavior to detect phishing attempts.

✅ Natural Language Processing (NLP) detects phishing email patterns

✅ AI flags spear-phishing attempts by analyzing sender-recipient relationships

✅ Image recognition detects brand impersonation in fake login pages

💡 Example:

AI-powered email security tools like Microsoft Defender and Google's AI spam filters block 99% of phishing attacks before they reach users.

12.2.3 AI & NLP for Dark Web & Threat Actor Analysis

◆ Natural Language Processing (NLP) for Analyzing Hacker Communications

Many cybercriminals communicate in encrypted chat rooms, dark web forums, and Telegram channels. AI-driven Natural Language Processing (NLP) models help investigators by:

✅ Detecting keywords related to cybercrime & attacks

✓ Identifying sentiment shifts & emerging threats in hacker forums

✓ Translating foreign-language discussions about exploits & vulnerabilities

💡 Example:

AI NLP models monitored Russian dark web forums and detected early discussions about the Colonial Pipeline ransomware attack before it became public.

◆ AI-Powered Facial Recognition for OSINT Investigations

Threat actors often use fake social media profiles or aliases. AI facial recognition helps OSINT analysts:

✓ Identify duplicate or stolen profile images

✓ Link fake accounts to real-world identities

✓ Detect impersonation scams & fraud operations

💡 Example:

AI-based OSINT tools like PimEyes and Clearview AI have been used to identify criminals using fake identities online.

12.2.4 AI-Driven Threat Intelligence Platforms (TIPs)

◆ AI-Powered Threat Intelligence Platforms (TIPs) & Automation

Threat Intelligence Platforms (TIPs) integrate AI-driven OSINT data into cybersecurity workflows. These platforms:

✓ Aggregate threat intelligence from multiple OSINT sources

✓ Use AI to enrich threat data & assign risk scores

✓ Automate the correlation of attack indicators

💡 Popular AI-Powered TIPs:

- **Recorded Future** – Uses AI to analyze threat actor activity across open & dark web sources
- **Anomali ThreatStream** – Automates threat intelligence gathering & IOC correlation
- **MISP (Malware Information Sharing Platform)** – Uses AI for STIX/TAXII threat sharing

◆ Predictive Threat Intelligence with AI

Advanced AI models can predict cyberattacks before they happen by:

✅ Analyzing historical attack patterns & threat actor behavior

✅ Identifying new vulnerabilities being exploited on the dark web

✅ Correlating geopolitical events with cyber espionage activity

💡 Example:

AI models detected increased nation-state APT activity before the 2022 Russia-Ukraine cyberwar escalated.

12.2.5 Challenges & Ethical Concerns of AI in OSINT

While AI-powered OSINT offers powerful advantages, it also comes with challenges and ethical risks.

◆ AI Bias & False Positives

- AI models can misidentify threats due to bias in training data.
- False positives can lead to misattributed cyberattacks or innocent users being flagged as criminals.

◆ Privacy & Surveillance Concerns

- AI-driven facial recognition raises ethical concerns about privacy violations.
- Governments and corporations may misuse AI-powered OSINT for mass surveillance.

◆ AI-Powered Cybercrime

- Cybercriminals are also using AI to automate attacks.
- Deepfake-powered scams & AI-generated phishing emails are becoming harder to detect.

💡 **Solution:**

OSINT analysts must validate AI findings manually and use ethical frameworks for responsible AI deployment.

12.2.6 The Future of AI & Machine Learning in OSINT

The future of AI in OSINT will see more automation, improved accuracy, and deeper integration with cybersecurity operations.

📌 **AI-Driven OSINT Trends to Watch:**

🔍 **AI-powered deception detection** – NLP models will detect deepfake scams & synthetic fraud.
🔍 **Self-learning threat intelligence** – AI models will adapt in real-time to evolving threats.
🔍 **Blockchain for AI trust & transparency** – AI-generated OSINT findings will be recorded on the blockchain for integrity.
🔍 **AI-enhanced cyber threat hunting** – OSINT analysts will use AI to proactively hunt emerging cyber threats.

🚀 **Final Thought**: AI is revolutionizing OSINT and cyber threat intelligence, but it must be used responsibly. The future of cybersecurity depends on the ability to harness AI-powered OSINT while addressing its risks and ethical challenges.

12.3 The Role of Automation & Big Data in Cyber OSINT

The scale and complexity of cyber threats have grown exponentially, making traditional manual OSINT investigations slow and inefficient. With millions of cyber incidents, dark web transactions, phishing campaigns, and malware infections occurring daily, automation and big data analytics have become essential for modern OSINT operations.

In this chapter, we will explore:

- How automation streamlines OSINT investigations
- Big data analytics in cyber threat intelligence
- The role of machine learning in processing large-scale OSINT data
- Challenges and ethical considerations of automated OSINT

By integrating automation and big data analytics, OSINT investigators can process vast amounts of cyber threat intelligence (CTI) faster, making investigations more efficient, scalable, and proactive.

12.3.1 How Automation Enhances OSINT Investigations

◆ Automating Data Collection & Threat Monitoring

Instead of manually searching for cyber threat indicators, OSINT analysts can use automated scrapers, bots, and API integrations to collect intelligence from:

✅ Dark web forums, marketplaces, and Telegram channels

✅ Threat intelligence feeds & cybercriminal underground networks

✅ WHOIS databases, passive DNS records, and malware repositories

✅ Phishing detection services & suspicious domain registries

💡 Example:

Recorded Future's OSINT tools use automation to collect and correlate cyber threat intelligence in real-time from over 1 million sources.

◆ Automated Dark Web Intelligence Gathering

Many cybercriminals operate on dark web marketplaces and encrypted forums. Automated tools can:

✅ Monitor cybercriminal discussions for mentions of new exploits or stolen credentials

✅ Alert analysts about emerging ransomware groups or malware-as-a-service (MaaS) offerings

✅ Detect leaked databases & breached credentials as soon as they are published

💡 Example:

Automated dark web monitoring tools like DarkOwl and Flashpoint continuously scan hidden marketplaces for leaked corporate data.

12.3.2 Big Data Analytics in Cyber OSINT

◆ Why Big Data is Critical for OSINT

Cyber OSINT investigations generate massive datasets, including:

✓ Breach data from billions of leaked credentials

✓ Threat actor discussions across thousands of forums & chatrooms

✓ Millions of phishing domains & malware samples

Big data analytics helps OSINT analysts extract meaningful patterns from this overwhelming volume of data.

◆ Big Data Techniques Used in OSINT

📌 **Data Correlation & Pattern Recognition** – Detects links between threat actors, malware campaigns, and cybercrime networks.
📌 **Predictive Analytics** – Uses past attack patterns to forecast future cyber threats.
📌 **Sentiment Analysis** – Analyzes hacker forum discussions to detect rising cyber threats before attacks occur.

💡 Example:

Google's Chronicle Security Operations applies big data techniques to detect cyber threats weeks before traditional methods.

12.3.3 Machine Learning & AI in Big Data OSINT

◆ AI-Driven Threat Intelligence Analysis

Machine learning (ML) models analyze massive OSINT datasets faster than human analysts by:

✅ Detecting anomalies in cyber threat trends

✅ Identifying hacker OPSEC mistakes (e.g., reusing aliases or email addresses)

✅ Recognizing hidden patterns in malware campaigns

💡 Example:

AI-powered OSINT tools like Maltego and Paliscope use graph analytics to connect cybercriminal identities across different datasets.

◆ NLP for Analyzing Dark Web Communications

Natural Language Processing (NLP) helps OSINT analysts:

✅ Translate hacker forum discussions in Russian, Chinese, and Arabic

✅ Detect cybercriminal slang & emerging exploits

✅ Analyze ransomware group negotiations on dark web sites

💡 Example:

NLP-powered OSINT tools detected pre-attack discussions about the Log4j vulnerability on underground hacker forums before the exploit became widely known.

12.3.4 Automated OSINT Tools & Threat Intelligence Platforms (TIPs)

◆ Popular OSINT Automation Tools

Many OSINT tools leverage automation and big data analytics to streamline investigations:

Tool Name	Function
Shodan	Scans the internet for exposed IoT & server vulnerabilities
Maltego	Uses graph analysis to map cybercriminal networks
SpiderFoot	Automates OSINT data collection from multiple sources
MISP	A Threat Intelligence Platform (TIP) for sharing cyber threat intelligence
VirusTotal	Analyzes malware & suspicious URLs using big data

💡 Example:

MISP (Malware Information Sharing Platform) allows organizations to automate the sharing of cyber threat indicators in real-time.

12.3.5 Challenges & Ethical Concerns in Automated OSINT

◆ Accuracy & False Positives

- Automated OSINT tools sometimes misidentify threats due to incomplete or misleading data.
- False positives can waste time & resources on non-existent threats.

💡 Solution:

- OSINT analysts must validate automated findings manually.

◆ Privacy & Surveillance Risks

- Automated OSINT tools scrape social media, forums, and personal data, raising privacy concerns.
- Governments and corporations may misuse OSINT automation for mass surveillance.

💡 Solution:

- Ethical guidelines should balance cybersecurity with personal privacy.

◆ Cybercriminals Are Also Using Automation

- Hackers use automation to launch large-scale phishing campaigns, scan for vulnerabilities, and generate deepfake scams.
- AI-generated phishing emails and synthetic fraud are becoming harder to detect.

💡 Solution:

Cybersecurity teams must evolve automated OSINT techniques to counteract AI-powered cyber threats.

12.3.6 The Future of Automation & Big Data in OSINT

As cyber threats become more complex and automated, OSINT must evolve.

📌 Future Trends in Automated OSINT:

🔍 **AI-powered deception detection** – New algorithms will detect deepfake scams & synthetic fraud.
🔍 **Self-learning OSINT systems** – AI-driven OSINT tools will adapt to evolving cybercriminal tactics.
🔍 **Blockchain-integrated OSINT** – Ensures transparency & data integrity in cyber threat intelligence.
🔍 **Cloud-based OSINT as a Service (OSINTaaS)** – Automated OSINT platforms will be scalable & accessible globally.

🚀 Final Thought:

The combination of automation, big data, and AI is revolutionizing OSINT and cyber threat intelligence. While these advancements bring efficiency and speed, they also introduce new challenges. The key is to balance automation with human oversight, ensuring accurate, ethical, and actionable intelligence.

12.4 How OSINT Will Adapt to New Cybersecurity Challenges

The world of cybersecurity is constantly changing, with new threats emerging daily. As attackers become more sophisticated, OSINT (Open-Source Intelligence) must adapt to stay effective. Cybercriminals are leveraging AI, automation, deepfakes, and advanced evasion tactics, making traditional OSINT methods insufficient on their own.

This chapter explores how OSINT will evolve to counter new cybersecurity challenges, including:

- The rise of AI-driven cyber threats
- The increasing role of automation in cybercrime
- Stronger anonymity measures used by hackers
- Regulatory and privacy concerns affecting OSINT investigations

By adapting to these challenges, OSINT will remain a powerful tool for cyber threat intelligence (CTI), digital forensics, and cybersecurity defense.

12.4.1 The Rise of AI-Powered Cyber Threats

◆ AI-Generated Phishing & Deepfake Scams

Cybercriminals are now using AI-generated phishing emails, voice deepfakes, and fake videos to bypass traditional defenses. AI-driven cyber threats include:

✓ Realistic phishing attacks that bypass spam filters

✓ Deepfake videos impersonating executives for fraud

✓ Automated scam chatbots that manipulate victims

💡 Example:

In 2019, criminals used AI-generated deepfake audio to impersonate a CEO, successfully tricking a company into transferring $243,000.

◆ OSINT's Response to AI Threats

To counter AI-powered threats, OSINT must evolve by:

✓ Using AI-driven pattern recognition to detect synthetic media (deepfakes, fake voices)

✓ Leveraging real-time AI models to analyze phishing and scam patterns

✓ Deploying automated OSINT tools to detect fake accounts and botnets

💡 Future Development:

OSINT analysts will collaborate with AI researchers to build deepfake detection tools for cybersecurity investigations.

12.4.2 Cybercriminals' Increasing Use of Automation

◆ How Hackers Use Automation

Cybercriminals are now automating attacks at scale, including:

✅ Mass phishing campaigns that send thousands of fake emails per minute

✅ Credential stuffing attacks using breached passwords to hijack accounts

✅ Automated dark web scraping tools to gather stolen data

💡 Example:

The Emotet botnet used automation to infect millions of devices worldwide, launching large-scale phishing and malware attacks.

◆ OSINT's Adaptation to Automated Threats

To keep up, OSINT must:

✅ Develop AI-powered scrapers to track cybercriminal forums in real time

✅ Automate breach data analysis to detect credential stuffing patterns

✅ Integrate machine learning for faster cyber threat detection

💡 Future Development:

OSINT automation tools will continuously monitor cybercriminal activity, detecting new attack trends before they become widespread.

12.4.3 The Challenge of Stronger Anonymity Measures

◆ How Threat Actors Are Hiding Their Tracks

Hackers and cybercriminals are using stronger anonymity tools to avoid detection, including:

✅ Tor, I2P, and decentralized dark web networks

✅ Cryptocurrency tumblers & privacy coins (e.g., Monero) for untraceable payments

✅ AI-generated fake identities that make tracking harder

💡 **Example:**

Ransomware gangs now demand Monero payments instead of Bitcoin to prevent OSINT tracking.

◆ **OSINT's Adaptation to Advanced Anonymity**

To counter these tactics, OSINT must:

✅ Use blockchain analytics to track cryptocurrency laundering

✅ Develop advanced metadata analysis to uncover hidden cybercriminal footprints

✅ Collaborate with cybersecurity firms to improve darknet intelligence gathering

💡 **Future Development:**

OSINT tools will integrate AI-powered identity verification to detect fake personas used by cybercriminals.

12.4.4 Privacy Regulations & Their Impact on OSINT

◆ **Stricter Data Privacy Laws**

With growing concerns over data privacy, new laws and regulations are limiting access to open-source data. Key challenges include:

✅ GDPR & CCPA restrictions on personal data collection

✅ WHOIS privacy masking, making domain investigations harder

✅ Social media platforms restricting API access for OSINT research

💡 **Example:**

The GDPR law forced domain registrars to hide personal details from WHOIS records, making it harder to track malicious domain owners.

◆ How OSINT Will Adapt to Privacy Challenges

To balance privacy compliance and cybersecurity, OSINT must:

✓ Develop alternative data collection techniques that comply with regulations

✓ Use legal data-sharing agreements for cyber threat intelligence exchanges

✓ Enhance ethical OSINT methods to prevent misuse of data

💡 Future Development:

Governments may introduce OSINT guidelines that balance security and privacy.

12.4.5 The Role of Quantum Computing in OSINT

◆ The Threat of Quantum Cyberattacks

Quantum computing has the potential to break traditional encryption, making current cybersecurity defenses obsolete. Cybercriminals and nation-state actors could use quantum technology to:

✓ Crack encrypted communication channels

✓ Bypass traditional authentication methods

✓ Access classified intelligence undetectably

💡 Example:

China and the U.S. are racing to develop quantum-resistant encryption to counter future cyber threats.

◆ How OSINT Will Evolve with Quantum Computing

To prepare for quantum threats, OSINT must:

✅ Monitor quantum research developments to anticipate future risks

✅ Support the adoption of post-quantum cryptography for securing OSINT data

✅ Develop new investigative techniques that remain effective in a quantum-powered cyber landscape

💡 **Future Development:**

OSINT analysts will partner with cryptography experts to ensure that future cyber threat intelligence remains secure.

12.4.6 The Future of OSINT in Cybersecurity

As cyber threats evolve, OSINT will need to adapt by:

✅ Embracing AI and machine learning for automated cyber intelligence gathering

✅ Developing advanced methods to counter stronger anonymity measures

✅ Navigating new privacy regulations while maintaining ethical intelligence collection

✅ Preparing for future cybersecurity challenges, including quantum threats

🖥 **Predictions for OSINT's Future:**

🚀 AI-driven threat intelligence will become standard in cybersecurity investigations.

🚀 OSINT automation will accelerate threat detection, reducing cyber attack response times.

🚀 Collaboration between OSINT analysts, AI researchers, and cybersecurity teams will increase to stay ahead of cybercriminals.

Final Thought:

As the cyber threat landscape continues to evolve, OSINT must remain agile, innovative, and proactive. By leveraging AI, automation, and advanced analytics, OSINT will continue to play a critical role in cybersecurity defense, cybercrime investigations, and threat intelligence operations.

12.5 Ethical & Legal Considerations in Cyber Threat Intelligence

Cyber Threat Intelligence (CTI) plays a critical role in identifying and mitigating cyber threats, but it also comes with ethical and legal challenges. As organizations, governments, and security researchers use Open-Source Intelligence (OSINT) to track cybercriminals, questions arise about privacy, surveillance, and responsible data collection.

This chapter explores the key ethical and legal considerations in CTI, including:

✔ The ethical boundaries of cyber intelligence gathering

✔ Legal frameworks governing OSINT investigations

✔ The risks of over-collection and mass surveillance

✔ The impact of privacy laws like GDPR and CCPA

✔ Best practices for ethical cyber investigations

As cyber threats evolve, CTI must find a balance between security, privacy, and compliance to ensure investigations remain both effective and ethical.

12.5.1 The Ethical Dilemmas in Cyber Threat Intelligence

◆ Where Do We Draw the Line?

Cyber threat intelligence requires collecting vast amounts of data, but not all data collection is ethical. Some key concerns include:

✔ **Surveillance vs. Security** – When does monitoring online activities cross the line into unethical surveillance?

✔ **Hacking Back** – Should security teams be allowed to retaliate against cybercriminals?

✔ **Privacy Invasion** – Is it ethical to collect personal data from leaked breaches, even for security purposes?

💡 **Example:**

Some companies scrape social media data to detect cyber threats, but this raises ethical concerns about monitoring users without consent.

◆ Ethical OSINT Principles in Cyber Investigations

To address these concerns, CTI analysts follow ethical guidelines:

✓ **Proportionality** – Only collect necessary and relevant data.
✓ **Minimization** – Avoid storing unnecessary or sensitive personal information.
✓ **Transparency** – Clearly define why data is collected and how it will be used.
✓ **Non-Interference** – Do not manipulate or engage with cybercriminals in a way that could be unethical or illegal.

♀ Future Development:

Organizations will likely adopt global ethical OSINT standards to ensure responsible intelligence gathering.

12.5.2 Legal Frameworks Governing OSINT & Cyber Investigations

◆ Key Cybersecurity & Privacy Laws

OSINT investigations are subject to various legal restrictions, including:

✓ **General Data Protection Regulation (GDPR)** – Limits the collection and use of personal data in the EU.
✓ **California Consumer Privacy Act (CCPA)** – Provides U.S. citizens control over their personal data.
✓ **Computer Fraud and Abuse Act (CFAA)** – Regulates unauthorized access to computer systems in the U.S.
✓ **Electronic Communications Privacy Act (ECPA)** – Restricts the interception of digital communications.

♀ Example:

GDPR forced cybersecurity researchers to anonymize collected OSINT data when analyzing cyber threats.

◆ What Is Legal in OSINT Investigations?

OSINT analysts must ensure their methods comply with the law by following these best practices:

✅ **Use only publicly available data** – Avoid unauthorized access to private systems.
✅ **Respect data protection laws** – Do not collect or store personal information without consent.
✅ **Obtain legal approval for dark web investigations** – Some jurisdictions require law enforcement collaboration.

💡 Future Development:

Governments may standardize OSINT legal guidelines, ensuring security researchers know their legal boundaries.

12.5.3 The Risks of Over-Collection & Mass Surveillance

◆ How Much Data Is Too Much?

Modern OSINT tools scrape and analyze vast amounts of data, sometimes crossing ethical and legal boundaries. Key risks include:

✅ **Mass Data Collection** – Gathering more data than necessary can violate privacy laws.
✅ **Storing Sensitive Data** – Leaked credentials and PII (Personally Identifiable Information) must be handled responsibly.
✅ **Government & Corporate Surveillance** – Some organizations use OSINT tools to monitor individuals without their knowledge.

💡 Example:

Some countries have used OSINT tools to track political dissidents, raising serious human rights concerns.

◆ Best Practices to Avoid Over-Collection

To prevent ethical violations, OSINT analysts should:

✅ **Define clear objectives** – Collect only what is needed for a specific investigation.

✅ **Anonymize data** – Remove PII when sharing intelligence reports.

✅ **Respect individual rights** – Do not use OSINT for unlawful surveillance or discrimination.

💡 **Future Development:**

AI-driven OSINT tools will implement built-in compliance filters to automatically remove unauthorized personal data.

12.5.4 The Impact of Privacy Laws on OSINT Investigations

◆ How Privacy Laws Limit OSINT Methods

Privacy laws are changing how OSINT analysts collect, store, and analyze data. Key impacts include:

✅ **Restricted WHOIS data** – GDPR removed access to domain registration details, making cybercrime investigations harder.

✅ **Limited social media access** – Platforms like Twitter, Facebook, and LinkedIn have tightened their APIs, restricting OSINT tools.

✅ **Stronger encryption laws** – Governments are limiting decryption efforts, making it harder to investigate cyber threats.

💡 **Example:**

Before GDPR, security analysts could easily identify domain owners via WHOIS records. Now, most domain data is redacted, making phishing investigations more difficult.

◆ Adapting to Privacy Regulations

To comply with new privacy laws, OSINT investigations must:

✅ Use legally approved data sources (e.g., sanctioned breach databases).

✅ Obtain consent when collecting sensitive information.

✅ Leverage law enforcement partnerships for deeper investigations.

💡 **Future Development:**

Privacy-focused OSINT tools will automate compliance checks, ensuring all data collection meets legal standards.

12.5.5 Ethical OSINT in Law Enforcement & Cybersecurity

◆ Law Enforcement's Use of OSINT

Law enforcement agencies rely on OSINT for cybercrime investigations, but they must follow strict legal and ethical rules.

✅ Tracking cybercriminal activities on forums and dark web markets.

✅ Identifying threat actors through leaked credentials.

✅ Gathering evidence to support criminal prosecutions.

💡 Example:

The FBI used OSINT to track ransomware groups by analyzing Bitcoin transactions linked to ransom payments.

◆ Ethical OSINT for Corporate Security

Companies use OSINT to protect their business, but they must avoid illegal surveillance or privacy violations.

✅ Monitoring brand reputation without targeting individuals.

✅ Investigating data breaches while respecting privacy laws.

✅ Detecting insider threats using only public and authorized data.

💡 Future Development:

Governments may introduce OSINT certification programs for ethical and legal compliance.

12.5.6 The Future of Ethical Cyber Threat Intelligence

As OSINT continues to evolve, ethical and legal concerns will become more complex. Future developments include:

🚀 AI-powered compliance tools that prevent legal violations in OSINT investigations.

🚀 Global legal frameworks to standardize OSINT data collection practices.

🚀 Increased transparency in cybersecurity investigations to prevent abuse.

Final Thought:

Cyber threat intelligence is a powerful tool in defending against cybercrime, but it must be used ethically and legally. By following best practices, OSINT analysts can ensure their work respects privacy, complies with regulations, and supports a safer digital world.

12.6 Preparing for the Future: Skills & Tools for Next-Gen Threat Intelligence

As cyber threats become more sophisticated, automated, and state-sponsored, the field of Cyber Threat Intelligence (CTI) must evolve to stay ahead. OSINT (Open-Source Intelligence) will continue to be a critical tool for analysts, but the skills and tools needed to conduct investigations are rapidly changing.

This chapter explores:

✅ The essential skills CTI analysts must develop

✅ The advanced tools shaping the future of OSINT investigations

✅ How AI, machine learning, and automation will redefine cyber threat intelligence

✅ The growing need for collaboration and intelligence-sharing

To future-proof their expertise, CTI analysts must adapt, upskill, and leverage cutting-edge technologies to stay ahead of cybercriminals.

12.6.1 Essential Skills for Next-Gen Threat Intelligence Analysts

◆ **Skill #1: Advanced OSINT Investigative Techniques**

Traditional OSINT methods like WHOIS lookups, social media analysis, and IP tracking are no longer enough. Future CTI analysts must:

✅ **Master dark web investigations** – Identifying cybercriminals operating in hidden forums.
✅ **Analyze blockchain transactions** – Tracking ransomware payments and illicit crypto activity.
✅ **Understand supply chain threats** – Investigating third-party vulnerabilities that cybercriminals exploit.

💡 **Example:**

Ransomware groups now use privacy-focused cryptocurrencies like Monero—CTI analysts must develop techniques to deanonymize illicit transactions.

◆ **Skill #2: Cyber Threat Hunting & Malware Analysis**

Threat intelligence is shifting from reactive to proactive. Analysts must:

✅ Hunt for Indicators of Compromise (IoCs) before an attack occurs.

✅ Analyze malware samples to understand attack vectors.

✅ Reverse-engineer cyber threats to predict future tactics.

💡 **Example:**

By studying code reuse patterns in malware families, analysts can connect new threats to known cybercriminal groups.

◆ **Skill #3: AI & Machine Learning for Threat Intelligence**

AI is transforming cyber intelligence, but analysts must know how to use and interpret AI-generated insights.

✅ Understand how AI-driven OSINT tools collect and process data.

✅ Identify false positives in automated threat detection.

✅ Train AI models to detect cyber threats faster and more accurately.

💡 Example:

AI-powered natural language processing (NLP) can scan thousands of dark web forums to detect early signs of cyber threats.

◆ Skill #4: Legal, Ethical & Compliance Knowledge

With growing privacy laws and ethical concerns, analysts must:

✅ Ensure OSINT investigations comply with regulations (e.g., GDPR, CCPA).

✅ Respect privacy boundaries while collecting intelligence.

✅ Avoid engaging in unauthorized hacking or surveillance.

💡 Example:

With WHOIS data now redacted under GDPR, analysts need legal alternatives for identifying malicious domains.

12.6.2 The Next Generation of OSINT Tools

◆ AI-Powered OSINT Platforms

Next-gen OSINT tools will leverage AI to automate threat detection. Some key advancements include:

✅ **Automated dark web monitoring** – AI can scan hidden marketplaces and hacker forums in real time.

✅ **Facial recognition for threat actors** – AI can match leaked images with known cybercriminals.

✅ **Deepfake detection** – As cybercriminals use AI-generated personas, OSINT tools must verify digital identities.

💡 Example:

AI-driven OSINT tools like Maltego and Hunchly are evolving to provide real-time intelligence correlations.

◆ Blockchain & Crypto Analysis Tools

As cybercriminals increasingly use cryptocurrency, CTI analysts will rely on:

✅ **Blockchain forensics tools** – Tracking Bitcoin, Monero, and Ethereum transactions.
✅ **AI-driven crypto transaction analysis** – Detecting suspicious wallet behaviors.
✅ **Crypto-ransomware tracking** – Identifying funds flowing to criminal organizations.

💡 Example:

Chainalysis and CipherTrace help analysts track illicit cryptocurrency movements.

◆ Dark Web Intelligence & Automated Threat Hunting

Accessing dark web markets and forums is essential for tracking cyber threats, but new tools will make it:

✅ **Safer** – Automated bots can collect intelligence without exposing analysts.
✅ **Faster** – AI can analyze millions of dark web posts for cyber threats.
✅ **More actionable** – OSINT platforms will correlate dark web findings with real-world attack data.

💡 Example:

Tools like DarkOwl provide live monitoring of cybercriminal activity on the dark web.

◆ Threat Intelligence Sharing Platforms

Collaboration is key—CTI analysts will increasingly rely on shared intelligence through:

✅ **STIX/TAXII frameworks** – Standardized formats for cyber threat intelligence sharing.
✅ **Threat Intelligence Platforms (TIPs)** – Tools like AlienVault, Anomali, and Recorded Future help teams collaborate.
✅ **Government & private-sector partnerships** – More real-time information sharing between companies, law enforcement, and researchers.

💡 Example:

The MITRE ATT&CK framework is helping standardize threat intelligence classification across organizations.

12.6.3 The Future of Cyber Threat Intelligence Careers

◆ The Demand for OSINT & Threat Intelligence Analysts

As cyber threats grow, the demand for skilled analysts will surge. Future careers include:

✓ **Cyber Threat Intelligence Analyst** – Investigating cyber threats for governments and corporations.
✓ **Dark Web Intelligence Specialist** – Monitoring underground markets and hacker forums.
✓ **Blockchain Forensics Analyst** – Tracking crypto transactions linked to cybercrime.
✓ **AI-Powered Threat Detection Engineer** – Training AI to detect cyber threats automatically.

💡 **Future Prediction:**

Companies will hire OSINT specialists to proactively defend against cyber threats, rather than relying solely on incident response.

◆ Certifications & Training for Future Analysts

To prepare for next-gen CTI careers, analysts should pursue:

✓ Certified OSINT Professional (COP)

✓ Certified Threat Intelligence Analyst (CTIA)

✓ MITRE ATT&CK Defender (MAD) Certification

✓ GIAC Cyber Threat Intelligence (GCTI)

💡 **Example:**

The SANS Institute offers advanced CTI training for analysts specializing in cyber threat detection.

12.6.4 Final Thoughts: Future-Proofing Cyber Threat Intelligence

Cyber threat intelligence is entering a new era—one driven by AI, automation, and cross-industry collaboration. Future analysts must:

🚀 Master advanced OSINT techniques to stay ahead of cybercriminals.

🚀 Leverage AI-driven tools for rapid threat detection.

🚀 Comply with global privacy laws to ensure ethical investigations.

🚀 Work with law enforcement and cybersecurity teams for stronger intelligence-sharing.

Final Thought:

The future of OSINT and Cyber Threat Intelligence belongs to those who adapt, learn, and embrace next-gen technologies. The digital battlefield is evolving—are you ready?

Cyber threats are constantly evolving, with hackers, cybercriminal groups, and state-sponsored actors launching attacks that target individuals, businesses, and governments worldwide. Open-Source Intelligence (OSINT) plays a critical role in identifying, analyzing, and mitigating these threats by uncovering digital footprints, tracking cybercriminal activities, and gathering intelligence on breaches and vulnerabilities.

OSINT Threat Intel: Investigating Hackers, Breaches, and Cyber Risks provides a comprehensive approach to using OSINT for cyber threat intelligence (CTI). This book explores advanced methods for investigating hackers, detecting security breaches, and identifying cyber risks before they escalate. Whether you're a cybersecurity professional, investigator, or analyst, this guide will help you strengthen your cyber intelligence skills and enhance digital security.

What You'll Learn in This Book

- **Understanding Cyber Threat Intelligence (CTI):** Learn the fundamentals of threat intelligence and how OSINT enhances cyber investigations.
- **Tracking Hacker Groups & Cybercriminals**: Use OSINT techniques to monitor underground forums, hacking communities, and darknet markets.
- **Data Breach Investigations**: Identify and analyze leaked databases, stolen credentials, and compromised corporate assets.
- **Threat Actor Profiling**: Learn how to build profiles of cybercriminals using digital footprints and behavioral analysis.
- **Malware & Phishing Investigations**: Discover how to track phishing campaigns, malware signatures, and command-and-control (C2) infrastructure.
- **Deep & Dark Web Intelligence**: Navigate hidden cybercrime networks to uncover emerging threats and illicit activities.
- **Digital Forensics & Attribution**: Use OSINT techniques to analyze attack vectors, trace IP addresses, and link threat actors to their real identities.
- **Cyber Risk Assessment for Businesses**: Learn how to evaluate the cyber risks facing organizations and protect sensitive data.
- **Social Engineering & Psychological Tactics**: Understand how hackers exploit human behavior and how OSINT can counteract these threats.
- **Ethical & Legal Considerations in Threat Intelligence**: Ensure compliance with cybersecurity laws and best practices while conducting investigations.

With real-world case studies, practical exercises, and expert insights, OSINT Threat Intel equips you with the skills to proactively detect cyber threats, investigate security breaches, and protect against cyber risks. Whether you're in cybersecurity, law enforcement, corporate security, or intelligence analysis, this book is an essential resource for modern cyber investigations.

Thank you for choosing OSINT Threat Intel: Investigating Hackers, Breaches, and Cyber Risks. Cyber threats continue to grow in complexity, and by investing in your OSINT skills, you are helping to strengthen digital security and protect individuals, organizations, and critical infrastructure from cyber risks.

We hope this book has provided valuable insights into cyber threat intelligence and investigative techniques. As always, we encourage ethical and responsible use of these skills—knowledge is a powerful tool, and using it wisely ensures a safer digital landscape for everyone.

Your curiosity, dedication, and passion for intelligence gathering make the OSINT community stronger. If you found this book helpful, we'd love to hear your thoughts! Your feedback helps us improve future editions and create more in-depth resources for investigators like you.

Stay secure, stay vigilant, and keep investigating.

Continue Your OSINT Journey

Expand your skills with the rest of **The OSINT Analyst Series**:

- **OSINT Foundations**: The Beginner's Guide to Open-Source Intelligence
- **The OSINT Search Mastery**: Hacking Search Engines for Intelligence
- **OSINT People Finder**: Advanced Techniques for Online Investigations
- **Social Media OSINT**: Tracking Digital Footprints
- **Image & Geolocation Intelligence**: Reverse Searching and Mapping
- **Domain, Website & Cyber Investigations with OSINT**
- **Email & Dark Web Investigations**: Tracking Leaks & Breaches
- **Corporate OSINT**: Business Intelligence & Competitive Analysis
- **Investigating Disinformation & Fake News with OSINT**
- **OSINT for Deep & Dark Web**: Techniques for Cybercrime Investigations
- **OSINT Automation**: Python & APIs for Intelligence Gathering
- **OSINT Detective**: Digital Tools & Techniques for Criminal Investigations
- **Advanced OSINT Case Studies**: Real-World Investigations
- **The Ethical OSINT Investigator**: Privacy, Legal Risks & Best Practices

We look forward to seeing you in the next book!

Happy investigating!

www.ingramcontent.com/pod-product-compliance
Lightning Source LLC
LaVergne TN
LVHW081751050326
832903LV00027B/1897